REPORTS AND REALITIES

FROM THE

SKETCH-BOOK OF A MANAGER

OF THE

ROSINE ASSOCIATION.

DECEMBER, 1855.

PHILADELPHIA:
JOHN DUROSS, PRINTER,
BLACK HORSE ALLEY.
1855.

PREFACE.

WELL, we are going to publish a book! What is the object? We have two motives. We desire to benefit those who may read, and we want them to aid us, by purchasing and circulating our book. Are people prepared for it? Will they not condemn it as an immoral publication? We know that many persons have full sympathy with us, but these are not they whom we hope to benefit. The well need no physician! We wish to reach those who are not prepared, whose faith in our work is only as a grain of mustard seed; and we want in this book to use the appliances that may foster it, to give our rain and sunshine, our spring-time and harvest, our faith and our hope, our belief that a class of society who have been considered hopeless and irreclaimable, have been, and may yet be reached, as the hands of Christian women may be extended to aid and encourage them, give them an opportunity of earning an honest and respectable livelihood, and are willing to act as teachers to point them Zionward, while in their own deportment they show that they themselves are followers of the meek and lowly Jesus, and that they are living out his Gospel.

We are surrounded by persons who rarely do their own thinking, who are influenced by the popular opinions of their own particular circle or ministerial teacher. Such people are never prepared to develope the humanity that is in their own hearts, or comprehend the feelings that lie buried in others, until something forcibly calls their attention to the subject, and then they are often quite astonished to find the world so much better than they had supposed it to be, and that men and women, however coarse and low, or vicious and degraded, have yet a portion of the same divinity in their souls which they themselves have inherited. They discover that the vices and follies of these individuals are but the outward garments placed upon them by circumstances, and, as they get at the inner man, they are surprised at the world of virtues and kind feelings that lie hidden there, and are only waiting for the fitting time and opportunity to give their outward manifestations. We would like to take some of these persons who are just awaking to the Rosine House, upon the entrance there of some of the unfortunates who have fallen among thieves, and have been stripped and bruised, and they would note in the sacrifice the inmates are willing to make, to add to the comforts of the stranger, that the true humanity is still living within them, and (we believe) may also be found in the hearts of the very thieves who stripped them.

We have been associating more than seven years with thieves, and vagabonds, and drunkards, and degraded women, and among them all we have found very few who have not manifested, amid their errors and follies, that there was still a divine principle and a consciousness of duty at times operating upon their minds, which only needed congenial circumstances to develope them. And this is one of the reasons why we want to send our little book into the world, that we may reach the unbelievers of the universality of the divinity in man, and may give them our experience, and instil into them our faith, that, as we become purified, we shall attract and develope the good that is in others, and, as we embrace opportunities to do them good, we elevate ourselves and become more capable of extended usefulness, and, consequently, of enjoying the increased happiness that springs from the devotion of our means and faculties for the benefit of others.

Our Reports have been circulated from year to year, and have gone as missionaries into many a family, and have awakened an interest that asks to have them gathered together, hoping that the collections of facts, and expressions of .sentiment founded on those facts, may stimulate our readers to examine whether they have extended their "walks of usefulness" into the highways and byways around them, and whether there may not be something for them to do in the field where we have been laboring.

In arranging our book, we felt the necessity of a little variety, that our readers might not grow weary of the sameness, and we have interspersed sundry extracts from our note and letter book, on various subjects—incidents of real life—expressing our thoughts as they arose from time to time, and *facts literally true as we have narrated them.* We may appear egotistical in having to say "*I*" and "*we*" so often, but we have not yet learned to tell our story without using the pronouns, and facts so occupy our thoughts and time, that we have neither leisure nor inclination to portray fictions, nor enter into imaginative speculations.

INTRODUCTION.

In January, 1847, a company of ladies met in a private parlor, to prepare a Petition to the Legislature of Pennsylvania for the Abolition of Capital Punishment, and to make arrangements for calling a *public meeting of women*, to consider the propriety of circulating the petition for signatures.

The public meeting was attended by about 500 women, many of whom were deeply interested in the subject. An Address was read, and arrangements entered into to obtain signatures to the petitions, and a committee appointed to have the charge of sending them to the legislative body. Within six weeks 1000 copies of the Address were circulated, and 11,777 names appended to the petitions were forwarded to Harrisburg, and presented by the different members.

The following poem to the Advocates of Capital Punishment, was inserted in several newspapers, and the efforts upon the subject only ceased at the close of the sittings of the Legislature.

TO THE ADVOCATES OF CAPITAL PUNISHMENT.

What ! would ye swing your Brother's form
  High up in Heaven's free air,
And place the image of your God
  A dangling victim there?
Who gave you pow'r to read his heart,
  Or know how deep his guilt,
Or judge what provocation came
  Ere blood by him was spilt ?
Can ye retrace the length of years
  Since he commenced this life,
And mark the coursing of events,
  His wrongs, his woes, his strife ?
His battles with untoward fate,
  His blasted hopes and schemes,
His longings for the pure and right,
  His visionary dreams?
Perhaps, from life's first early dawn
  Ill nestled by his side,
His teachings may have been in wrong,
  And sin his childhood's guide ;
No mother's voice, perhaps, for him
  Sent up an earnest pray'r;
No father at the mercy seat
  Asked his acceptance there ;
No sister twined around his heart
  A soft and gentle spell,
Which made an atmosphere of love
  Wherever he might dwell;
Virtue, perhaps, to him was known
  But as an empty name,
And truth, and justice, but the guise
  Of cowardice and shame;
Religion's winning, earnest tones
  May ne'er within his soul

Have spread their influence divine,
  To purify the whole—
Then, would ye swing your Brother's form
  High up in Heaven's free air,
And place the image of your God
  A dying victim there?

With all his sins upon his head
  Before his destined hour;
Is yours the fiat of his days,
  Yours the avenging pow'r?
Did not *that Eye* that saw his deed
  Take note when it was done,
And read the thought that caused the act
  Ere yet it was begun?
And could He not, with vengeance swift,
  Have laid the culprit low,
If, in His wisdom, He had seen
  It meet to deal the blow?
Think you His hand less strong than yours?
  Are you more just, more wise,
That ye with daring hands unrobe
  The soul that never dies?
He whom your God in mercy spared
  No mercy meets in you,
And yet we pray—"Forgive us, Lord,
  As we all others do."

Perhaps, no guilt your pris'ner knows,
  Although for crime arraigned,
And proofs may cluster thickly round
  By circumstance maintained;
He may be innocent, and stand
  Before his Maker's sight
A spotless one, more pure than you,
  Who *think* you act the right—

And can ye give him life again,
Or mete him right for wrong,
If future time should prove the guilt
May somewhere else belong?
Then, *dare* ye swing your Brother's form
High up in Heaven's free air,
When time may tell, an innocent
Has been suspended there?

Suppose he did it—and suppose
Your priests around him placed,
Teaching, repentance may atone,
And sinners may be graced—
Suppose he does repent, and lies
Washed clean before the throne,
Becomes a saint, and purified,
And Heaven he feels his own;
With anxious zeal his spirit craves
To fill life's little span
With calling all to turn and see
God's love to guilty man.
And who, than he, once sunk in sin,
Can more that love portray?
Who preach more truly—Sinners, turn,
Crime may be washed away!
Then, could ye hang that saint redeemed
High up in Heaven's free air?
Is earth so full of righteous ones
That ye have some to spare?

And where your Father mercy showed
Can ye no mercy show?
Have ye ne'er sinned, that ye must thus
Deal the avenging blow?
But, if repentance should *not* come
Before his hour of doom,
If, unregenerate you should send
Your Brother to the tomb,

Think you that ye will guiltless stand
  Before your Father's eye?
Did ye not *murder* when ye said
  Your prisoner should die?
Or, are your prison-houses full?
  Have ye no room for one?
Is bread so scant ye cannot feed
  Till life's short course is run?
Have ye not bolts and bars enough
  To hold the victim fast,
When burglars with their thousand wiles
  Are there securely cast?
And are ye sure, no changing fate
  May give to you *his* place?
Are ye so sanctified in good
  Ye cannot fall from grace?
Can no temptation have the pow'r
  To urge the hasty blow?
Have ye so conquered evil thoughts
  That sin no more ye know?
Or, may not circumstances charge
  Your innocence with crime?
Full oft we know it has been thus
  From immemorial time.
Then, by the danger all must share
  That his may be our lot,
By all the bonds of human kind
  Aid to wipe out this blot!
Cease not from striving, till our law
  Is clear from bloody stain,
And *reformation,—not revenge,—*
  In principle sustain!

At the last meeting of the committee, one of the ladies mentioned a subject that had been resting upon her mind, to which she desired to call their attention. It was the formation of a society to open a house for the reformation, employment, and instruction of females, who had led immoral lives. The subject at once arrested the attention of the ladies, and feelings of sympathy were expressed, and a willingness to unite and give their aid in the prosecution of the undertaking. Within a few days afterwards, the proposition to form such an association was laid before the members of the Dorcas Society of Friends, of Cherry Street Meeting, and also the Vaughan Sewing Circle, at Mr. Furness's church. A general interest was expressed, and several ladies gave their names as members, if such a society should be formed. Some gentlemen were also called upon, who expressed their approval of the effort, and eight hundred dollars were subscribed.

Notices were then published, inviting women of all denominations to attend a Meeting in the Museum Building, to consider the subject and prepare for the formation of such a society. A large meeting of women convened in accordance with this invitation, on the afternoon of March 20th, 1847. Sarah Peter was called to the chair, and Lydia Gillingham and Elizabeth Townsend were appointed secretaries.

The following address was read:

ADDRESS.

In preparing an address for a meeting like this, for the purpose of forming an association to endeavor to rescue a portion of our female community from a life of shame and misery, we are impressed with the great responsibilities of the undertaking, and our minds would naturally shrink from engaging in it, were it not that we remember that they are our sisters. We may turn our backs upon them, we may withdraw (as the most of us have ever done) our sympathies, our kindness from them; we may cast upon them the cold look of scorn; we may give them the words of reproach and condemnation—but they are yet our sisters; and ought we not to endeavor to inquire in what respects do they differ from us? Can we suppose they are another class by nature? Were they not formed by Providence with as kind, as gentle feelings as ourselves? Were they not endowed with the same physical and mental organization as the brightest and best amongst us? Do not the springs of love and affection gush forth as freely from their hearts as from our own? Are they not as susceptible of as high moral and intellectual cultivation? and are they not capable of the same desires for a higher and better life? Are we prepared to reply to these questions? Shall it be negatively or affirmatively? If our answer may be in the negative, can we then condemn our less favored sisters, and cast them from us? Have they not an increased demand upon our kindness, our forbearance, our sympathies? Ought not the strong ever to protect the weak, and guard them with every care and precaution that the higher, stronger, purer mind can suggest? But, if we cannot adopt this view, if we do not believe that the beneficent Creator has bestowed upon them mental or physical disabilities to follow the path of right, to live the true life, does it not lead us into other investigations, and cause us to desire to trace the evil to its source? to fathom the deep mysteries that have shrouded so large a portion of our population in unutterable, indescribable misery?

We are told there are six thousand women in our city, who are leading lives of shame and crime, and yet we have been sleeping calmly and quietly in the midst of these scenes of horror; or, when the knowledge of some of these circumstances have been forced upon us, we have shrunk from them with disgust—but where is the hand that has been stretched forth to stay the evil, to remove the plague spot from our community? Can we come up, with clear consciences, to this tribunal? Can we say, we did all that we could? Do we not feel that, in some degree, we are all of us concerned in the guilt of our sisters? We know the majority of those who are thus living in violation of the laws of God and man, are of what are considered the lower classes of society, those whom too many of us are in the constant habit of oppressing. At this charge, do we not instinctively feel the glow of indignation? and is not the denial ready to spring from our lips? But let us examine into this matter! We are aware of the small reward female labor receives under usual circumstances, and the temptations consequent upon this into which young women are thrown; while too many of them have neither moral nor religious training to imbue them with a principle to withstand the inducements of a life of greater apparent ease, and more enlarged pecuniary acquisitions. With this knowledge, which we have received in various ways, can we bring forward any efforts, any attempts on our part to remedy the evil? Have we labored, in the families of this class, to implant a proper principle in the minds of either parents or children? have we sought to give to women's labor the true compensation? or, are we and ours enjoying what ought to have been the meed of their honest industry? These are important questions; and, as we can answer them, will be the reward of our consciences. There is another point on which we ought to reflect with deep earnestness. Young girls have been placed in our families. Have we endeavored to give them the same moral and religious training as our own daughters? Have we clothed them in the garment of virtue, and made them perceive it was beautiful? Others, of more advanced age, have dwelt with us! have we treated them with forbearance, kindness, and sympathy, and sought to reconcile them to their lot of labor, by removing, as much as possible, the barrier of caste, that too often separates the employer and the employed? or have we, by our coldness and haughtiness, endeavored to impress them with the idea, that there was a marked line between us; and, by our conduct, wounded spirits, perhaps, as proud as our own, and urged them to abandon our firesides for the greater equality in a home of vice? and, when our sister (owing, perhaps, to our treatment) has sought to escape from what she felt to be the tyranny of wealth, and yielded to temptation, what have been our efforts to reclaim her? Have we gone to her wretched habitation, and sought to win her back to virtue? Have we offered her a happier home, and told her we had wronged her, and perhaps prompted her to err? have we opened to her the avenues by which she might regain a degree of respectability, and consulted her taste and feelings in the occupation we offered her? Have we compared her fate with ours, and owned that, under the circumstances in which she had been placed, we, too, might have fallen? These are all considerations which are necessary to fit us for the work of this day, and there are many others of vast importance connected with the subject, but our time is too limited to enlarge more fully upon the causes that tempt to crime. We must now turn to the remedy, hoping that our future conduct may atone, in a degree, for the omissions and commissions of the past.

Some of us have been impressed for a long period with the necessity of an effort in this cause, but the prejudices of society have been so powerful, that woman has not dared to step forward to snatch her erring sister from a life of crime, and endeavor to reclaim her and sustain her, kindly and lovingly, through the paths of honest toil to noble independence. To this work have we now come, and we propose to you to form an Association, which may, under right influences, lead to the happiest consequences. We ask you to assist in this labor of love—to join us in the endeavor to instruct and employ these wanderers, and show them the pleasantness of the paths of virtue—to aid us in introducing them into a new life, and sustaining them in it by the moral and religious attractions we may cast around them. We feel the importance of the movement. We know there are great responsibilities attending it—but we believe, as we seek to walk rightly in the path of duty, and ask for wisdom from above, to govern and guide our actions, we shall triumph over the difficulties that may surround us, and enjoy a consciousness that our efforts have not been in vain.

Many of us have been led to inquire, as we have met the poor degraded victims of vice, who have passed us in our walks, can nothing be done for them? With some of us, this has been the oft-recurring question. We have looked around us in vain—and when we would have spoken to them of reformation, reproved them for their continuance in their sadly erring course, and pointed them to a path of propriety and virtue, our lips have been closed; for we have known there was no suitable home that could offer them the sympathies and genial influences which their circumstances demanded.

For some years past there has been an institution in operation (founded and conducted by benevolent persons, who saw the necessity of an effort to provide a shelter for those who desired to reform), which has given a home to many for a period, and some have been reclaimed—but, in consequence of being under the superintendence of men, its labors have been in a degree inefficient, and the reformation of this class has been considered almost as a hopeless effort; but we believe, that with woman's sympathy, woman's guiding care, her quick perceptions of the necessities of woman's nature, a regenerating influence may be brought into operation, which may show to the world that even the poor degraded prostitute is not irreclaimable.

We believe that asylum has done much good, and the Directors of it have labored faithfully to promote what they considered the best interest of the inmates; but to us it appears, that an institution, conducted upon a different plan, will more effectually promote the desirable object of restoring such individuals to usefulness and respectability. With those concerned in this asylum, we desire to preserve the best feelings—there is a large field of labor for each of us. To the idle or to the sick *we* cannot offer a home; but to the industrious and energetic we hope to open the avenues to a useful, independent life, while we shall endeavor to cast around moral and religious influences, which may sustain them in their upward and onward career.

With these views, we lay before you an outline of our plan; but the experience which time must bring can alone fill up the more minute details.

We propose to you to form an Association—the objects of which shall be, the reformation, employment, and instruction of females who have wandered from the paths of virtue, and who are desirous to return to respectability and usefulness.

We have, at this time, an opportunity of obtaining a house, which is considered in a suitable situation, and as conveniently arranged as any building could possibly be, that was not built especially for the purpose. The price at which it is offered is one that is believed by gentlemen, who are competent to judge of its value, to be such as to warrant a belief, that if at a future time there should be a desire to dispose of it, there would be no loss sustained upon the property. The front room of the building can, without much expense, be altered into a store, which will greatly assist us in our designs, as we propose to make it a means of convenience, and believe it would be one of profit to the institution. There are fourteen rooms in the house, all having a good light and cheerful appearance, suitaable for work rooms and chambers. It has only been built six years—the front building is four stories high and the back three, making four rooms on a floor in the three lower stories. The store will be sufficiently large; and, having a parlor, dining-room, and kitchen on a level, it will be exceedingly convenient. Thirty women may be comfortably accommodated in it without using three fine rooms on the second floor, which should be appropriated to the business department.

Having thus described the house, we will lay before you our idea of the manner in which it may be suitably and profitably occupied. We propose to have a competent, discreet woman as housekeeper, and well qualified teachers of the trades of tailoring, mantua-making, straw-work, and other pleasant and profitable employments, as the family may increase, and the managers consider it can be done with propriety.

The girls, upon entering the institution, should be permitted to choose the trade they may prefer, of those in operation in the house, and be considered as apprentices until they shall be so far perfected as to be able to work without further instruction, during which time they should take their turns in performing the cooking, washing, and household duties, with which branches we consider it is absolutely necessary that every woman should be familiar. As soon as they become proficients in the trades they have chosen they shall be considered as boarders in the family, and a regular debtor and credit account be kept between each individual and the institution; they being credited with the amount received for the work they have accomplished, and a regular charge made of their board and other accommodations, at the price which experience shall enable the managers to decide may be consistent with the economy of the establishment. This arrangement, we believe, will be productive of much advantage, as there will be a constant stimulant to exertion; and every individual must feel they are laboring for themselves, and preparing a fund from their own earnings, which, when they leave the establishment, shall enable them to re-enter society under favorable auspices, and assist in establishing them in a respectable station in life.

A suitable time each day should be devoted to mental instruction—subject to whatever plan the superintendents may find to harmonize in the best manner with the interests of the inmates; and, while the motto of the house shall be, "You shall support yourselves honestly by the labor of your own hands," the health, the comfort, and a proper degree of leisure for recreation, must ever claim the attention of the managers—but experience alone can give judgment in regard to these arrangements, and from season to season they must be subjected to alterations.

It will be necessary to employ a person in the store; but, by keeping a small assortment of trimmings, which may be a great accommodation to the family as well as to the neighborhood, and also to customers bringing work to the house, the expenses of the woman who attends it may be paid, while at the same time it may afford an opportunity for the sale of any articles manufactured in the establishment; and this person be made the medium of communication between those who may call upon business and the inmates, so as to prevent unnecessary exposure, or disturbance to the family. We have also reason to believe, that many benevolent young women, whose circumstances will prevent them from assisting in the labor or management of the house, will gladly spend some of their leisure time in working at fancy articles for the benefit of the concern, and will thus add their mites in the cause of humanity. These articles may be disposed of in the store, and be a source of profit, while the consciousness of a benevolent purpose will increase the happiness of the donor.

Having thus given a general outline of our views, we are sensible there are many details which may be of great interest to ourselves, and to the objects for whose benefit we propose these arrangements, but which time and experience alone can develope.

Of our interest in this subject we need not speak. Time, money, and labor must all be appropriated in the enterprise, to insure its success; but we believe the consciousness of performing our duty will animate us to exertion, and cheer our onward path, and if what is now deemed an experiment should be productive of the benefits at which we aim, the reward of our efforts will be reaped in our own increased happiness, as well as by those who are the objects of our care and solicitude. We have not entered into this work lightly, or without reflection; but a strong consciousness of its great responsibilities induces us to seek the co-operation of all those who feel that it is in the treasury of good works we can alone find true riches. Already have we met with those whose hearts responded at once to our appeal upon this subject, and we are encouraged to believe that, if we enlist our own sympathies in this cause, and feel that we are the advocates of those who cannot, dare not speak for themselves, we shall be heard with feelings of interest by others, who will pour into our treasury those gifts of which they are the almoners of Heaven.

We are deeply impressed with the greatness of our undertaking, and ardently desire that our minds may be clothed with wisdom, that we may be enabled to fulfil in this great work what we believe to be the designs of Providence.

An appeal was then made by the President on behalf of those alluded to in the call for the meeting, and the proposition was adopted to form an Association for the reformation, employment, and instruction of females, whose habits and situation have precluded them from the sympathies and respect of the virtuous part of the community. Several ladies gave their views of the necessity of such an institution, and statements were made of some cases that had come under their knowledge, of young women who had committed suicide, who might probably have been saved had such a society been in operation.

A Committee of five was appointed to prepare a Constitution, viz.: Sarah Peter, Eliza Parker, Susan Dorsey, Maria M. Davis, and Mira Townsend. Also a Committee of thirty, to collect subscriptions from persons whose feelings responded to the efforts in this cause, and who might be willing to associate in this benevolent enterprise.

Women of all denominations were earnestly invited to attend a meeting, to be held March 25th, (five days after).

Pursuant to this notice, a large assembly of women met at the appointed place, when a constitution was adopted, and twenty managers elected for the ensuing year. There was considerable discussion in reference to the name to be given to the Society, and a sketch was read of the life and labors of Rosa Govona, an Italian girl, who had founded several institutions in her own country for poor and unfortunate girls, where they were taught to labor, and qualified to earn a respectable living by the labor of their own hands. An objection was made to the adoption of any name that might be considered a term of reproach to those who might come under the care of the Society ; and the name Rosine Association was preferred to any other title, as it commemorated an excellent and virtuous woman, whose whole life was devoted to benefit the poor and unfortunate of her own sex.

The name *Rosine Association* was therefore adopted.

The meeting adjourned to meet again on the 4th of April. Since that period various public meetings have been held, at which the progress of the Society in the prosecution of the objects for which it was formed has been reported by the Managers.

PREAMBLE.

When we consider the present state of society, the many instances that come to our knowledge of deviations from the path of virtue and propriety, of woman, losing first her self-respect, then becoming indifferent to the opinion of others, casting off the restraints of decency and morality, and abandoning herself to a life of crime and shame, we feel we are called upon to inquire, why is it so? and also, can no remedy be applied? We know they are questions of grave importance, and while we are led to perceive that a deficient education, the want of proper remuneration for services, and the neglect of suitable maternal and sympathizing care on the part of parents and others, in whose charge young girls are placed, exposes them to temptation; we also discover that the prejudices and habits of social life are often the causes of woman falling into error, and afterward yielding fatally to the despair, caused by the influences around her; she feels she has lost her caste; she can no more be received into respectable society; the finger of scorn and the word of reproach are now to be her portion, and in her hopeless misery she abandons all that has been dear to her, and becomes an alien to her friends, and an outcast from the sympathies and charities of the good and the virtuous. But we cannot suppose that, sunk as she may be in vice and degradation, she has lost all the finer, better feelings of woman's nature;—we believe there are few such instances. The customs and prejudices of society have, after the first fatal step, accelerated her downward course, and we, who are her sisters, whose hands ought to be stretched forth to support the fallen victim of error, have heartlessly abandoned her in her misery and guilt. But a better day is before us! We believe that the lost may be reclaimed; the fallen one may be restored to society and usefulness; that we may say, as did our blessed example, "Go, and sin no more!" we feel we may cast around her elevating influences; we may teach her to estimate herself properly; inspire her with principles of integrity, industry, and independence; and, while we surround her with moral advantages and religious instructions, which may animate her to live a right life, we may awaken her faculties to perceive the dignity of her nature, and her duties as a responsible being to her Father, and her Creator.

With these views we propose associating ourselves together, that we may establish an Institution, for the reformation, employment, and instruction of females, whose habits and situations have precluded them from the sympathies of the virtuous part of the community.

CONSTITUTION.

To secure from vice and degradation, a class of women who have forfeited their claim to the respect of the virtuous,—to prepare and maintain for them an asylum, which, by its system of religious instruction, shall elevate their moral nature,—to teach them how to gain an honest living "by the work of their own hands,"—and, eventually, to render them useful members of the community—an association has been formed, and denominated the *Rosine Association* of Philadelphia, for the government of which the following Constitution is adopted.

Article I.

Every woman, on the payment of not less than one dollar, annually, shall be admitted as a member of this society; or, by paying the sum of twenty dollars, shall be a member for life. Every *person* may become an annual contributor.

ARTICLE II.

This Society shall meet on the first Fifth day (Thursday) of the fourth month (April) each year, at which meeting thirty members shall be competent to transact business. At this meeting there shall be chosen twenty managers, in whom shall be vested the whole concerns of the Society.

ARTICLE III.

The Managers (being duly notified by the officiating Secretary) shall meet within three days after their election, and shall choose from among their number a President, Vice-President, Secretary, and Treasurer. They shall have power to make by-laws for their own government—to fill vacancies in the board, and to call special meetings of the Society, whenever, in their judgment, it may be expedient. They shall make an annual report of their proceedings.

ARTICLE IV.

Every alteration of this Constitution must be proposed at a meeting preceding the one of its adoption.

Managers: Sarah B. Corbit, Margaret Griscom, Rebecca S. Hart, Emily Taylor, Annis P. Furness, Anna Williamson, Elizabeth Pugh, Elizabeth Hunt, Sarah Tyndale, Anne Price, Harriet M. Ogden, Eliza Parker, Ellen N. Baldwin, Maria M. Davis, Susan H. Dorsey, Caroline Cowperthwaite, Mira Townsend, Rachel S. Evans, Sarah Lloyd, Elizabeth Hughes.

At a meeting of the Board of Managers held Fifth month (May) 15, the following officers were appointed:

President, Sarah B. Corbit; Vice-President, Elizabeth Pugh; Secretary, Sarah Lloyd; Treasurer, Mira Townsend.

REPORT OF THE BOARD OF MANAGERS.

November, 1847.

Since the formation of the Rosine Association the Managers have been engaged in forwarding the objects of the Society. The house alluded to in the Address, read at that time, which it was proposed to purchase, has since been rented on a lease for five years, with the privilege of buying it at that period if it should then be considered desirable and our funds should warrant it. We obtained possession of it in August, since which time we have had a bath-room and out-kitchen built, shutters made for the back buildings, a cooking range and warm-air furnace inserted, and various alterations and improvements added, to fit it for our purpose. In making these alterations it was exceedingly gratifying to us to find that an interest upon the subject pervaded all classes of our citizens. The lumber merchants and carpenters, the brickmakers and bricklayers, the plasterers, paperers, and painters, have all aided in their different departments, so as considerably to lessen our expenses in altering the building; and a number of kind friends have contributed articles of furniture, which have enabled us to get into operation at a comparatively small amount of expenditure. But several of our rooms are still unfurnished. We would therefore appeal to the benevolent for aid, in money or goods, as may best suit their convenience, so that we may establish the institution on a permanent basis, and make a home for the friendless, where the best feelings of their nature may be cultivated, and habits and sentiments acquired in harmony with the spirit of Christianity.

We have now the names of 253 women as annual subscribers. Many benevolent persons have contributed to our funds ; but in starting an institution of this kind, means are necessary, not only to commence operations, but to continue them, that a fair trial may be made of the efficacy of a system that proposes not only the reformation of the objects of its care, but to qualify them, mentally, morally, and physically, to maintain themselves in an honest and respectable manner by their own labor. We must, therefore, continue our appeal to those who are interested in good works, and who desire that an attempt may be made to benefit the most depressed and hopeless part of our community. We invite every woman who loves the cause of virtue, and can feel for the miseries and degradation of her unfortunate sisters, to become a member of our Association, and thus pledge her name and interests for the support of correct principles and practices; and we ask the sympathy and assistance of every man who believes that moral and religious influences may operate beneficially in the restoration of fallen humanity, and who feels that he has a duty to perform for those who may truly be called the most wretched of our population. Thousands of dollars are given annually in this city to send missionaries among the heathen of distant lands, while our own heathen—those who are living without the knowledge or fear of God, without any definite idea of their duties here, or hope of happiness hereafter—are in our midst, deserted and neglected. Let us then unite in this work, and by every means in our power assist in the reformation and regeneration of that unfortunate class, who, like the intemperate, may be redeemed by kindly influences, and become new beings.

We solicit your assistance, therefore, in funds, or in goods of any description, which we can either use or sell, and in giving employment to the family in *dressmaking and tailoring*. Our institution *must* be a House of Industry. Our motto is, "You shall support yourself honestly by the labor of your own hands."

ANNUAL REPORT OF THE MANAGERS OF THE ROSINE ASSOCIATION.

April, 1848.

A year has elapsed this day, since we met, and agreed to unite together as a Society, to promote by our efforts the cause of virtue, and prepare a home and asylum for unfortunate females, who, having yielded to habits of licentiousness, had found the ways of sin to bring shame, disease, poverty, remorse, and unhappiness, and who might be induced to enter an institution where reformation, employment, and instruction should be combined in such a manner that they would be convinced that a right path is preferable to a wrong one, and a life of virtue and industry produce more happiness than a course of idleness, vice, and depravity. We met, not to ask in the spirit of judgment why our sisters had erred; not to cast upon them the term of reproach because they had deviated from propriety and virtue; but to acknowledge that the customs of society, the small remuneration for female labor, and the frequent neglect of the proper cultivation of the moral and religious sentiments of the youth of both sexes, and of all classes, had produced in a great degree the evil we lamented, and to endeavor, as far as might be in our power, to apply a remedy.

We then associated ourselves together, hoping the Divine blessing might rest upon our efforts, and, being regularly organized, we assumed the name of the Rosine Association, in honor of a poor but estimable young woman, of the name of Rosa Govona, who founded several establishments in Italy, where the destitute and unfortunate of her own sex were enabled to earn a decent and respectable living.

The Society being thus formed, considerable exertion was needed to collect funds to enable us to get into operation. This required a great sacrifice of time, labor, and feeling; but we have been cheered on our way by the consciousness of the rightfulness and importance of the great work we had undertaken, and the sympathy and benevolence which encouraged and assisted us. A house was rented, repaired, and altered to suit our convenience. Mechanics of various kinds gave us their aid, so as considerably to lessen the expenses we should otherwise have incurred. It was opened in the early part of October, 1847. We have now been six months in operation, and feel that much has been accomplished considering the apparent hopelessness with which many viewed our enterprise, and the working by faith alone of our members. We were all inexperienced in the labor we had undertaken, and every department seemed to claim able heads and hands; but we believed in the righteousness of our cause, and what we lacked in ability, we gave in heartfelt devotion to it.

A suitable Matron, Tailoress, and Mantuamaker were engaged, and a small store opened, hoping it might be a source of profit and convenience.

Our Institution is yet in its infancy. The Managers themselves require a training to fit them for their important duties; and the arrangements of the family have been, and must be varied, according to circumstances, and as experience determines their wisdom and necessity. When our house was opened, we had in view the general outline presented in the address at our first meeting, and we have endeavored to pursue the plan devised there, only increasing our regulations as occasion seemed to demand them. Considerable exertion was made to procure employment for the inmates, that they might be instructed in the most important and profitable branches of female labor; and, as soon as the number in the house seemed to warrant it, our school was commenced, and they have received instruction in orthography, reading, writing, arithmetic, grammar, geography, and physiology. These branches have been taught by our members, and we have been highly gratified by the interest that has been shown, both by teachers and scholars; and also by the industry in the work-room. These facts are very cheering, as they prove clearly to us that an institution so conducted, must produce incalculable benefits, as the knowledge and habits of industry acquired in the house must be productive of advantage to every individual throughout their whole lives. Owing to our inmates having been so short a period employed at the trades they have been learning, we have not had an opportunity of testing the benefits to be derived from the stimulation of working for their own pecuniary advantage; but we believe, as they increase in competency, and profitable business flows into the house, we shall find it a powerful assistant in adding to the happiness of our pupils, and increasing their moral and industrious propensities, by convincing them that they can procure an honest and respectable living by their own labor, and that the capacity for enjoyment and usefulness is much increased by added knowledge. By the introduction of trades into the house, we do not contemplate making all mantua-makers and tailoresses, but to give such as have the capacity and inclination the opportunity, and to qualify all to do the usual sewing in a family, in addition to a knowledge of housework and cooking, so that, when they leave the Institution, they may be enabled to enter into a life of general usefulness wherever they may be located. We are fully aware of the importance of making our work-room as lucrative as possible, so as to assist in bearing the expenses of the family; but we must remember that the majority of those that come under our care are ignorant, and unaccustomed to restraint or application ; that, in their former mode of life, amusement was the great business, and excitement the daily necessity. The change, therefore, must be great, and we feel the importance, while we cultivate habits of industry, also to appoint intervals of recreation, and introduce modes of amusement. Battledoors and graces have been furnished, and innocent cheerfulness encouraged. We desire, in the round of business and instruction of their present life, the memories of the former one may be dimmed and fade away, and better, brighter, and happier images fill their minds, and banish the sad past with its harrowing reminiscences. Nor have we been unmindful of endeavoring to cultivate their higher and holier feelings and sentiments. The Scriptures are read daily in the family; they are encouraged to learn and sing hymns; and, as opportunity presents, the importance of striving to live in the spirit of prayer, that they may be strengthened and assisted in their desires to lead a better life, is impressed upon them, and an endeavor made to awaken feelings of gratitude towards Him who hath opened a way for their deliverance from a course of sin and misery, and given them an opportunity to atone for the errors of the past, by the well-spent present and future. We have also been sensible that the best mode to banish evil or unpleasant thoughts, is to present to the mind others that may be instructive and amusing. We have, therefore, been endeavoring to collect a library of suitable books, in which we have been kindly assisted by several contributors, and also by the Bible Associations, who have furnished Bibles and Testaments.

The Education Committee, on the afternoon of the Sabbath, have Bible and other reading, and suitable conversation with the family, endeavoring to make the Sabbath school interesting and instructive. Ministers, and other religious persons, who desire to hold meetings in the house, are admitted upon these occasions, by the invitation of the Managers, or upon application to the Visiting Committee.

Our Board has been divided into four standing committees: on the store, house, work, and education, and a fifth, alternating committee, composed of one member of each, who have the general superintendence of the whole, and are denominated visitors. By this arrangement, each member, by being in turn a visitor, is interested, not only in her own particular department, but in every one in the Institution.

We have also had another committee appointed to visit among the houses where the unfortunate objects of our solicitude reside. The duties of this committee have been important and painfully interesting. Many hours have been passed by them in these sad abodes of heartless gaiety and unenjoyed revelry, and it is with pleasure they acknowledge the general kindness and respect with which they have been received, and their mission understood and appreciated. During these visits, their former impressions have been confirmed; that ignorance, the want of proper moral and religious culture, and wholesome restraints, have been the fruitful causes of the demoralization of the young, while to those more advanced in life, have been added the low prices of woman's labor, and the general unhappy influences arising from the example of the immoral, intemperate, and debased, in some portions of our city. Indeed, as they have pursued their mission in some sections, they have felt that the whole moral atmosphere was corrupted, and have been led to wonder how any could escape contamination, of either sex, while they breathed the malaria that issued all around them from the dram shops, and the varied sinks of infamy that are clustered together. The committee have visited in one square, thirteen houses; in another neighborhood, in half a square, nine houses; and, within a short distance, in a block of one quarter of a square, fourteen houses; in all of which, young, unfortunate and degraded females reside, and in the most of them the bottle, with its poisonous draught, is the daily companion, constantly sinking them lower, and lower, by increasing their debasing habits, until their short and sad career is closed in the almshouse, or the prison—the victims of disease and of every species of vice. While we speak thus of these sad facts, we do not wish to convey the idea that these miserable and wretched women are more vicious or depraved than the men, who, in many cases, wickedly allure them to a life of sin, or are their companions during its generally brief continuance, but the prejudices of society, which have deprived woman of caste and respectability, for the offence which has too often been lightly visited upon man, has had the effect to paralyze her energies, and make her a hopeless, reckless, broken-hearted creature, living a life of deception, assuming a levity that is foreign to her feelings, and seeking associations that are utterly repugnant to her nature. While thus we dwell upon these painful circumstances, we have also to remember, that those who are the visitors and supporters of these houses and their inmates, are many of them the husbands, the fathers, the brothers, and the sons of the virtuous women of our community, and that in these abodes of vice, surrounded by enticements of every kind, the youthful mind is corrupted by the exhilarating glass, the exciting game of cards, the profuse expenditure of money, and the cultivation of habits which produce an utter laxity of morals, and lead to dishonesty, disgrace, disease, domestic infelicity, and spiritual death. Do not these reflections call us to self-examination? Have we performed the duties incumbent upon us, by condemning and shunning the known libertine, by candidly warning and cautioning those within our influence, and endeavoring, by our own pure and gentle spirits, to keep them in the magic circle of home, and its holy elevating sympathies and affections? Have we, who are mothers, endeavored to instil those true and correct principles into the minds of our children that would lead them to reflect upon their social and religious duties, their responsibilities to their fellow beings, and to their Creator, and to consider the violation of the seventh commandment a species of moral insanity, which is sure to bring in its train a depreciation of character, health and happiness, and of that self respect which is the cherished companion of the virtuous, and entitles them to that most glorious promise that was given upon the Mount, "Blessed are the pure in heart, for they shall see God."

But we hope a new era is dawning in the moral world; and the existence of this Society, claiming *three hundred and forty-six members* within one year from its formation, is a cheering token that "there is a good time coming." The spirit of inquiry is abroad, and woman's heart, with all her sympathies, is awaking, and as she meets the poor degraded ones in the street, decked with their sadly gained finery, or hears the story of deception, vice, and woe that has made them what they are, the question is asked—what can we do? This Society gives the answer. We have associated for the reformation, employment, and instruction of these. We have openly avowed that we will be the friends of the erring and the unfortunate of our own sex; that we will give them our sympathy, to win them from evil; our assistance, to show them they can support themselves honestly and respectably; our encouragement, that they too may feel that the day of progress is come, and that they may be sensible of the elevating influences of that spirit, that, while it says, "Daughter, sin no more," will add, Let us go up to the house of the Lord together.

Since the organization of the Society we have had twenty-five individuals under the care of the managers, but they have not all been inmates of the house. Of these, seven are now situated in respectable families; four have been restored to their parents; and one, through the influence of one of the Board, has been married to the person who induced her to err. Two were sent to the Almshouse after a few days' residence, not being in a state of health to be benefited by this institution. One was discharged, not being considered a hopeful case. Two left voluntarily. There are now eight in the house learning trades, receiving an education, and becoming acquainted with cooking, house-work, and the different branches of the usual employments of women. Of those still under our care, we must express our approbation of their general conduct. They appear desirous to gain instruction in the different departments of business knowledge; and we have reason to believe, they feel they have a happy home; and some of them have been led to desire a progress in better things, and to inquire, "What can I do to be saved?"

At our last public meeting it was stated, that some cases had come under the notice of the managers, of women who had children, and who felt they must continue in an evil course of life to gain a support for them. There were many interesting remarks upon the subject, and a statement was made of some facts, which induced the Society to pass the following resolution:

Resolved, That the managers of the Rosine Association are empowered to make what arrangements they think necessary in each particular case that presents, and make suitable provision for the children of such mothers as they consider will be hopeful members of the Rosine family; such provision to be discontinued as soon as the mother can support it or them by her own efforts, or upon her leaving the house.

A proposition was then made to start a fund, to be called the Children's Fund; which, being approved, fourteen dollars sixty-seven cents were contributed. One child, with its mother, has been under care, to the support of which part of the sum subscribed has been appropriated.

A collecting Committee was also appointed, to invite *women* to become members of the Association, and to call upon persons generally, to give them an opportunity to contribute to our funds.

Since that period we have applied to the Legislature for an Act of Incorporation, which we have reason to believe will be granted. The Society will then be qualified to hold property for the benefit of such objects as may be embraced in the charter.

This will afford an opportunity to the benevolent to make an investment, that must ever be satisfactory to themselves; as the interest arising from it will not only be received in *time*, but continue throughout *eternity*. It is very desirable that the Institution may be placed on a permanent basis, and that we may be enabled to complete the purchase of the house, upon which we hold a mortgage of thirteen hundred dollars.

Neither our store nor work-room has been as profitable as we could desire; but we hope our members and friends will assist us, by the purchase of goods in the one, and bringing their tailoring, mantua-making, and plain sewing to the other, and also inducing their friends and domestics to bring their custom to the establishment.

Considerable sewing has been done to furnish the house, and also to prepare clothing for the inmates, several of whom have been almost entirely destitute of suitable apparel. The number of articles made for the use of the house, comprising bedding, toweling, &c., is two hundred and thirty-nine. Garments for the inmates, seventy-seven. For customers, one hundred and eighty-six.

The year of our service, as managers, has now closed, and we resign our commission to the Society with deep and varied feelings. We have been treading in a new path—one that has awakened powerful emotions within us. We have constantly felt the necessity of a higher wisdom than our own to guide us, that we might be qualified to judge rightly what might be for the real advantage of the immortal souls intrusted to our care. In the spirit of prayer we have earnestly desired to be gifted with wisdom, and to be endowed with that loving charity that might fit us properly for our work; and we would ask for our successors, that they may have increased ability to forward the purposes and intentions of this Society, that of rescuing the vicious, the miserable, and the degraded female from a life of sin and shame, placing her in a situation where she may become useful, respectable, and happy here, and assist, as far as possible, in aiding to prepare her for that better world, where she may be a redeemed angel in the presence of her Father forever.

But while our feelings have been deeply interested for those who have deviated from a virtuous course of life, we have not forgotten they were once innocent, and that many of them might have been preserved in that purity, had better, happier influences been around them in their more youthful days. The past we cannot repair—but we can alleviate the sufferings of the future; and we would solemnly appeal to those who have the charge of young immortal beings to remember, that if more care had been exercised in the faithful, moral, and religious training of our youth, there would be less occasion for this Society. We desire, also, to call the attention of our members, and others, to the necessity there is of a suitable home being provided for young friendless and destitute females, many of whom are cast upon the world without suitable guardians or protectors, and subjected to all the temptations incident to such a situation. Within the last year the Female Moral Reform Society, in New York, has opened a house, where friendless and destitute women and children are received, maintained, and instructed, until suitable homes are provided for them. Such an institution is needed in this city; and we hope an increase in our funds may enable us, at no very distant day, to have a branch under the care of our Society that may give a suitable asylum to such, until they may be qualified for usefulness, and hearts prepared to adopt them into a true and happy home. We wish not only to save the lost, but to preserve the innocent.

In concluding our report we may add, that we consider we have cause to feel encouraged in the important work into which we have entered. We are convinced that great good may be accomplished, and we believe the Divine blessing has rested upon our labors, while we hope the schooling we have had may help to make *us* both wiser and better.

TREASURER'S REPORT.

Mira Townsend, Treasurer, in account with Rosine Association.

Fourth Month, 1st, 1848.

DR.

To amount of cash	received from sundry persons,	$4,970 38
" "	Received from Work Committee for work done in the house, - - - - -	75 00
" "	Received on account of Children's Fund, - - -	14 67
" "	Interest on Money loaned, -	81 00
		$5,141 05

CR.

By amount paid salaries, rents, repairs, house expenses, &c., - - - - -	$1,371 11
" Loaned at interest, - - - -	2,700 00
" Invested in store, - - - -	1,000 00
" Cash on hand, - - - - -	60 94
	$5,141 05

LIST OF MEMBERS.

Abbot, Elizabeth
Abbott, Mrs.
Acton, Hannah
Agnew, Mrs. Jehu
Agnew, Eliza Jane
Adams, M. M.

Brindley, Mrs.
Bunting, Elizabeth
Bujac, Anne W.
Boggs, Margaret
Burkhart, Sarah
Bradford, Mrs. S.
Badger, Mrs. William
Barker, Sarah W.
Boyd, Mrs.
Barton, Susan R.
Bonsall, Mary M.
Bonsall, Naomi
Brown, Hannah
Badlum, Jane A.
Badlum, Sophia
Black, Rebecca
Bedford, Louisa
Brooks, Elizabeth
Bennett, Mrs. Jas. M.
Buzby, Maria
Benner, Sarah
Benner, Rebecca
Buckley, Eliza
Burleigh, Gertrude K.
Brainard, C. C.
Brainard, Mary
Barton, Catharine
Butcher, Mary
Bradfield, E. W.
Barry, Mary H.
Bloomfield, Isabella
Baldwin, Ellen N.
Boon, Sarah
Baker, Elizabeth

Cowperthwaite, C.
Clarkson, Sarah
Conway, Ann
Caron, Eliza A.
Chandler, Caroline
Campbell, Mary
Cox, Lavinia
Cotringer, Mary
Canby, Eliza
Corbit, Sarah B.
Clark, Mrs.
Crowley, Eliza C.
Carter, Mrs. W. I.
Cooper, Hannah
Crawford, Jane
Corbit, Emma
Clapier, Theresa
Cheesborough, Sally
Clendenin, Anne
Copper, M. H.
Churchman, Sarah
McCall, Elizabeth
Cavender, Eliz'th M.
Collins, Mrs. T. B.
Collins, Mrs. Eliz'th
Campion, Elizabeth
Cameron, J. K.
Colliday, Mrs. S.
Cox, Margaret
Creswell, Elizabeth
Campion, Mrs. T.
Castner, Mrs. Sam'l
Carter, Sarah
Colket, Elizabeth

Davis, Maria M.
Dorsey, Susan H.
De France, Caroline
Davis, Lydia C.
Davenport, Susanna
Duane, Mrs. Wm.
Davis, Elizabeth M.
Dodge, Mrs.
Dunlap, Sarah

Elder, Sarah
Evans, Rachel S.
Ellis, Rebecca
Ellis, Margaret H.
Ellis, Hannah W.
Eckel, Mrs. M.

Evans, Mary Ann
Ellis, Martha R.
Ellis, Mrs.
Elliot, Eliza T.
Eddowes, Miss
Ewing, Miss
Emory, Susan

Furness, Annis P.
Farnum, Mrs. B.
Furness, Mrs. James
Fussell, Maria D.
Fisher, Mrs. John
Ferris, Bridget
French, Elizabeth B.
Foster, Mrs.
Franklin, Mary
Fry, Anna
Field, Rachel

Griscom, Marg't A.
Grim, Rebecca C.
Green, Lydia E.
Gillingham, Mary K.
Gilpin, Anna
Gillingham, Sarah K.
Gillingham, Lydia
Griffith, Jane S.
Goodwin, Phebe
Graeff, Miss
Goeller, Margaret
Gratz, Rebecca
Green, Sarah
Guest, Rebecca
Grew, Mary

Hart, Rebecca S.
Heiskill, Frances
Hanson, Ellen
Hanson, Gulielma M.
Hunn, Elizabeth A.
Hancock, Esther
Horton, Maria W.
Hewlings, Sarah
Hance, Sarah J.
Halloway, Emeline
Howell, Mary
Hall, Mrs.
Harper, Eliza
Harding, Mrs.
Hazletine, Mrs. Ward
Haddock, Mrs. Dan'l
Harding, Mrs.
Hollingsworth, Miss
Hildeburn, Sophia
Hodge, Mrs. Dr.
Hunt, Elizabeth
Hastings, Mary M.
Hagar, Mary
Harkness, Esther
Hayhurst, Esther
Hunt, Elizabeth
Harvey, Mrs. J. G.
Heisse, Mrs. R.
Hallowell, A. P.
Hinchman, Anna W.
Hathaway, Mrs.
Hough, H.
Hallowell, Han'h P.
Howe, Mrs.
Hallowell, Ther'sa K.
Hill, Elizabeth

Ingham, Florence

Johnson, Mrs. R.
Johnson, Nancy M.
Jackson, Jennette
Jackson, Rachel
Jordon, Jane
Jenkins, Hannah J.
Justice, Huldah
Jenkins, Elizabeth
Jones, Ella
Jeanes, Mary
Johnson, Mercy
Johns, Hannah

Kaley, Mary Rowland
Kroll, Deborah Ann
Kay, Mrs. Elizabeth
Kirkland, Mrs.
Kelsey, Mary
Kimber, Susan

Lewis, Sophia
Lang, Jane
Latimer, Eliza
Lloyd, Sarah
Lye, Mrs.
Larcomb, Anna S.
Lincoln, Mrs.
Lord, Mrs. G.
Lex, A. F.
Lewis, Sidney Ann
Lapsley, Mrs. David
Lownes, Mary P.
Lovering, Ann C.
Lyman, Mrs. Charles
Denning, Mrs. F.
Lamborn, Anne
Lewis, Mary D.
Lea, Susan M.
Longstreth, Mrs. J.
Lang, Anna

Massey, Anna
Miller, Hannah
Mott, Lucretia
Murphy, Lydia A.
Mitchell, Mrs. James
Mitchell, E. V.
Milligan, Julia
Morrison, Anna
Miller, Mrs. John
McClellan, Mrs. S.
McMurtrie, Mrs. Dr.
McConnell, Mary
Moore, Mrs. B. H.
Macey, Jane
McCall, Elizabeth
Morrison, Caroline
Miles, Catharine C.
Mott, Mary Anna P.
Matthews, Ann
McCutcheon, Mrs. C.
Maris, Louisa
Milliette, Mary

Mercer, Mary D.
Martin, Susan
McIlhenny, Eliza W.
Morris, Catharine
Morris, Catharine W.

Neidhardt, Isabella
Needles, Anne M.
Norris, Dolly
North, Miss
Newall, Mrs. T. A.
Nancrede, Mrs. Dr.
Newbold, Emma

Ogden, Harriet
Ogden, Prudence

Pugh, Elizabeth
Parker, Eliza
Palmer, Sarah
Pancoast, Tacy R.
Paxson, Deborah
Pratt, Elizabeth
Porter, Elizabeth D.
Pugh, Sarah
Perot, Elizabeth
Plumley, Rebecca
Paul, Elizabeth
Porter, Emma
Pierce, Mrs. Charles
Perot, Caroline R.
Paleske, Susanna
Pepper, Sarah B.
Peal, Mrs. Rembr'ndt
Peters, Mary B.
Peters, Miss S.
Phillips, Ellen
Petit, Mrs. Dr.
Parker, Elizabeth
Price, Anne

Robertson, Mrs. A.
Rand, Mrs.
Reeseford, Mary
Rogers, Mrs. Wm.
Rogers, Mrs. Evans
Robinson, Mrs. D M.
Ruther, Mrs. C. J.
Rossiter, Margaret
Ruddick, Mrs.
Rouzee, Mary E.
Rowland, Elizabeth
Rankin, Jane
Riehle, C.

Stratton, Caroline
Sherman, Agnes G.
Smith, Ann
Smith, Sarah W.
Sully, Sally
Sexton, Maria
Smith, Mrs.
Skillman, Ura
Sill, Mrs. Joseph
Smyth, Elizabeth
Slade, Mrs.
Smith, Miss
Stone, Anna
Sleeper, Edith
Singer, Mrs. John
Smith, Mrs. W. R.
Spearing, Mary Ann
Saunders, Elizabeth
Sleeper, Mary
Shapley Mrs.
Somers, Eliza

Townsend, Mira
Townsend, Ann A.
Tyndale, Sarah
Taylor, Emily
Townsend, Hannah, Jr.,
Townsend, Beulah P.
Troth, Henrietta
Thompson, Adeline
Townsend, Elizabeth
Turner, Susan
Thorne, Mary S.
Todhunter, Mrs. Wm.
Towne, Mrs. J. Henry
Tiers, Mrs. Frank
Turner, Mrs. Fred'k
Turner, Mrs. Wm.
Tete, Mrs.
Taylor, Rebecca
Tyson, Martha H.
Town, Mrs. John
Thackara, Mrs. S. F.
Thatcher, M.
Tomlin, Abigail
Trotter, Eliza H.
Twitchel, Emily
Tyson, Mary J.
Tyler, Mrs. G. F.
Townsend Emily S.
Townsend, Elizabeth
Turner, Abbey
Twaddell, Mrs. E.

Wood, Susan
Williamson, Anna
Williamson, Mary
Walborn, Ellen
Webb, Maria
Webb, Sarah J.
Wharton, Anne
Wood, Mrs. G. A.
White, Lydia
Williams, Martha P.
Wager, Mrs. P.
Wescott, Mrs.
Worrall, Elizabeth
Wharton, Hannah
Wirt, Mrs. Wm.
Woodruff, Mrs.
Wyeth, Mrs. S. D.
Ward, Mary Ann
Wilson, Clarissa S.
Wallace, Margaretta
Williams, Sarah T.
Winslow, Emily
Wister, Elizabeth
Wood, Mary F.
Webb, Harriet

Yocum, Susanna

NAMES OF CONTRIBUTORS IN MONEY, GOODS, OR LABOR.

Alsop, A. E.
Adams, Samuel C.
Addicks, Vandusen & Smith
Alexander, Hugh
Archer, Ellis S.
Abbott, Redmond
Amanderson, Jr.
Ashton, John, Jr.
Anspach, Bro. & Co.
Allison, David A.
Adamson & Heins
Anderson, Mrs. W. V.
Ashurst, Richard

Brown, Joseph D.
Barton, Susan R.
Brady, P.
Brown, David S.
Barclay, Mrs. Andw.
Brown, Washington
Budd, Henry
Baldwin, Thomas
Baldwin, M. W.
Brock, John
Barker, J. R.
Boswell, James I.
Boyd, William S.
Barton, Isaac
Bullock, Martha
Burr, Joseph
Burling, B. S.
Bolden, George
Barron, George
Bailey, Lydia R.
Badger Mrs.
Brown, Ann T.
Bacon & Dilks
Bockius, J.
Bibighaus, ——
Bowlby, ——
Biddle, Anna
Blakiston & Wallace
Brown, J. D.
Branson, Samuel
Barnet, Nesbit & Garretson
Bringhurst, John
Baker, Henry
Biddle, W. & R.
Biddle, Clement
Buck & Morgan
Busch, ——
Bennett, Altemus L.
Baker, Elizabeth
Bartis, ——
Burton, Isaac
Brunner, M.
Bitting, Thos. R.
Bailey, J.
Baggs, James B.
Bailey, David
Barber, Edward
Barger, William
Bley, ——
Bowers, H. A.
Burton & Finn
Burton, Henry A.
Beans, Mary
Brand, Albert C.
Brown, Hannah
Bankson, ——
Bryan, George S.
Bain, Mrs. M.
Bryan, Ellen
Bland, Samuel
Bradford, Mrs. Saml.
Belrose & Faye
Bowen, B. B.
Butler, Thomas
Bowdle, Tristram
Bryan, C.
Berens, Dr. B.
Brown, Samuel

Corbit, Joseph
Corbit, Henry C.
Clark, Jane
Cope, Thomas P.
Cuthbert & Wetherill
Chur, A. Theodore
Conrad, Matthew
Carrigan, Jacob
Claghorn, John W.
Cassin, John
Cattell, Alexander G.
Collins, Wm. M.
Campbell, Alex. H.
Cooper, Hiram T.
Collins, Joseph
Clause & Griffith
Cluley, William
Clark, Jacob W.
Chapman, William
Collins & Robinson
Campion, Thomas
Cowpland, Joshua
Carter, C. J. H.
Cooper, Hannah
Chandler, Jos. R.
Clark & Cunningham
Cole, Edward
Cummings & Brodie,
Cummings, ——
Canby, Caleb
Clay, George
Cox, Gideon
Clark, ——
Clothier, Caleb
Chandler, Marine
Campbell, Mary
Connor, Mrs.

Campbell, Mrs.
Conrow, Nathan H.
Cavender, John H.
Caufman & Wolf
Campbell & Pharo

Davis, Edward M.
Davis, Isaac R.
Davis, Samuel N.
Derbyshire, A. I.
Dodson, Harriet
Dallett, E.
Dickson & Brother
Davis, Samuel H.
Dreby, Christian
Dallam, J. W.
Daniels & Smith
Dickinson, Sally N.
Dixon, Caleb I.
Donnelly, John
Dyott, Dr.
Dowler, Jacob
Dorsey, William
Dreby, Christian
Dorigo, F.
De Bequier, Miss
Dutton, Mrs.
Dilks, Miss
Dilworth, Wm.
Draper, Wm.

Esherick, Joseph
Eckel, John
Eckstein, John
Ellison, W., & Co.
Esher, Jacob
Ely, Kent, Brock & Co.
Eldridge, Levi
Ellis, N. & W.
Euston & Wier
Eiserman, D. & G.
Ellis, Amos
Ennion & Hopper
Elfelt, Simon, & Son
Ellis, David
Ellis, R.
Elliot, Hugh
Evans, Oliver
Eyre & Landell

Farnum, Henry
Farnum, Mrs. B
Fales, Lathrop & Co.
Furness, James T.
Felton & Zimmersling
Farr, John C.
Freeman, James A.
Flemming, Geo. M.
Field, Mrs. John
French, Wm. H.
Fitler, Theophilus
French & Richards
Fryer, William
Flint, Thomas
Fell, ——
Furniss, Brindly & Ash
Ford, John M.
Faust & Winebrenner
Fricke, H. & G.
Finley & Co.
Fisher, Mrs.
Field, Mrs.
Feinour, Mr.
Fortnum, Wm.

Grigg, John W.
Gilpin, Anna
Grew, Henry
Godley, Mrs. Jesse
Gillilan A. Hudson
Gibbs, John W.
Garrison, John
Gemmill, James R.
Gumbs, Mrs.
Goff, J. W.
Gray, Orlando
Gladding, M.
Gilpin, Mrs. Charles
Groves & Brother
Gaskill, Aaron W.
Golder, Robert
Gibbs, Mrs.
Gladdings, John
Gardiner, Dr.
Gillingham, Deborah
Griscom, Dr. John
Gibson, John
Goodwin, P.
Grum, Mrs.
Gendell, John A.

Hallowell, Hannah P.
Hartley & Knight
Heald, Bucknor, & Co.
Hankins, Wm. H.
Hillborn, Cyrus
Hudson, Thomas
Hinchman, Anna W.
Hart, A.
Howell, Joseph
Hunt, Uriah
Hays & Walter
Howard, James W.
Hoopes & Andrews
Hayes, Samuel
Hall & Boardman
Hobensack, J. N.
Hammett & Hiles
Hamaker & Earley
Hammersley, George
Hart, Valentine
Harned, John
Hieskill, Ferdinand
Hieskill, Colson
Hoskins, Francis
Heintzleman & Co.
Hart, Samuel
Hancock, Biddle
Howard, William
Howell & Brother
Hibbs, J. G.

Henry, John W.
Hays, Samuel
Harley, J. S.
Hill, John
Hankins, W. H.
Hartshorn, Anna
Hazard, Alexander
Harper, Mrs.
Hartley, ——
Hover, Joseph E.
Harper, Benjamin
Hall, Mrs.
Harker & Caldwell
Hanson, A. F.
Horstman, Mrs.

Ingleby, J. Campbell

Johnson, Robert
Jordan, Jane
Jeanes, Samuel
Jackson, Dr. Samuel
Jenkins, Hunn
Johnson, Topliff
Jenkins, Jabez
Jones, William
Johnson & Sterrett
Justice & Kenderdine
Jordan, Jacob
Jones, Joseph W.
Jones, Wm. D.
Jones, Col. Sidney
Jones, J.
Johnson, Jane
Jones, S. B.
Johnson, Mrs. Laurence
Jones, Dillwyn
Jones, Mrs. Caleb
Johns & Payne

Kneedler, Jesse
Kennedy, J. M., & Co.
Keyser, P. A.
Kent & Santee
Keen & Coates
Kirkpatrick, James Y.
Kennedy, Harriet
Kenderdine, Charles
Koons & Heilman
Klett, Frederick
Kendall, R. G.
Kellar, ——
Kerr, ——
Kugler, Dr.
Knight, A. L., & Co.
Kenny, S. G.
Klapp, Dr.
King, Mrs.
Keats, Miss

Lovering, J. S.
Livingston, Mrs
Lukens, Reuben
Lennig, Charles
Lewis, A. J.
Louton, William T.
Longstreth, M. H.
Lewis, William
Lord, Mrs.
Lewis, Joseph S.
Lister, Samuel
Lippincott, J. B.
Legget, R.
Lybrand, C. D.
Leeds, Nathan, & Co.
Landreth, D.
Levick, Eben
Levy, G. J.
Lippincott, Aaron S.
Lipman, Hyman
Laws, George
Lothrop, Mrs.
Lyons, Mary
Langstroth, Thomas
Loud, Mrs. Thomas
Levering, Mrs.
Longstreth, Charles

Mott, James
Mellor, Thomas
McKean, H. Pratt
Myers, John B.
Mitchell, Mrs. James
Moore, Heyl & Co.
Murphey, James
Megarge, Samuel
Morgan, William C.
Mason & Kirkland
Mackey, C. C
Mentien, J. W.
Martin, Oliver
Maison, P.
Metler, G. W.
Moore, James T.
Morton, S. C.
Mentz & Rovoudt
Mount, E.
Meany, Thomas
McDonald, Wm.
McEwen & Sheetz
Morgan, Joseph
Mitchell, J.
Mench, C. B.
Moyer & Hazard
Moore, C. M.
McQuaid, Felix
Moore, J. W.
Mitchell, S. Augustus
M. A. M.
Miller, Daniel, Jr.
Moore & Campion
McDonough, A.
Morris, Charles M.
Megarge, Charles
McCurdy & Co.
Meredith, Edwin
Matsinger, ——
McNeal, Charles
Morgan & Co.
McCallment, J. W.
Moore, Mary
McKeever, Mrs.
Middleton, Samuel

Moore, Gabriel
McDowell, Joseph
Middleton, Charles

Neal, Daniel
Nesbit, Alexander
Newbold, Emma
Newberry, John
Newland E.
Newkirk, H.
Neal, William
Neff, R. K.

Ogle, Williams
Oat, George
Ogden, John M.
O'Brien, Laurence
Orne, J. B.
Ogden, ——
Ogden, Jesse

Price, Richard
Pugh, Isaac
Parker, Joseph, Jr.
Price, Joshua L.
Parrish, George D.
Parrish, Dillwyn
Patterson, ——
Phipps, Stephen
Porter & English
Potts, M. B.
Potter, W. A.
Parker, John
Parker, Joseph
Peters, James
Perrine, Mrs.
Phipps, Sarah
Parry & Randolph
Phipps, Charles
Price, Eli K.
Patterson, Rutter & Co.
Parker, Charles
Patterson, Dr. H. S.
Pratt, ——
Peters, Miss
Peddrick, Geo. L.
Potts, Lawrence
Pugh, Samuel
Porter & English
Poulteny, Letitia
Parke, Hannah
Perkins & Co.
Patton, John W.
Pepper, Henry J.
Pleis, J. F.
Pond, J.
Potts, W. B.

Reynolds, McFarland & Co.
Ridgway, Thomas
Robbins, Thomas
Remington, William
Rowand & Walton
Richardson, Wm.
Robertson, William
Rowland, James & Co.
Rowland, James
Reeves, Biddle
Ridgway, Samuel H.
Rice, John
Ritter, J. L. & B. J.
Repplier & Co.
Rohrman, J. V.
Ridney, H. F. & W.
Reid, John
Reeve, Robert
Reeve, Joel
Rochefort, ——
Reeve, Elwood
Rock & Blanchard
Randall, Mr. B.
Robins, Samuel
Ripka, Joseph
Robb, Mrs.
Raguel, Mrs.
Rosenthal, Zadoc P.
Richards, Thomas
Reed, Jacob
Reed, T. S.
Roussel, Eugene

Stemmill, Benj. B.
Sykes, Mrs. Robert
Sharpless, Townsend
Sharpless, Samuel J.
Sharpless, Dr. J. T.
Sharpless, Maria
Strawbridge, George
Stoever, F.
Stuart, George W.
Simpson, E.
Soutter, Robert, Jr.
Stewart, H. B.
Simes, S.
Sanderson, Wood, & Co.
Snyder, George
Shinnick, L.
Stewart, B. D.
Siter, James, & Co.
Smith, Charlotte A.
Shoemaker, Charles
Snowden, Benjamin
Sell and Walter
Stein, H. G.
Stetler, John M.
Smith, Hugh
Smith, George K.
Savage & James
Stoutenberg, J.
Stevenson, Wm.
Smith, ——
Shoemaker, Robert
Spear, J. D.
Sickel, J.
Sprague, James H.
Smith, Hugh
Snowden, Edward
Stradling, ——
Stratton, John
Shinn, Asa
Sargent & Gustine
Sherborne, ——
Stotesbury & Ayre
Smith, Mrs.
Sharpless, H. G.
Sharpless, Charles J.

Shee & Worrell
Swain, Eliza
Smithers, Richard
Schenck, Dr.
Smith, T. B.
Stackhouse, P., Jr.
Stroud, James
Scull, David
Smith, Mrs. J. R. C.
Slade, Mrs.
Schrack, Christian

Townsend, Samuel
Tingley, B. W.
Taylor, Levi
Townsend, Solomon
Toppan, Charles
Turner, Joseph
Taylor, Benjamin
Taylor, N. & G.
Trotter, Nathan
Townsend, Edward
Thompson, Benjamin
Thorne, Charles
Thomas, John
Tatum, Daniel
Taylor, Mrs.
Tiers, J.
Thomason, John
Tucker, John
Thouron & Co.
Tustin, J. E.
Thompson, J. Edgar
Tarr, Henry S.
Thum, ——

Vanderkemp, C. D.
Vezin, Charles
Vandeweer, W. &. S.
Vaughn & Davis
Vanstavoren, C.
Vanmeter, ——
Vansant, Mary

Wetherill, John P.
White, Josiah
Williamson, I. V.
Wood, Joseph
Warner, Joseph
Webb, Reuben
Wood, Richard D.
White, Thomas
Wright, John
Wetherill, George D.
Weaver, George J.
Watson, George W.
Whitecar, Ware &
Walley, Samuel S.
Wolfe & Rantenburg
Wickersham, Eliza C.
Williams & Brown
Williams, T. & Co.
Warner, F. V. & Co.
Webster & Patterson
Wetherill, J. M.
Williams, John
Williamson, Jos. D.
Williams & Lasher
Wheeler, J. J.
Whilden, Alexander
Whitall, John M.
Walsh, Robt. F.
Whelan, J. G.
Warnock, Mrs. Wm.
Warnock, Mrs. Robt.
Williamson & Davis
Williams, Reed & Co.
Wayne & Simmons
Wainwright & Gillingham
Wetherill, John M.
Woolridge, J. W.
Wright & Hunter
Wayne, William
Wainwright, William
Watson, Brock
Watson, Thomas & Sons.
Wharton, Deborah
Worrall, Mrs. A.
Wright, Joseph
Williamson, Passmore
Welling, Charles H.
Wallace, Robert B.
White, Miss
Whitman, S. F.
Walmsley, Wm.
Wilson, C. T.
Wildman, Dr.

Young, Alexander
Yarnall, Benjamin H.
Young, James
Yerkes, Wm.
Young & Randolph
Young & O'Farrell
Young, A. R.
Yarrow, Mrs. John
Zeiber, G. B.

We are indebted to the kindness of several persons for anonymous contributions, and to $9 43 from some little girls, from 5 to 12 years of age, pupils at Miss James' Academy.

Form of a Bequest of Personal Estate.

I give and bequeath to the Rosine Association of Philadelphia, and their successors, the sum of dollars, towards promoting the objects of said Society.

Form of a Bequest of Real Estate.

I give and devise to the Rosine Association of Philadelphia, or their successors, all that (here describe the property), together with the appurtenances, to hold to the said Rosine Association of Philadelphia, and their successors, forever, for them to dispose of and convey in any manner which will promote the objects of said Society.

VISITS TO HOUSES OF IMMORAL CHARACTER.

Extract from a Letter to H. P.

Amid the various duties arising from our efforts to save some of the poor, erring children of our city, we have felt it right to visit some of the houses where they cluster together, in hopes that a word dropped in season may find a place in some heart, and awaken feelings that may lead them to abandon their present condition, and have faith, that we can be useful to them, and accomplish for them what they feel is altogether impossible for them to attain by their own efforts,—namely, a restoration to a life of usefulness, and of comparative happiness. Persons often ask, Are you not afraid to go to such places? Why should we be afraid? We go, hoping to do them good; and, though we speak plainly, yet they know we mean only kindness to them; and we have rarely met with any rudeness, even among the most degraded. Accompanied by Mrs. F., I went to the house of a woman whom we had been cautioned against visiting, as being so coarse and rude, that she would probably be uncivil to us. When we knocked at the door, she came to it, and only opened it a few inches wide, and, seeing we did not look like her usual visitors, said, roughly, "What do you want?" We told her, we wanted to pay her a visit. This she unceremoniously declined. We said, we wished to inform her what we were trying to do for the unfortunate, that we wanted her to help us, and, if she would let us come in, we thought we could interest her. For some time she kept the door very nearly closed, but, as we talked, it seemed unconsciously to open, until at last she bade us come in. We entered. Her tone and demeanor were defiant and repulsive, and her attitude, as she took her seat, indicated that she had steeled her heart, and was determined that we should not creep into it. Of all this we took no notice, but spoke with her gently and kindly. After a time, she assembled her family, and we conversed with them altogether. Of the inmates of the house, I cannot speak now, but they inspired us with feelings of deep interest, and our remarks were principally addressed to them, while we observed, that, as the conversation progressed, the attitude and manner of the mistress changed, until at last she sprang from her chair, and, seizing a stool, placed it at our feet (as Mrs. F. and myself happened to be sitting together on the sofa), and, seating herself upon it, laid one of her hands on each of ours, and looked up in our faces, with the simple earnestness of a child that is listening to the loving words of its mother. There was a world of wealth in that woman's heart, and she laid it all open before us, and told us her story of her good and evil deeds, of her changing her name, that those she loved might not be disgraced by her conduct, of her resentment and embittered feelings because society had placed its foot upon her, and sentenced her to a life of misery, as the penalty for her transgression, while her tempter stood amid the princes of the land, covered with honors. We shall never forget that woman. We could have shed tears with her, as, welling up from her heart's deep fountain, came the emotions and tenderness that had been buried for years. And there is many another heart besides hers, that is so covered up and obscured by the miseries and vices by which it has been surrounded, that the superficial observer thinks, that if there was ever goodness there, it must have died out long ago. But, it is there still! The weeds may cover it, and the poisonous malaria that surrounds it may produce only noxious influences, but if one sunbeam can only reach down into those depths, where the memories of early years and loving and gentle affections lie sleeping, they may spring again into life, and the hidden germ, warmed and invigorated, may blossom once more with renewed beauty.

Many of these visits have been deeply interesting, and we always feel the great necessity of a proper qualification to speak wisely and rightly on such occasions. Some time since, one of our ladies accompanied me to a house, where I had been once before, to see a young girl, whom we hoped to be able to save from the abandoned life she was leading; and, after our interview with her, we were passing away from the house, when, in a back room, we saw a party seated at a table playing cards. We stopped, and I opened my bundle, and laid before each of the young men the tract, headed, "The Young Man from Home;" saying, "Young men, I wish to give you some better employment than spending your time in that way." One of them read the title, and said, "He was at home anywhere!" and another remarked, "That times were dull; they had nothing else to do." I replied, "That times must be dull indeed if they could find nothing better to do. I was fifty years of age, and had never found a day yet that I had not something better to do than playing cards in a house of ill-fame." When we first spoke to them, they answered in a jesting tone and manner, probably amused at our addressing them, though mortified at our finding them there; but, as the conversation progressed, they became serious, and one of them entirely silent. The other one said, "It was a difficult thing for a young man to know what to do, there were so many faiths, and so many churches—so many false professors of religion, that he believed that there were as good people in these houses as in the churches; and the principal difference was, that here they were more honest, and showed what they were." Our reply to this was, "It matters not to thee how many faiths, or how many churches there are—whether Catholic, Methodist, Presbyterian, or Quaker—whether we are true or false to our religion, or even if the whole world be hypocrites; it is all nothing to thee. There is that in thy own mind that tells thee what is right and wrong, and that is all that is important for thee. Obedience to that consciousness of right will never lead thee into such a house as this, or into such society." "Ah!" said he, in a saddened tone, "I fear I shall never do any good. I have had a great deal of good advice from a Quaker gentleman, T. S." "He is my brother," I remarked, "and I know he never advised thee to frequent such places as this. Where did you meet?" thinking perhaps he might have been an apprentice, or in his employ. "Oh," he said, "at Frankford, or Germantown, or somewhere." By this evasion, with some of his previous remarks, it struck me, that perhaps my brother, who is a prison visitor, might possibly have met him there, though his appearance was very respectable, and I quickly asked, "Was it at the Eastern——?" I there stopped. He replied, "No, no, I never was that low." Considerable was then said on the proper employment of time, of the evils attending a course of licentiousness, of our duties to our Creator, and to one another. Meanwhile, the game of cards had gone on slowly; occasionally one was thrown down, but evidently all were deeply interested in the conversation. Our visit was ended; but, as we turned to go, I said to the young man, "I would like to know thy name." In a moment his head was bent to the table, and we could see the blood suffuse it to the deepest hue. In a tone that bespoke my feelings, I said, "Oh, how sad it is to see a young man place himself in a position where he is ashamed to tell his own name." The cards were dashed upon the table, he sprang from his seat, and, with his cheeks covered with tears, rushed out of the house. We silently followed.

May the heart that was touched at that period by the visitation of the feeling within himself, to which we had referred him, suffer its refining influence to operate upon his soul, until he can know a proper appreciation of that time, that was given for better, higher, and holier purposes. Sisters, this is our missionary work; we need not go to the land of the distant heathen, the heathen may be found at our doors. There are thousands around us to whom the Gospel is never preached. We want no doctrines, we want no sects, but we need that living Gospel of "doing justice, loving mercy, and walking humbly," that will go to the lowest haunts of vice and misery, and snatch the victims there from the enthralment of their own sins and those of others; convince them there is a better way, and that we will help them to attain it; and let our faith, by speaking through our actions, show that we believe we have one Father in Heaven, and that we all are brethren.

A year after this visit, a young woman who had come into the Rosine said, she had met a young man a few days before in the street, with whom she had formerly been acquainted, and asked him to come and visit her. "I don't go to such places any more," he replied; and, upon her inquiring how that happened, he related the conversation that had taken place a year before with two ladies whom he met at the house of Mrs. H. She repeated almost literally the remarks that had been made.

THE SEMI-ANNUAL REPORT OF THE MANAGERS OF THE ROSINE ASSOCIATION.

October 7th, 1848.

At our Annual Meeting in April, the Managers of the Rosine Association presented to you a statement of their transactions to that period, with a history of our progress in the great work in which we are engaged. Since then we have endeavored to advance as much as possible towards that degree of usefulness in the cause of humanity which your feelings, as well as our own, desired, and for which we were appointed your agents. In pursuing our vocation our labors have not been confined to our house and family. Upwards of one hundred and sixty visits have been paid in houses of immoral character. Many of those visits have been deeply interesting, and while we have been sensible that this missionary work is one of vast importance, we have earnestly desired that we might have the proper qualification for it, and that a blessing might rest upon our endeavors to convince those unfortunate women that Providence had assigned to them a higher, nobler station than that, in which the mental endowments were sunk in the gratification of the low animal propensities, and that a higher, better destiny awaited them, if, breaking from the thraldom of the debasing fetters that bound them, the more elevated feelings of their nature were allowed to resume their proper control. We must acknowledge the kindness and politeness that have greeted us, and the expressions of gratitude that have flowed from many who had long been unused to kindness from those, who, clothed in the garments of virtue, should have remembered that their duty was not to sink to lower infamy those who had fallen, but to endeavor to follow the example of Christ, who associated with sinners that he might speak to them the words of life and love, and show them by his bright example the beauty and purity of holiness.

Since the opening of the Rosine School, we have had forty women under our care, fifteen of whom are still in the house, learning trades, and increasing their knowledge of all kinds of business. Of a number of those who have left us, we have very favorable accounts, and have reason to believe their conduct has been satisfactory to their employers, and creditable to themselves. We would fain have all who come to us firm in their resolves to continue in the path of rectitude; but the habit of inebriation—which is the usual companion of other vices—is so powerful, that in many cases the good resolve, and the aspirations after better things, yield to that thirst which is never quenched, and the wretched victim sacrifices hope, happiness, and salvation, physically and mentally, for that draught which has ever proved the greatest curse of the race.

Six of our number have gone to the almshouse; indisposition rendering them unsuitable inmates in our family—the institution not being a hospital, but a house of industry, to qualify those who are able and willing to support themselves in a respectable manner by their own labor, and a home, where the penitent may know that kindness will greet her, and where the desires of her better nature will meet with sympathy and encouragement, education and instruction in various employments prepare her for usefulness, and she will be sustained in her efforts to regain her self-respect, and that of mankind.

Until within the last two months, our school has been conducted by our members; but our various engagements rendering it impossible at all times to attend to the duties, we have thought proper to employ a teacher, who devotes four evenings in each week to the task of instruction, in which she is occasionally aided by others. We have been highly gratified by the progress of many of our scholars, fourteen of whom could not read when they came to us, and several did not know a letter.

Two evenings in the week are devoted to keeping their clothes in order, and attending to the necessary weekly duties. On the Sabbath afternoon we have a meeting for worship, which is attended by professors of various denominations, and one of our members usually spends the Sabbath eve with the family, which is occupied with suitable reading and conversation.

As it is now a year since the opening of the house, it is proper to report the amount of work done by our inmates, within that period. Owing to the extreme ignorance of many, great care and exertion have been required in this department, and we have watched with pleasure and satisfaction the desire of improvement that has been generally manifested, and the struggle to overcome the idle habits that are the usual accompaniments of a life of irregularity and vice. In some of the institutions for the same class of persons, the girls are occupied in sewing buttons on cards, and similar employments, which are more profitable in a pecuniary way than making clothing; but we consider it of the greatest importance to qualify them for general usefulness in families, and therefore have thought it right to sacrifice the pecuniary advantage of the Institution, for the increased benefit of the inmates.

We wish to interest our members to bring their tailoring and mantua-making to the house, as we have had to procure work from tailors, and the compensation is so small, that our work-room has not availed the profits it might if our members had more generally become our customers. Many of those who come into our family are exceedingly bare of clothing, and we have thought it right to give to all the privilege of wearing the clothing belonging to the house (while with us); and, in many instances, propriety requires that we should give them various articles when they leave, which adds considerably to our expenses. Contributions of clothing would therefore be very acceptable. The number of articles made for the use of the family amount to 540: 21 bed-ticks, 98 pillows and cases, 7 bolsters and cases, 23 bed-spreads, 68 sheets, 8 table-cloths, 38 comfortables, 71 towels, 55 dresses, 50 chemises, 32 skirts, 46 aprons, 27 handkerchiefs, and 2 bed-gowns.

For customers, 473 garments have been made:

124 vests, producing - - - -	$63 12
46 pairs of pantaloons, - - -	27 00
70 shirts, - - - - - - -	43 74
55 dresses, - - - - - - -	38 25
Sundry articles, numbering 178, - -	43 20
Total, 473 for - - -	$215 31

The amount of our expenses, including rent, furnishing, salaries, alterations and repairs to the house, and family expenses, has been, $2,113 99.

What our expenses will be in the future we cannot say, but they will probably average $1,600. To meet this, we have the interest on the

Mortgage on the house, - - -	$78 00
On $1400 loaned, - - - -	84 00
Annual subscriptions from members, -	415 00
Probable income from employment of inmates, - - - - - - -	300 00
Annual subscriptions from gentlemen,	140 00
	$1,017 00

By this statement, we shall yet need an increased income of $600 to balance our accounts.

How this can be raised, we must leave to your wisdom to devise. We have now four hundred members, who are annual contributors, generally paying $1 00. If those among them, who feel their circumstances will warrant it, will pay two dollars per annum, this will probably raise two hundred more, and if every member will feel bound to obtain at least one or more among her friends, we might soon feel that our family is permanently established.

Efforts have been made at our meeting to organize an efficient collecting committee, to invite our citizens to become subscribers to a fund that would enable us to purchase the house, and insure the permanent support of the establishment. To some of the members of this committee we are indebted for considerable assistance, but the labor has fallen in a great degree upon the managers, to make collections and procure subscribers. This, in connection with their other duties, has absorbed considerable time, more at some periods than they felt they were altogether warranted in bestowing. We therefore propose, that our members generally be invited to procure contributions and subscriptions, and that some others may be added to the collecting committee, whose hearts are in the work, and who are willing to speak for those who cannot speak for themselves.

At the period of our annual meeting we had applied to the Legislature for an Act of Incorporation. This was obtained soon after, and we are now legally qualified to act in a society capacity, and receive legacies. One of our friends, who attended our annual meeting, and became deeply interested, was taken sick a few days afterwards, and looking forward to a change, made her *will*, and left the Rosine Association one hundred dollars. Soon after she passed away to that region where, we hope, she will be numbered with those who will welcome the redeemed Magdalen to heaven. The legacy will be paid in a few months.

Several cases coming under our notice of females desiring employment having been sent to houses of ill-fame from Intelligence Offices, and through advertisements in the newspapers; and knowing that women are always liable to be thus drawn into the haunts of sin, and exposed to temptation through deceptive allurements, the managers have thought it right to open an Intelligence Office for women and children, believing the usefulness of the Society may thus be increased, and many perhaps saved from ruin. Situations have already been procured for forty-five women and children.

Applications have been made to us on several occasions to receive women who have been inebriates, but who have not been in habits of licentiousness; and also to take charge of young girls, who were in imminent danger of being drawn into a course of vice, if the Society did not give them the protection of a home, and the influence of educational and other advantages. Acting upon the principle that "prevention is better than cure," we have taken some such individuals under our care. How far this may be in accordance with the views of the Society we know not, but we desire to be advised on the subject.

We feel it to be a matter of great importance, that a house should be open for the reception of virtuous but destitute women and children, until homes in suitable families could be procured for them. In this Asylum, girls out of place, but who have some means, could be boarded on moderate terms, and thus safely protected until situations could be obtained. We believe that many might thus be saved from the temptations to which they are subjected in their homeless and friendless condition.

REPORT READ AT THE SEMI-ANNUAL MEETING OF THE ROSINE ASSOCIATION.

Since our Annual Meeting, one of our members, believing that a more thorough knowledge of the labors of the friends of humanity in other cities, would enable us to act with increased judgment in our own Institution, visited New York and Boston, to gain information relative to the various Associations that have been formed to correct and reform the vicious and degraded, and also to assist the innocent, the virtuous, and the destitute children of poverty and misfortune. In this journey, she saw much to convince her, that though everywhere (if we search below the surface), we find we are more or less guilty, by our penuriousness, thoughtlessness, and indifference, of causing or contributing to the poverty, and often the consequent depravity of many of our sex, yet the Almighty is ever prompting his children who desire to walk in his ways, to devote their energies, their leisure, and their funds, to the relief of those who have been the victims of oppression, or neglected moral and religious culture.

A display of eloquence may warm the fancy, and interest the feelings, may excite our admiration and approbation, but a simple narrative of facts speaks to our hearts, awakens our sympathies, and prompts the hand and the tongue to action—such facts press upon the mind of the writer, and urge her to lay before you in the simplest manner the information that others are up and doing—their hands are to the plough, and their motto is—"We will do what we can."

The first visit paid was to the Tombs, in New York, to which place several others were made subsequently. The Report of the Prison Society of 1845, states the average number of women in that prison, is 60 or 70, and that in the past year, 1970 were committed, all of whom were without any employment whatever. Here, we found in the upper rooms a number of young girls, from ten to twenty years of age, associating together. It was a sad sight to see the little vagrant of ten or twelve years, committed for the want of a proper home, cast into companionship with those, whose habits had taken from them a name in respectable society, and whose corrupting influence must be powerful over those neglected and unfortunate children. In the yard of the prison were about thirty women, seated on benches, many (perhaps the greatest number), showing by their wretched, bloated faces, a proof of the cause of their incarceration. Others were in the cells, or walking in the entries, but with every opportunity to circulate the poison that festered their own minds, and created a malaria wherever they moved or breathed.

On the Sabbath afternoon, a temperance meeting was held in the prison, which, under other circumstances, might have been profitable, but under the existing ones, the beneficial effect is exceedingly doubtful. The men and boys, a motley crew indeed, stood in the galleries of the corridor where the meeting was held, and the female prisoners were seated on the benches below, exposed to the gaze of those above, and also, to that of a number of spectators, whom curiosity alone appeared to have drawn to witness the exhibition. This exposure of the prisoners to each other, and to the public, must have a disastrous effect, particularly on the women, if only one particle of shame yet lingered in their minds, or they should be recognized after leaving the prison.

But sad as these circumstances are, they have been worse. Formerly these women and children were under the charge of men only (doubtless sometimes illy fitted for the station), and no female voice spoke to them in tones of condemnation, instruction, or encouragement. But Providence raised up a band of devoted women, opened for them the doors of that prison, and through their influence a matron was introduced, and a regular series of visits made to the miserable inmates. They have now the opportunity of hearing the Scriptures read, the utterance of heartfelt prayer, and the words of inquiry, of admonition, and of sympathy, from female lips. The writer met several of those ladies there, and understood some of them devoted part of every Sabbath to this blessed mission.

Blackwell's Island was also visited. To this prison women are sent, who are sentenced to periods of confinement of from one to six months. A large majority of these cases are from disorderly houses; women (many of them young), to whom the glass, profane oath, and licentious practices, are the habits of daily life. To some of these, the constant changes are from the abode of drunkenness and debauchery to the almshouse, and the prison. Cases have been known, where women have been thus imprisoned *forty* times, and in their midst were several young girls, whose countenances, manners, and histories, told that the blight of the destroyer had but lately passed over them. From the Matron we learned, that there were 260 women there; one hundred in the hospital; and one hundred and sixty in a frame shantee, shut up together during the day, often without employment, and corrupting, by this dreadful association, the good that might yet remain in a single inmate. It was a distressing scene to witness, and to know that so little effort was made to cultivate industrious habits, or reform the morals of that degraded company; to the most of whom, perhaps to all, Providence had given the capacity to be useful, respectable, religious women. From occasional visits to these prisons, benevolent, earnest minds have seen the necessity, not only of efforts to remedy these evils, but that a preventive power could and would effect great benefits to the unfortunate daughters of poverty, ignorance, and crime. Prompted by these feelings, two societies of women have arisen, whose labors are enlisted for that unfortunate class. The female branch of the Prison Association has a temporary home, prepared for such as they may have reason to believe, can be benefited by being under their care; and for whom situations are found as soon as practicable. From the Annual Report of 1847, this society has had in charge ninety-nine individuals, for many of whom places have been procured. Of these, they have had favorable accounts of thirty-eight, and twenty were still at the Home.

The Female Moral Reform Association have also an Institution called "The House of Industry, and Home of the Friendless," for the reception of virtuous, but destitute women and children, until situations are provided for them. These ladies have entered into an extensive field of labor. From May 1st, 1847, to April 31st, 1848, six hundred and five women and children have been under their care; of this number 334 have been adults, and 271 children; 150 of these women could not read.

They have also opened an Intelligence Office, that they might, through their efforts, save the innocent from being sent to the abode of "her whose steps lead down to hell," or betrayed into the power of the destroyer, and that the destitute and the stranger might have their wandering steps guided to homes of respectability and usefulness. During the past year 1415 women applied to them for situations. Of these 541 obtained employment; many others applied, but not being of that class that could properly be placed in families, their names were not registered. In consequence of so many more persons applying for situations than of housekeepers desiring domestics, many have continued to resort to the office, week after week, until their funds were exhausted, and the watch-house became their only home, if, in their desperation, they were not tempted to turn as a last resource to a life of crime. These facts coming daily before the managers, they felt the absolute necessity of more enlarged facilities to extend the great work Providence had given them.

Auxiliary societies have been formed throughout

the state, and money raised, and clothing sent to aid them, not only in New York, but from other states. During the past year, 197 boxes, barrels, etc., containing clothing, bedding, fruit, and vegetables, designed for the use of the Institution, have been received from the auxiliaries and other friends, and eleven thousand seven hundred dollars contributed to enable them to build a suitable house, and prepare a temporary abode, where the helpless orphan, and the destitute and friendless woman, may fly for a season, and feel that there they may truly find a home. A lot has been purchased, and the building commenced.

In addition to these extensive operations in the cause of humanity, the Society publishes a paper called the "Advocate of Moral Reform," of which they send 10,000 copies to act as missionaries in as many families, and 40,000 pages of tracts emanate from that office, speaking their words of advice and consolation to the thoughtless, the vicious, or the distressed. They have also published 10,000 copies of the "Walks of Usefulness," a valuable work which ought to be read in every family.

To this account we may add that woman's heart has been so awakened to the necessities and capability of this noble enterprise, that one thousand and six women have become life members of the Society.

The Magdalen Society of New York (also under the care of females), has been fifteen years in operation. In the past year, forty-seven women have been under the care of that association, and seventeen are now inmates of the Asylum. Like ourselves, they have had their trials and discouragements, but with us they can rejoice in believing that though as formerly, some seed may be thrown upon stony ground, and some may be choked by briers, yet some has fallen on a fertile soil, that is bringing forth good fruit, with a hopeful promise for the future.

In Boston, the society for the same class of persons, has at present a fine large new building, called the Penitent Females' Refuge. For a number of years they struggled with pecuniary and other difficulties, which they have now surmounted, and the society appears to be placed upon a permanent basis. When visited in July, they had 18 inmates. In the comparison between the Institutions in New York, Boston, and our Rosine, they have the advantage in having more extensive buildings, and the opportunity to accommodate each individual with a separate apartment, but in other respects we congratulate ourselves, that, with our plan of operation, we feel we can do more good than we could in pursuing theirs.

By the introduction of trades, OUR HOME may be truly called a school, as besides the usual branches of English education, every individual who wishes may become thoroughly versed in tailoring, mantua-making, plain sewing, cooking, and house-work.

In the Asylums, both in Boston and New York, occasional cases have been received, of women who have been the victims of intemperance, but, who have not deviated from the path of virtue, and of young girls, whose situations of danger called for protection, instruction, and care, which, if not bestowed, the Divine power alone could have saved from degradation and vice.

We, too, have had similar applications. The intemperate woman has flown to us, asking us to protect her from her own debasing habits, and the innocent girl, whom circumstances had placed upon the brink of ruin, have been brought to us, even by those whose houses were the abodes of licentiousness; and the shelter of our house and the benefits of our institution have been craved by them, with all the earnestness of supplication, for the poor child, who, unconscious of the dreadful horrors of that gulf before her, thoughtlessly and carelessly approached the awful precipice, over which, if she fell, infamy and moral and spiritual death would be her portion. How far propriety may warrant us in receiving such into our home, ought now to be the subject of consideration.

By the 10th Annual Report of the Moral Reform Society in Boston, we find they are following in the footsteps of the New York Society, in publishing a newspaper called the "Friend of Virtue," forming auxiliary societies throughout the state, keeping an intelligence office, and providing a temporary home for the orphan or neglected child, and the destitute and homeless woman.

They, too, have struggled with pecuniary and other discouragements, but, as their objects became known, and the public interested, their difficulties are decreasing, and they are gaining that appreciation and sympathy that will enable them to work more effectually in the cause of humanity.

The number of individuals received into their temporary Home, during the past year, was 193, of whom they say 86 are known to be doing well.

Some have not been heard from, and others are bad, or doubtful cases; 12 infants have been born in the house, and 12 received after birth. The Intelligence Office is credited with $527, received from applicants, and 800 women and children have been provided with respectable homes.

They have lately removed to a large and commodious house, and eleven auxiliary societies have each contributed materials to furnish one room. Their address to their friends is worthy of quotation, being equally applicable to them and to us. "After having done so much, will our contributors suspend their efforts? There can be no rest from paying our rent; no rest from sustaining the Home; no rest from clothing the destitute; no rest from giving bread to those who devote all their time to the cause; and there is no rest for those who feel bound to this labor of love, for the neglected, the destitute, and the wretched."

Another society in Boston claims our notice. It is the Needlewoman's Friend Society; 175 women have been employed during the past year, and sixteen hundred dollars expended in the payment of their labor. They have a store where garments made by these persons are disposed of, and also fancy or other articles are sold on commission for those who need support, yet are reluctant to have their wants known. This Society also performs an incalculable amount of good, but the low prices paid for woman's labor, in every department, renders it impossible for the weary, worn-out seamstress, with the greatest exertion, to do more than gain a bare subsistence.

In referring to the statistics of these different associations, we are led to reflect upon the causes of crime and destitution, and though various influences are powerful to effect the wonderful amount of vice and misery with which our land is deluged, yet we rise from this examination with the full conviction, that in woman as in man, the same causes produce the same effects, and that if careful reports were kept in these institutions, they would stand in about the same ratio as those presented by our prisons. These tell us that ignorance, intemperance, and the want of early industrious business habits, bring shame, ruin, and misery in their train. From reports of different institutions, we make some extracts, because they are matters of which women generally know little, and because they are important, as they ought to influence every one in our community to exert themselves to remove evils which are the parents of every degree of vice.

Robert Wiltse, agent of the Sing-Sing Prison, states, that in 1834, the convicts there numbered 842; 170 of whom could not read; 34 had never been at school; 85 could read but not write; 42 had a common English education; 38 had been in college; 510 could read and write, but many very imperfectly; 485 of these were habitual drunkards, and one-third of the whole number had committed their respective crimes under the influence of liquor; 161 were orphans at 18 years; 48 before they were 5 years; 72 between 5 and 14 years. The convictions of a large majority of these cases may be traced to a total neglect on the part of their parents or guardians in educating them, and confining their attention to some regular systematic business; 257 had intemperate parents; 397 had lost, or left parents before they were 21 years of age; 48 before 10 years of age; 352 had been married; 86 had deserted wives.

The Rev. Mr. Smith, Chaplain of the Auburn Prison, New York, states, that in 1834, the convicts in that prison numbered 670; of these, 188 were without education; 267 with very little; 204 with common; 8 with academical; 3 with collegiate. Of these 670, but 8 were total abstinents; 492 were under the influence of liquor when their crimes were committed.

Mr. Pillsbury, Warden of the Connecticut State Prison, states the number of convicts to be 180. No convict there has ever received a college or classical education. The proportion in this prison of those who could not read has been 22 in 100. Who could read but not write, 32 in a hundred; could do both, 46 in 100; read, write, and cipher, 8 in 100; never learnt a trade, 72 in 100; began to learn trades, but abandoned them, and did not follow any, 24 in 100; have followed regular trades, only 4 in the 100; committed crimes while intoxicated, 44 in 100; who could read, write, and were temperate, 2 in 100; of convicts who could read, write, are temperate, and followed a trade, *not one;* could read, write, and worked at trades, 4 in 100; owners of real estate, 6 in 100; owners of real estate and temperate, 2 in 100; habitual drunkards, 75 in 100; deprived of parents before ten years of age, 32 in 100; the average age of criminals is 25.

These proportions are taken in the cases of 1118 prisoners, convicted from 1790 to 1834.

Their crimes may be ranged under three heads: Violence, 190; theft, 716; fraud, 207. Average of cost of conviction to the State, $75 00.

From the annual report of the Maryland Penitentiary we find that in 1847, 89 convicts were received, 49 of whom were under 21 years of age. Of 281 now in the prison, 121 cannot read, 50 can read but not write; 116 were left orphans, 139 were not bound out, or left before they were of age, and 118 were either habitual drunkards, or were in liquor when their offences were committed. In 1843, in that prison, on 290 convicts there was inflicted as punishment for various offences, 9537 lashes, and they were subjected to 463 days of confinement in the cells on bread and water.

In an institution in New York, similar to our House of Refuge, for the reformation of juvenile delinquents, which has been in operation 22 years, they have received 4,167 children. By the annual reports of the last three years, we find they have admitted within that period 543. Of these, 400 were foreigners, and but 143 Americans.

The police records of New York state, that in one year 480 were committed to prison under 25 years of age, many of them between 9 and 16.

The Inspectors of Moyamensing Prison report, that in 1847, 175 convicts were sentenced to hard labor. Of these, 9 only were temperate, 36 moderate drinkers, and 130 intemperate; 92 had not learned a trade; 42 were under 20 years of age; 83 could not read, and 27 could read very imperfectly. In our Eastern Penitentiary in 1845, of 138 convicts received, 33 could not read, 66 could not write, 18 were under 20 years of age, and all but 15 had been in the habit of drinking. Of these, only 21 had served out apprenticeships, and 96 had never been bound to trades. The Rev. Thomas Larcomb states, that of 962 prisoners who had been under his care, 515 had been deprived of one or both parents in early life, and 830 professed to have received no religious instruction, 406 were concerned in manufacturing ardent spirits, or lived in houses where it was sold, 151 could be called temperate, 13 commencèd their course of crime under 10 years of age, and 328 under 20. The first cause of crime of 168 was intemperance, of 182 licentiousness.

The whole number of convicts in the Eastern Penitentiary since 1829, has been 2300. Of these, 283 were under 20 years of age, 594 could not read, 517 could read, but not write, 1408 drank to intoxication, and 516 were moderate drinkers, 1929 had not been bound to trades, or had not served out apprenticeships.

From the opening of our House of Refuge in 1828 to 1845, 1800 children were received. The average has been 14 years of both boys and girls, when they were admitted. In referring to the reports of seven years, we find 704 children received. Of these, 560 could not read intelligibly, and many did not know their letters.

Since the opening of the Rosine Institution, last October, we have received 40 inmates. Of these, 14 could not read, and several had not learned a letter. A number of the others were poor readers, none could spell correctly, and only two or three knew the multiplication table perfectly. Three had attempted to learn trades, but abandoned them without making much progress; 28 were natives of this country, and 12 were foreigners.

These statistics unfold to us convincing proofs that ignorance and intemperance are the demons, whose victims people these institutions, either directly or indirectly, and whose influence operates to prevent the cultivation of those moral and religious sentiments that can alone lessen the number of their sorrowful inmates. With such records before us, can we rest, and feel we have nothing to do? While our prisons, our almshouses, and our asylums, tell the same story, can we sit idly without making an effort to prevent or remedy the evils that surround us? Have we nothing to do in the way of private labor, or in giving our aid to such societies as may trace these evils to their source, and strive to remove them, and in place of the malaria that produces crime and misery, create a healthful atmosphere glowing with the light of intelligence, and purified by mental and religious culture?

Let us reflect upon this subject, and let those thoughts be the parents of actions that will lead us into useful life. Then, indeed, shall we feel we have not lived in vain. Everything around us is unceasing action, and we, too, will find it a busy world if we fulfil all our duties.

☞ The members are requested to call with their subscriptions at the Store of the Association, No. 204 North Eighth Street.

It is desirable that payments should be made soon after the Annual Meeting, which occurs the first Thursday in April.

MAMMY, DON'T CRY.

A TALE OF THE TIMES.

The other day to Bedford Street I went—and wandered there
In search of a poor homeless one, who needed friends and care;
I found her not, but in her stead I saw a sight most sad;
A woman kept that garret-room in filthy tatters clad;
A bed of straw laid on the floor—a table, and a chair,
A charcoal furnace—and these formed the whole possessions there.
On some dark rags, in one recess another woman laid,
She was a boarder—and a third—(also a boarder) staid,
With two small children, in that room—no other home had they,
Her landlady had turned her out, for she had nought to pay—
Her husband had been dead three months—her furniture was sold—
Her clothes were gone, and little left to keep them from the cold,
She sat upon the bed of straw—her babe was at her breast—
A lovely child, scarce three years old (in dirty tatters drest),
Was by her side—and when she told her tale, with many a sigh,
The little cherub, nestling close, said, "Mammy, do not cry!"
I oft have heard the plaints of woe, and seen the tear-drops start,
But rarely have I heard a voice that so unnerved my heart,
As that young child's, when, looking in her mother's bloated face,
She showed, in "Mammy, do not cry," such tenderness and grace.

Days passed—but still upon my mind that scene—those children staid—
So I returned, and sad at heart, another visit paid;—
The woman who had owned the room, and took the boarders in,
They said, had been to prison sent—*Drink, her besetting sin*—
The bed, the table, and the chair, the furnace, too, were gone;
The whole, most probably, had been for liquor put in pawn;
No article of furniture was in that dismal room,
Save one—*it was a knife*—which had escaped the general doom.
The boarder, who on rags had laid, was crouched upon the floor,
But such an eye, and such a face I never saw before.
A brutal wretch, who bore the name of Man, had struck the blow,
And in her streaming blood had laid his drunken victim low.
And there, on that uncovered floor, the children's mother laid;
"She has been drunk since yesterday,"—the other woman said;
She was asleep—upon her side—her bosom open—bare—
Her arm outstretched—the little babe was closely nestling there,
The lovely little cherub girl, whose tones had won my heart
Was seated by her mother's side, who bore no mother's part.
No shoe, nor stocking, either had—one shoe the mother wore,
And concentrated wretchedness was pictured on that floor,
"The down stairs lady, yesterday, had given a piece of bread—
No food the child had seen that day"—by angels only fed.

I roused the mother up, and tried to make her comprehend
That I would take the cherub home, and prove myself
her friend.
But no! the native instinct sprang impulsive to the
heart:
"You cannot—must not take my child—from her I will
not part!"
Tears freely flowed—again that voice said, in its earnest
tone,
"Mammy, don't cry!" I could have clasped the cherub
as my own.
Some food was brought—the children's eyes bent on that
loaf of bread;
More keen delight I never saw, than when those lips
were fed.
Yet, all my eloquence was vain. Of food, of bed bereft,
Of raiment, fire, no comfort near—no hope nor credit
left—
Degraded, drunken, without strength her duties to fulfil,
The woman sunk—yet in that form there lived the
mother still.
I left them on that cold bare floor, and sadly turned
away,
Wishing the legislative power had been with me that day;
I would have closed each dram-shop then—no tavern,
nor hotel,
Should keep a bar—*the druggist's shop alone should poi-
son sell.*
Then, can we give one wondering thought why vice and
crime should reign,
When with the mother's milk, the babe imbibes the
liquid bane—
When all around, by license free, is deadly ruin wrought,
*And human beings turned to brutes, by Rum for six-
pence bought?*

REPORT OF THE MANAGERS OF THE ROSINE ASSOCIATION.

Managers:—Annis A. Furness, Anne Price, Sarah Tyndale, Elizabeth Pugh, Margaret Griscom, Eliza Parker, Ellen Lord, Ann Campion, Mira Townsend, Lydia Gillingham, Sophia Lewis, Mary Kaley, Susan Grew, Annabella L. Townsend, Eliza Yard, Margaret Kelton, Elizabeth Hunt, Mary M. Hastings, Elizabeth Allen, Eliza Parker.

President, Annis P. Furness; Vice-President, Anne Price; Secretary, Margaret Griscom; Treasurer, Mira Townsend.

May, 1849.

The revolution of another year brings us again together, and the question arising in every mind is, what have we done during the past twelve months to realize the idea which was the means of associating women of different tastes and pursuits, and of various denominations, in one band, to act as with one mind. Is that idea a living element growing with the progress of time, expanding the good and kindly feelings of our nature, and working the redemption of those who have been placed under circumstances which have made them differ from ourselves, by their vices or their misfortunes?

We cannot flatter ourselves by believing that *we* would have been stronger, or more elevated than they are, had no better principles been instilled into our minds, no purer, higher associations surrounded us, no holier influences beamed upon our path than were shed upon that of the generality of the fallen ones.

If we admit this view to be true, the question recurs to us with double force, what have we done to repair these disadvantages, caused by the unequal state of society, and to create a more correct feeling in the community?

What have we done? Sixty-four women have been received into our house, taken from scenes of vice and pollution, from the gaming table, and the drunkard's bar; from courses leading to the almshouse and the prison, and placed in a position where they had the opportunity of receiving a degree of education, a knowledge of tailoring, mantuamaking, and sewing generally, and of being instructed in household duties. To these have been added the advantages resulting from the almost daily association with our members, familiar reading of the written Gospel and the spoken Word, through the living instrument. Many of these have appreciated their privileges, and we hope their future may be an enduring record of the blessings that may be derived from a residence for a season in the "Rosine Home."

We could not rationally expect, that in a class who have hitherto had so little to hope, so little to stimulate their better feelings, that all should be prepared to abandon at once every debasing practice, and corrupted habit, and estimate as we do, their present benefits, and future advantages. They have been cast off by the virtuous community; we have perhaps all felt at times a secret horror of their very presence, and have shown it in our words and actions. Our efforts now prove that a change has been wrought in *us*, but *they* feel that *we* are a small part of the community, and that the stain once upon them can never be washed away. We may forgive, but they know we will not forget. Hope therefore with them is, and must be small. Doubtless, in some cases it has been the deficiency in that organ, that during adverse circumstances induced them in a despairing moment to add crime to misfortune.

Again:—Where no principle has been instilled, impulse will rule. Let us trace the course of one, and it will be that of many of that hapless class. The offspring of parents whose habits have sowed the evil seed, whose principles being corrupt could bestow no other upon their child; perhaps at ten years of age sent through the streets to sell matches, or to beg; at twelve, hired as a child nurse, or errand girl, from family to family, and at a more advanced age seduced to the path of evil by such associates as chance may throw around her, and here is the girl who seeks her home in the brothel.

A representative of another large class may also be drawn. The orphan child of the victim of poverty and destitution is placed in a family, who (though doatingly careful of their own daughters), think not, care not, feel not for the poor little drudge in the kitchen, who receives barely the stipulated schooling, and is considered careless and stupid for not making equal progress with the well-taught children of the family, to whose mistress it never occurs, that the mind, like the vegetable world, must have its sunlight, and its dew to capacitate it for improvement. Of the rain-drops caused by punishment mayhap it may have full acquaintance in the cheerless kitchen, or half-furnished garret, but of that sunshine in the heart that overflows in the romping children in the parlor, she has small experience. She sees the social habits there, and feels her own desolation. She longs for something, for somebody to love, and is therefore prepared to give the affection of an overflowing heart to whoever may claim its sympathies. Unguarded by principle (for none has been instilled), she becomes the victim of vice, not because she is naturally worse than others, but, that she has been more unfortunate, and there was no protecting hand, or warning voice, to save her in the hour of temptation.

We have met with some cases of girls, who, not having had proper care, have been sent to the House of Refuge, perhaps as vagrants, or for small offences, and while there, have been initiated by some of the older ones into such details of immoral life, as prepared them to become, in their turn, the same abandoned characters. The managers of that institution are fully aware of the importance of classifying their inmates, but the want of room has hitherto prevented them from making many arrangements which they deem important.

It is certainly a subject worthy of consideration by those who have the disposal of such persons, whether the "Refuge" is the proper place (under existing circumstances), for those who have been in licentious habits.

Another class to which we may refer, is that of girls, who have been sent from Intelligence Offices to immoral houses, and have thus innocently been thrown into the power of those, by whose arts they have been betrayed, through whose misrepresentations and persuasions they have been yielding victims, or even in some instances, the forced companions of pollution and crime.

Were it proper to detail some circumstances that

have come to our knowledge, in which the innocent and unwary have been thus led into scenes and practices of vice, the recital, while it awakened the sympathies, would shock the feelings. The question naturally arises, will not the law award the due retribution ? But we must remember, in such cases, the injured individual is pōor, and friendless, while the authors of her ruin, through their pecuniary, and other advantages, even when brought to the courts of justice, have the power (if not entirely to screen themselves), to cast such imputations upon her character, or her weakness, that the charges however true seem triumphantly refuted. Here again arises the inquiry :—What are we doing ? Are we instructing the youthful minds around us in regard to the temptations and dangers to which they may be subjected, warning them against evil books, and associations, and instructing them in those principles of morality and religion which will give them strength to resist seductive influences, and lead them when under discouraging circumstances, to put their trust in Him, in whom confidence was never reposed in vain.

Are we endeavoring to instil habits of industry, not only in accordance with the necessities of our families, but with the taste and genius of the individual ? Providence has not made all alike, but has given us intellectual inclinations, which must be in a degree consulted, to promote our happiness. Some of us believe, there would be few idle people, if every one could follow the dictates of those faculties with which they have been endowed. We acknowledge this difference in ourselves, but who remembers that the inmate in the kitchen may have her tastes and her aversions ? that though stern necessity may place her there, her employment may be distasteful to her, and while we accuse her of idleness and inattention; who thinks of inquiring in what lies her gift, and endeavors to facilitate its profitable indulgence?

The idea is spreading in society, and we believe it to be a true one, that if the field of useful employment for women was extended, and pecuniary remuneration in accordance to the labor, and not the sex that performed it, we should have a far more virtuous community, and females would not be tempted as they are at present, after struggling in vain to gain a miserable living by sewing, to cast off their painfully earned pittance, for the apparently greater gains of the idle prostitute.

Are we considering these subjects as we ought, and while we are awakening the minds of others to think, and to act, are we preparing the young females around us to qualify themselves for whatever business may open for them, and by their integrity, industry, and virtue, adorn and elevate their profession, whatever it may be.

We must recur again to the question.—What have we done? Of the sixty-four women who have been in the Institution, we should rejoice if we could say, all were still pursuing the rightful path; but habits of inebriation in many instances undermine the good resolve, and that impulse ungoverned by principle which first impelled them to err, as suddenly perhaps induced them to seek the shelter of our home, and in some cases has prompted them as hastily to abandon it.

But in several instances they have returned, and brought others with them, showing that though weak and impulsive, the aspirations after a better life were not extinct, and that they appreciated the benefits they had received, by inducing others to become candidates for the same privileges.

One of our present family, who has been several months with us, was told by one of the Managers that a situation would be procured for her, with which at first she seemed pleased, but after a little consideration she inquired if she might not be permitted to stay awhile longer, remarking, "I feel my soul is safer here." Another, who has been living in a family six months, in a conversation with a friend remarked, "the Rosine is a blessed home! had it not been for that, where would I have been at present? I feel that now there is a chance for me to rise once more into a respectable station in life, and earn my living in creditable independence." This is the feeling evinced by others who have been under our care; and those among us who have been most deeply engaged in the work, and have known most intimately the histories and feelings of our unfortunate inmates, can unite in the expression that the Rosine is indeed a blessed home. But while we rejoice in the evidences that Providence has in many respects blest our efforts, we must acknowledge we have had our trials, and our disappointments. Some who have claimed our interest and sympathy, and who for awhile promised well, have fallen again in the moment of temptation; but we have reason to believe that even a few days spent in the Rosine are not without their benefit, and that the poor erring one, though she may return to her evil course, has in most cases had the witness awakened in her soul, and felt she was left without excuse to her conscience, and in several cases, they have returned, begging to be again received in the home they had deserted. In two instances they brought others with them, and one of our present family was brought to us by one, who though she had not strength of principle to continue herself in the rightful course, yet urged another to come and solicit our shelter and protection.

Five months since a woman was brought to us by one of our members in a most wretched condition, without any clothing but a miserable dress. She had been sleeping in the barns below the city, and came up in the day, and wandered from place to place among the vile traffickers in the gin shops, for a mouthful of food, or a glass of that enemy that had wrought her ruin. She was received, and in a few days her history became known. She is the wife of a gentleman in a neighboring city. During a long-continued spell of illness her physician had ordered her to take her medicine in brandy to make it more palatable. She soon discovered that when under the influence of liquor her domestic afflictions and bodily sufferings were not felt so severely, and without reflecting that the draught that now soothed her, might become her worst enemy and her master, she unresistingly became a slave to that destroyer of souls, and sacrificed husband, children, and home. She had wandered to Philadelphia, had associated with abandoned wretches who had robbed her of her clothing, and for months had been a homeless, friendless, outcast. A week in the Rosine made her a new being. The better feelings of her nature awakened, she became sensible of her lost condition, and it was delightful to those who witnessed it, to watch the progress of this unfortunate woman, as from day to day her countenance altered, indicating that she was rising from her state of degradation, and the hallowed influences around her were restoring to her her self-respect, and the desire to gain the respect of others. She applied industriously to sewing, and became an able assistant in the Work-room. After being some months with us, her husband was informed of her being in the Rosine. He came immediately to the city to see her, and a correspondence ensued between them, which resulted in his sending her money, and permission to return to him. She left us three weeks since, and some of us felt it ought truly to be a thanksgiving day for husband, wife, and ourselves. She has been kindly received by her friends, is living with the mother of her husband, and has hopes once more of fulfilling her duties as a wife, a mother, and a Christian.

Some of you may remember, at the first meeting of the Society, one of our members spoke of having visited some houses of immoral character, in order to ascertain the sentiments of those women respecting the usefulness of such an Institution, and the probability of their desiring to be benefited by it. The first house at which we called was kept by two sisters, one of whom we saw. In conversing with her, she exclaimed, "You cannot imagine the horror of mind that I feel when I lie down at night; but what else can I do? no one would take me into their family. I have lived six years in this house, and have no character to sustain me in any other situation." When we had been in operation about six months, this woman came to us to know if we would receive her. Under an agreement to submit to more close regulations than we had then required of any one, she became one of our family, and was six months with us. She was one who might truly be called a heathen ; she knew not a letter in the alphabet, and the words and spirit of the written gospel were to her as though they were not. But the Father had not left himself without a witness in her soul, and that horror of mind that had shown her the evil of her ways, had convinced her there was something higher, better, and holier, that might yet be attained. She became as a child in our house, and faithfully performed the domestic duties assigned her, and with persevering application attended diligently in the school, and evinced the delight of a child as she marked her own progress.

She is now located in the family of a friend a few miles from the city, and the accounts we have had from her have been very favorable, both from them and herself.

Within the past year one of our inmates has married respectably, and gone West; another is supporting herself by taking in sewing; two have been received again by their friends, and are living with married sisters, and a number are situated in families where their good conduct entitles them to respect, while the future opens brightly before them. Three who have been under our care, are now church members; two of our inmates became qualified to work upon their own account, and have received a compensation for their labor. About eight months since, a mother brought her daughter to us, a girl of seventeen, whose unrestrained habits had led her into improper society. After some consideration, we received her as an indentured apprentice, until she was eighteen years of age. We have now the satisfactory belief that we have rescued this child from ruin, and the hope, that her future life will atone to her friends for their past trials, and her good conduct prove to the world, the benefits of a year's residence in the "Rosine."

We consider an Act of Indenture in such cases to have an excellent restraining influence, and believe that if parents and others having *such* minors under their charge would adopt the plan of this mother, the children might in many instances be saved.

Amid our varied duties, we consider our missionary labors in the homes of these poor misguided women as very important. We have paid upwards of two hundred visits in such houses, and a number of those with whom we there conversed have since claimed our care and protection. It may appear to some, that the benefits arising from these visits may be few; but we must remember the progress of truth is always slow—the seed must be sown before it can bring forth fruits; and that Gospel that was delivered by Jesus, thousands of years since, is not yet fully received, even by professing Christians. We may therefore feel encouraged, though as formerly all are not prepared to receive the proffered mercy; yet the Almighty has awakened many hearts to abandon their life of profligacy, and strive after better things.

In our reports, and at our meetings, we have spoken of the necessity of an asylum, or low-priced boarding-house, for women out of employ, until situations or business could be procured for them. We increasingly feel the necessity of such a home, and in a few instances have had to give a temporary shelter to individuals, or cast the friendless stranger into the street—although we are fully sensible that our house is not the proper refuge of virtuous women. Through our Intelligence Office we have procured situations for one hundred and seventy-seven women and children, without including those who have been inmates of the Institution. Upwards of three hundred applicants for situations have had their names recorded, and many of them have returned day after day, exciting our sympathy by their looks and words of disappointment.

It appears by a communication received from the Secretary of the Emigrant's Friend Society, that they also have felt the necessity of a temporary "Home," or cheap boarding-house for emigrants, as there are no boarding-houses for such persons except low dram-shops, where temptations of various kinds beset the stranger, and the funds that might support and convey them (if properly managed) to situations in the country, where they might be profitably employed, are drawn from them, and in a short period they are turned upon the public in a destitute condition. Under these circumstances the Secretary of the Emigrant Society appealed to the Rosine Association, hoping to meet with co-operation in this benevolent project. The subject being laid before the managers, they resolved, that, *as* the Rosine Association, we could not unite with the Emigrant Society; but, as individuals, *we* approved of their proposition for such a "Home," and would be glad to aid them in their much-needed enterprise. The plan of that society embraces a temporary home for men and families; while ours is only for women and children, who are waiting for situations or employment.

Hoping that some of the wealthy and benevolent individuals in this city may incline to appropriate a portion of their funds towards forwarding this object, we beg leave to revive the subject occasionally in your hearing.

During the year, the school in the Rosine has been continued, with great benefit to many of our inmates. Some of our members have a Bible class on the morning of the Sabbath. In the afternoon a religious meeting is held; and on the fourth day (or Wednesday) of each week, we have either a Bible-class or meeting. These meetings are attended by many of our members, and by persons of different religious denominations, whose feelings have been awakened to come and sit with the Magdalen in the spirit and under the teachings of Jesus.

The garments made for the family during the year amount to - - - - - -	400
For customers, including 49 dresses, 137 shirts, 31 chemises, 158 vests, 28 coats, 67 pairs of pantaloons, and sundry other articles, numbering altogether - - -	601
Total number, - - -	1,001

The amount earned in the work-room is -	$325 61
We have received in subscriptions from members, - - - - - - -	500 00
Annual subscriptions from gentlemen, -	170 00
Interest on money loaned towards the purchase of the house, - - - - -	138 00
Total, - -	$1,133 61

This may be considered our regular income; yet, owing to deaths, removals, and other circumstances, it must be subject to change.

In addition, we have received

By legacy from Deborah Phipps, - - -	$95 00
From an unknown Friend, through the Editors of the Inquirer, - - - -	5 00
From the fund for a set of plate for Gov. Johnson, - - - - - - - -	20 00

Anonymously, from different persons, -	$20 00
Solicited donations, by the Managers and other Members, - - - - -	614 50
Total receipts,	$1,888 11

Our expenses have been,—

Rent, - - - - - -	$400 00	
Water-rent for bath-room, - -	3 00	
Salaries to officers, - - -	371 00	
Clothing, &c., - - - - -	150 74	
Marketing, groceries, &c., - -	485 52	
Advertising, and printing pamphlets, - - - - - -	55 55	
Shoes, - - - - - -	16 25	
Museum-rent for public meetings, - - - - - -	7 50	
Incorporation expenses, - -	10 75	
Carpenter-work, - - -	36 40	
Beds, bedsteads, and other furniture, - - - - - -	74 51	
Painting, bricklaying, stationery, insurance, postage, locksmiths, and other incidental expenses, - - - - -	124 76	
Balance of cash on hand, - -	152 13	
Amount collected		$1,888 11

This statement shows our probable income to be one thousand one hundred and thirty-three dollars, sixty-one cents, while our expenses have been one thousand seven hundred and thirty-five dollars, ninety-eight cents; leaving a deficiency of six hundred and two dollars, thirty-seven cents, to be raised annually, if our expenses continue about the same.

We have now the names of four hundred and eighty ladies as members. If each member who pays one dollar would double her subscription, or interest a friend to become a member, we might soon be relieved from the unpleasant necessity of begging to support our family, and might then collect subscriptions towards purchasing our house, and preparing (if it should meet the sanction of the Society) to make the proposed effort for a temporary home, or asylum for virtuous women.

In addition to the above-named donations, one of our subscribers paid for printing two thousand copies of our semi-annual report, and we have received a number of contributions of coal, groceries, soap, brushes, &c., which have lessened our expenses considerably.

When we opened our store, we placed in it one thousand dollars worth of goods, and from that period the accounts of the store have been kept entirely separate from the treasury accounts. The amount of sales have been about two thousand dollars. We are pleased to find our customers are increasing, and hope another year will show an improved business.

The close of the second year of the Association awakens many reflections; and the retrospect of the past time brings with it a solemn feeling, as we again ask ourselves—what have we done?

We cannot expect ever to be able to do all that we would; but the consciousness that the Divine blessing has, in a degree, rested upon our efforts, has cheered us onward, and we feel that as yet we are but on the threshold of the great work to which we are called. We believe the time to be coming, when woman shall stand side by side with man in every noble effort—that she shall cease to be satisfied with being his toy, or his slave—that she shall require of him the same degree of purity that he now claims from her—that she shall feel the business of life to be her business; and that man and woman, as with one mind and one spirit, shall co-operate in the great and sacred duties of life, and hand in hand go up to the House of the Lord.

THE PLEDGE.

Husband and I were sitting one evening very cosily, talking over the events of the day, when the bell rang, and we were told a gentleman desired to see me at the door, but refused to come in. Accordingly, as he would not come to us, we went to the door to him, and found a respectable-looking young man there, who informed us he wished to get an order for the clothing of A. C., who, we knew, had left the Rosine some days previously, and returned to the house of B. (an abandoned woman), with whom she had been living. He said, Anne wished to leave the city, and needed her clothing. We replied, she could not have them without she came for them herself, and asked where she was? The youth hesitated, seemed embarrassed, and then said, he did not like to tell; but upon our informing him that we knew where she was, he acknowledged that she was at the house of B., and that he had become acquainted with her there. We then asked, if he thought it right to frequent such places? He unhesitatingly answered, "No, it is not right!" "Why then does thee go there?" "Oh, only for amusement!" "Does thee ever go to church?" "Yes, I attend my church regularly!" "What good does it do thee?" After reflecting a moment he said, "I do not know that it does me any good!" "Does it profit thee to frequent the house of B., and mingle in the associations of such a place?" "No, it does not!" "What then is thy reason for going to either place?" "I do not know," he replied. It was a bright moonlight night, and as the beams fell upon his face, disclosing an intelligent countenance, our interest was deeply awakened by his ingenuous replies, and we felt urged to continue the conversation, and pointing upward we said, "If neither the church nor the company at the house of B. have profited thee, would it not be well to try to know something of the great Church up there?" "Yes," he said, "it would!" We had then considerable conversation on the subject of evil society, and the indulgence of bad habits; he was told of the consequences that must result from such a course, in the loss of time, money, character, and health, and the final loss of both soul and body, and a contrast was drawn between such a life, and that of a man who, by correct habits, industry, and economy, could prepare a comfortable home for a virtuous, good wife, where he might realize true domestic happiness, and by the moral elevation of his character be entitled to rank among the best men in the community. He acknowledged the picture drawn to be a true one, and then said, "I have never done any one harm; I have never wronged anybody!" We rejoined, "Thy hand may be unstained by murder; the world may consider thee an honest man; the guilt of seducing a young and innocent girl, may not be upon thy soul, but is it much better to frequent such houses, and encourage practices that destroy the miserable victims, and heap upon them that ignominy that is a living death? It matters little how the unfortunate one is placed there, whether seduced by man or woman, or by her necessities,—her degradation is the same; but let her be as low as she may, the man who associates with her is as low, and equally as debased. The sin is not in the sex, but in the actions. Society may excuse the man, and condemn the woman, but in the sight of the Almighty, there is no difference between them; the guilt is the same; and both are on one level." "I see it," said he, in a reflective tone, that bespoke the inward monitor was impressing his mind with the truth of the views thus unexpectedly brought before him. Seizing the opportunity when his feelings were thus awakened, we inquired, if he had a mother? "I have!" "Is she a religious woman?" "She is!" "Does she feel interested for the welfare of her son?" "She does!" "What would she think were we to go to her, and tell her, her son frequented the house of the notorious B.?" "I would not for the world she should know it!" said he, convulsively. "It is well to spare the feelings of thy mother, but if she never knows it, there is an eye," (pointing upward as we spoke), "from which nothing can be hidden; that eye sees every act, and knows every word and thought;" "I know it," he rejoined. "But if thy mind was fully impressed with the consciousness of that, could thee dare visit such a place?" "I did not think about it then." After some further conversation, in which the subject of temperance came up, we asked, if he had ever taken a pledge, and upon his replying in the negative, we inquired, whether he would be willing to sign one. Again he hesitated. A contrast was then drawn between the character and happiness of a sober, moral, good man, and the wretchedness of a drunken, abandoned profligate, and we closed by saying, as we pointed to the bright sphere above us. "Let that moon be the witness of thy resolution, that from this night, the purpose of thy life shall be a right one; that from this hour, evil companions and practices shall be abandoned." "I will give you my pledge," said he, solemnly. "Then, come into the parlor!" We entered, and he was seated by the centre table, the large Bible was laid beside him, and his hand placed on it (for we desired the scene to be as impressive as possible). He was told we did not wish him to take an oath, for this Book said, "Swear not at all, neither by Heaven nor earth, but let your yea, be yea, and your nay, nay;" but we wanted him to remember that he was in the presence of the Almighty, and that a pledge taken there, would be equally as solemn as any oath in a court of justice. The pledge was then written and read, and he was desired to consider it seriously; it might be a hard one to keep. "I will keep it," said he, firmly. He then repeated it, and signed his name.

The whole conversation was serious, calm, and impressive, and the latter part solemn, and deeply affecting.

Here was a young man, who had come from the house of one, "whose steps lead down to hell," and who expected to return immediately there, arrested suddenly in his career of vice, brought to a sense of his condition by a stranger, at the street door; his heart tendered, and brought to see the iniquity of his conduct, and in the full consciousness of the presence of the Almighty, made willing to enter into a solemn promise of a change and amendment of life. Some suitable tracts were given to him, and he was urged to remember, that though he was *apparently* sent there by a bad woman, it was in reality his Heavenly Father, who took this mode of bringing him to a sense of his state and condition. He seemed to understand it thus, and we parted, with expressions of gratitude on his part, and feelings of the deepest interest on ours.

Our hearts were filled with wonder, love, and praise, and we felt truly, "Lord, thy ways are above finding out! thou workest by whom thou wilt!"

A year had passed away, when one evening we received a call from the same young man. He came to tell us he had kept his pledge, and to thank us for the interest we had shown for his welfare. That evening he had grown a wiser—now, he was a better man.

SEMI-ANNUAL REPORT OF THE MANAGERS OF THE ROSINE ASSOCIATION.

November, 1849.

Another period of six months brings us again together, and the feeling that attracted us then prompts every mind now to repeat the question, What have we done? and with your Executive Committee arises the same desire to reply, We have done what we could? Some of us have been precluded by our situations from devoting as much time to the work as we could have wished; but others have remained upon duty, so that very few days have passed without our Home being visited by some of our number. It is indeed a labor of love, and those who desire to be efficient must come to the work, resolving to be ready in season, and out of season, whenever duty calls. With some of us it has been no butterfly employment. The cause of humanity claims the industry of the bee, and the perseverance of the spider of Bruce. Patience must have its perfect work, and hope and faith be our constant companions. Yet we come to you with a word of cheer. Many of those who have been under our care are still pursuing the path of rectitude; and upon some of their minds we have reason to believe the Divine blessing has rested.

Several individuals have claimed our attention that have not become inmates of our house; as in some cases where there had been little exposure, we deemed it best that they should remain unknown to our inmates. To some of these we have given a home in our own families, until an opportunity presented to gain for them suitable permanent situations. To this class we desire to call the attention of our members. Many of us, perhaps, have known individuals, or at least, known those who had erred once, and who might have been saved, if a kind hand, a soothing and encouraging word, and a temporary asylum had been given them in their hour of need; but lacking these, and feeling the world was against them, remorse in their own minds, and no sustaining power around them to buoy them up, they have sunk into the degradation they loathed, and became hopeless, reckless, and abandoned. Here is our appropriate work. It is more easy to reclaim from one error than many; and to instil a high and noble principle in one who has deviated from the path of right merely because no principle of right has been implanted, than to uproot the habits of years, and destroy the careless hardihood which familiarity with vice must ever present.

In our last Report we told you of one young girl who at seventeen had been apprenticed to us by her mother. She had been led into improper society, her friends could no longer control her, and to save her from utter ruin she was taken to the House of Refuge. The managers there, with a proper regard for the well-doing of the younger children, refused to shelter her for more than a short period. In her grief and hopelessness the mother then turned to the Rosine. After due consideration, the managers concluded to receive her, on condition of her being indentured until she was eighteen. She was a child of ungoverned temper, and wayward in the extreme; and at times, in her fits of passion, had she not known we had power to enforce obedience, we too, might for the period have lost our control over her. There was often a trial for our patience, and great opportunity for the labor of love; but the year passed away. Three months since she left us, and we have reason to believe her desires now are to act a daughter's part, and in the bosom of her grateful family prove that our exertions for her have not been lost. Seeing thus the good effects of continued care in the cases of minors, we have had four others indentured to us, and we hope the result will be generally satisfactory, though we know, in such instances, great responsibilities rest upon us; and when they are brought by parents or friends, we cannot expect them to have strong convictions of the impropriety of their past conduct, and therefore have little repentance for the groundwork of amendment. But we have faith in patience, forbearance, and kindness, and in the gradual influence of those principles that we desire to inculcate, and that should mark us, as examples to them.

One of these children is but fifteen years and six months. She had been enticed from her home in Jersey by the misrepresentations of a cousin, who pretended she would procure a situation for her in a family, with high wages and many advantages. This cousin took her to a house of abandoned character, and then deserted her. Six weeks afterwards she was brought by one of our members from the Prison, where she had been thrown on a charge of abuse, by the wicked mistress of the miserable mansion, where she had become the victim of the basest crime. With her own entire consent, after having been several weeks in the house, she has been apprenticed to us by the Judge before whom she was brought when on trial.

Another was lured from her father's dwelling by a villain, and then left to mourn the folly of believing one who taught her disobedience. A young man met her in the street, and accosted her as she was wandering about, homeless and unprotected. He was one in whom a high sense of integrity among men had been instilled, but whose friends had probably given him no warning against the most prevalent vice of the age. They had deemed it immodest to tell him that his health, his physical well-being, his duties to man, to woman, and to God, required his strict adherence to virtue. Therefore he had sinned, not through ignorance that it was sin, but his moral sense had been so little impressed upon this subject, that he could excuse himself to his conscience, because most young men were equally guilty; and he hardly felt it as more than a fashionable folly. He was "sowing his wild oats;" and who, among all the ladies of his acquaintance, had looked coolly upon him, uttered a word of remonstrance, or given him a word of advice? Ah who? Yet even in his case there was a good feeling at work, and Providence raised for this poor child a friend to rescue her in an unexpected manner. Her youth, her beauty, her artlessness interested him, and awakened feelings he was unaccustomed to. She told him her simple story. All night long he thought of it,—sleep was banished. He compared her as she then was, to the being she must become in the downward path she seemed doomed to tread, and he was horror-stricken. This young creature, so guiltless now, must she become the victim of every loathsome vice, the companion of only the false and the depraved, and lead a life of shame and misery, until disease claimed his prey—probably in the almshouse or the prison? He arose a better man. He had resolved to perform a good action—to save, if possible, this child who had wandered from her father's house. He reasoned with her as his conscience prompted. She felt his words were the words of truth, and she consented to go anywhere he would advise, save to her home. She thought *there* she had committed the unpardonable sin. He made considerable effort to place her in a suitable situation, but in vain. His inquiries at last led him to the Rosine. He asked and obtained permission for her reception. She is now one of our children, and her father, since then, has gladly ratified the contract made with us by herself and this young man. May the good resolutions he formed during that sleepless night be sanctified to him, and may he be sensible that they came not from himself, but that God talked with him.

AN APPEAL TO MOTHERS.

Mothers, to you must we turn,—with you would we plead for your own children. Are you performing your duties to them faithfully? Are you warning them against evil associations and immoral practices? Are you treating them as rational beings, acknowledging you are aware of the weakness and temptations of humanity, laying before them their moral and physical responsibilities, and teaching them that the violation of these laws are sins against their Creator? Let no false modesty keep you a stranger upon these subjects with your children. Very early in life they know there is some mystery to be learned, and if the judicious mother does not, as an opportunity presents, speak candidly and truly with her children, and thus secure their confidence, they will gain their knowledge, most probably from corrupted sources, and the poisoned stream run through their whole lives, producing grief and misery, not only to themselves, but to the mother also, who shrank from her duty through a very mistaken view of the subject.

What would be your feelings, if you had reason to believe that in consequence of your neglect to impress upon the mind of your child the common principles of honesty, he should steal from your neighbor's daughter her purse, containing a thousand dollars that were to be her marriage portion, and consequently he would be arrested, and thrown into prison, and himself and family disgraced for life. You would be overwhelmed with grief, and lament unceasingly that any consideration prevented you from fulfilling a mother's part. But, what is the theft of a thousand dollars, or of countless thousands, in comparison to the crime that son may commit, in robbing her of the virtue that can never be estimated by dollars and cents; that can alone be known or measured by the omniscient eye that sees her agony of spirit, when she sinks the scorn of mankind, the victim to disease and intemperance, and dies upon the straw pallet in the poorhouse, or wrapped in her blanket on the floor of the prisoner's cell. Mothers, here is work for you! The reform of the age lies in your hands. Upon your child's mind you may write what you will. True, the good seed may sometimes seem choked by briers, or cast upon stony ground. Yet we believe, that though the child of the wise and pious mother may be led astray, yet, in the hour of temptation, her counsels may rise upon his memory, her warnings still his wild passions, and his mother's eye (though perhaps thousands of miles away), arrest his steps, subdue him in his mad career, and she be thus the saviour of her child. The law would sentence him who stole the thousand dollars to years of imprisonment, while the wretch who ruins the happiness and corrupts the principles of one "who is but a little lower than the angels," walks unscathed through life, and is called the good fellow—the gentleman. This plainly shows we estimate money higher than virtue or happiness. We would not associate with the thief, or admit him into our houses or families, but the libertine is received into the social circle. He who is a thousand-fold worse than a thief is too often our companion, and the friend of our husbands, our sons, our daughters. Shall it continue to be so? Our fiat can make it otherwise. Our refusal to speak to or associate with such men would soon produce a change in society. We must be consistent. It is vain to *talk* of virtue, while our conduct shows we are insincere; and that mother who seeks to train up a child in the way he should go, must avoid the man of libertine practices as she would the serpent in her path, or the child will not believe her, and reverence her as a model of purity and truth. *We must be what we wish our children to be.*

Some of us may think our influence cannot affect the world; we can do nothing in the way of reforming it: but, if we can implant proper principles in the mind of our child, he may become the parent of many children; and the good impressions made upon him may be engrafted upon them, and thus descend through many generations. In the meanwhile we are giving our example, our influence in the circle around us, and we know not how many minds may be operated upon by that example. A ray of light through a pin-hole is small, yet it diverges widely; thus the truth that is shown in our life, however circumscribed our circle, may extend its impressions we know not where, and be reflected through innumerable beings,—influencing each in their eternal welfare.

ENCOURAGING RESULTS.

Within the past six months the Rosine has received twenty-one inmates, which make the whole number eighty-five since the house was opened. Some of them, from various motives, have not had strength to continue in the better way, and have resumed their former mode of life. In several instances, after leaving, they have again sought admission, showing, that though easily tempted to go astray, yet the struggles of their better feelings still prompted them to make another effort. To be able to understand how they can return after once escaping from such a course of iniquity, we must remember that, in many cases, moral or religious principles have never been instilled. These cannot at once be engrafted, and, consequently, the criminality of their conduct does not appear to them as to us. Many of them have never been taught to work properly, therefore habits of industry must be slowly acquired, and often distastefully. They have never submitted to control, and the necessary order and restraints of our house are irksome to be borne. They have felt they were held in society as more degraded than their male companions, who are equally guilty, and their hope is small of ever being able to rise again in public estimation. Their uncultured minds are governed alone by impulse, while the shocking habits of inebriation and chewing snuff, in which they too generally indulge, to deaden the mentality and awaken sensuality, draw them back with (to them) an irresistible force.

But we have cheering evidences that our house has been a blessing to some even of the most hopeless cases, apparently; and, were it proper, we could refer to a number who show, by their continued good conduct and propriety of behavior, that we have not labored in vain. The writer of this Report was present last Sabbath at the baptism of one of the early members of our family. She had lived a number of years in improper habits, but in the Rosine her feelings had been awakened, and her spirit baptized into that repentance that brings amendment of life, until she could truly say,

This to me has been a blessed house. She has now been eighteen months living in the same family, and their testimony is, that they believe she is endeavoring to walk in the footsteps of Him in whose name she has given her vows to the church. Two others who have been under our care, have also become church members, and another, who was fourteen months with us, has been restored to her family, after being separated from them several years, and we believe her desire is to be a consistent Christian. Her friends joyfully acknowledge the lost is found. One, of whom we have spoken as being again received by her husband, and who, during her separation, had become very degraded, we learn is still doing very well; and another whom we mentioned in our January Report, as having been mistress of a house of ill fame for six years, and who had been considered as utterly abandoned, is still living in the country, and is considered by her employers an honest, faithful domestic, of truly respectable character. We might tell you of several others, who, by their continued industry and propriety of conduct, evince that they have been snatched as brands from the burning, and with gratitude own that the Rosine has been to them father, mother, friend, and home.

We have lost one of our inmates by death, but her repentance appeared to be so sincere, and her spirit so peaceful during her latter days, that the change seemed merely a translation from the sufferings of time to the enjoyments of eternity. We have never witnessed a more solemn and interesting scene, than when our inmates, forming a circle around the coffined Magdalen, sang the hymn,

"Were not the sinful Mary's tears
An offering worthy Heaven,
When o'er the sins of former years
She wept, and was forgiven?"

One of our members spent, during the summer, a few weeks visiting among her friends in New Jersey. She knew that many who needed our care were from that state, and therefore made an appeal not only to the sympathies, but to the duties of those residing in the country. Upon her return, she delivered to the treasurer $54 25, collected during this visit. Who of us can give a similar account of our remembering and pleading for the poorest of the poor in the season of our leisure and recreation? She was not only doing good for those for whom *we* labor, but to herself and all those whose better feelings she awakened and led to reflect upon their duties and responsibilities.

We have still occasionally to receive homeless and friendless females under our care for a few days, until situations can be procured for them, but we have never counted such as inmates.

With great pleasure we announce to our members that a Society, to be entitled the Temporary Home Association, has been formed, the object of which will be to give a temporary home to women out of employ, at a moderate board, where those who are able and willing to work, but who are without funds, may be received for a short period until they can get situations, under the condition of paying the stipulated board as soon as their circumstances will admit. This Society also proposes to give a temporary shelter to destitute children, of ages and circumstances to be placed in families.

Of the necessity of such a Home we have frequently spoken, and hail the formation of this Society as an important era, believing that the benefits that may be derived from it can never be calculated. There are doubtless, at this time, hundreds of women in this city in houses of ill fame, or living in more private circumstances, who would still be virtuous, respectable, and valuable members of the community, had such a home been open for them, where they might have been received in their hour of desolation and friendlessness, and protected from the temptations of evil associates, until employment presented to them a brighter hope of the future.

But while we are endeavoring to make a provision for those who are homeless in our city, is it not our duty to spread information throughout the country, of the risks and dangers to which every young woman is subjected in coming to the city to seek employment. Of many it may truly be said, "they know not what they do," when, for increased amusements or wages, they leave their peaceful country homes, and cast themselves into the temptations of an ever-fluctuating city. To our country members and friends we would also say, does not the ruin of these young women lie partly at your doors? You are accustomed to consider your own skirts to be clear, but we do not. You, with ourselves, have thought that it was immodest and improper to speak to young persons under our care upon the subject of immoral conduct. We have, therefore, implanted no principles of virtue, no detestation of vice. We counsel them about honesty, for they might steal from us if we did not. We warn them about indulgence in many of their evil propensities, for we might suffer from their outbreaks, but have we labored to impress upon their minds the importance of purity in every thought, word, and deed, and made them feel that the happiness and usefulness of their whole lives depended on their avoiding the first false step, or, perhaps, in allowing personal freedoms, that may lead, however, indirectly, to it.

There is another subject to which we would call your attention. It is the low wages given in many parts of the country. This produces constant difficulty with the employers, and dissatisfaction with the employed. Girls are consequently scarce in the country; while hundreds, who come to the city for higher wages, are led on step by step until they receive no other than the wages of iniquity. We desire to call attention to this subject, and believe our country friends will find an increased salary will provide them with more settled domestics, and they will evince more fully that they consider the laborer is worthy of her hire, while many young women will be retained in innocence and usefulness in their rural homes, who are now tempted, unsuspecting the dangers in which they may be surrounded, to cast themselves into this whirling vortex, in which health, happiness, and virtue may all be sacrificed.

In our missionary visits to houses of immoral character, of which we have the record of 260, we find a large majority of the inmates are from other places. Many are from the South, but an alarming list could be made of the natives of our own state, of New Jersey, and of Delaware.

Since our last meeting in this house, we have had three others—one in the Northern Liberties, one in Southwark, and the third in Camden. They were held at the request of some of our friends, who believed that occasional meetings of the Society in other neighborhoods would be beneficial, by spreading the knowledge of our operations, and enlisting other women to labor in this cause. By these meetings we gained an accession of forty members, and have reason to believe an interest was awakened in many minds that had heretofore reflected but little upon the subject. We have now 530 members.

Among such a number of women, there must be many well-qualified ones, who could spare some hours to devote either to soliciting funds, paying missionary visits in the houses, or uniting with us in the labors connected with the Institution. There are now some vacancies in the Board, and we hope no false modesty will prevent such from offering their services. Their company and assistance would also be highly valuable in our evening school, and our Sabbath morning and midweek exercises. We have no right to hide our light under a bushel—no right to bury our talents in a napkin. All of us are good for something, and it is only by using and cultivating our gifts, be they large or small, that we can expect them to increase, or be to the glory of God.

PLEDGE NUMBER TWO.

Returning home one summer's afternoon from the Rosine House, I passed down Wood Street, and on my way saw a boy, about 12 or 13 years of age, sitting on a door step, *smoking*. I have often spoken to boys, and girls too, on the street, when I felt I had a word for them, and on this occasion,

I was impressed to stop, and said to the boy, "What a young lad to be smoking segars! Does thee think it a good habit?" He replied, "It don't do any harm!" "How many does thee smoke a day?" "Not more than one commonly!" "Well, one a day comes to 365 in a year; but I find if people begin on one a day, they are apt after a while, to want more. A great many persons smoke six, and I have heard of some who smoked 20 a day. A young lad like thyself, with good habits, may stand a chance to live seventy years, and if thee should never use more than one a day, I want thee to think how many that would be in a lifetime, and how much money they would cost, even in a few years. Now, if all this money was saved, and placed at interest, it would amount to quite a clever sum to help start thee in business at the age of twenty-one, but if it is all wasted in smoke, what good will it do thee?" "None at all," said the boy. While we were thus talking, two other lads (who probably were neighbors), came along, and seeing us conversing, stopped to listen. After a few minutes, I asked them, "Boys, do you smoke?" One replied he did, the other, he did not; "But there," said one of them (pointing up the street), "is a *real fellow* to smoke!" Immediately he called out, "Bill! Bill!" but "Bill" not coming, he started off, and brought the wondering lad to see what the lady wanted. I then repeated our conversation, and told them they "had seen the rowdy young men about the streets, and these rowdies had all been boys like themselves, and perhaps commenced on one or two segars a day. But all bad habits grow rapidly when there is no principle to correct them, and lads who use segars, generally begin to grow thirsty, and are apt to frequent taverns; this, of course, leads to bad society, and soon they are seen lounging about the corners of the streets, annoying persons; next, they frequent houses of bad character; get into mobs and fights; curse and use profane language, and after a little while they are found in the prison. I often go there, boys, and see good-looking young men shut up, who ought to be a credit to the country, in consequence, perhaps, of having, at your ages, learned to smoke one segar a day, and giving way to the bad practices that smoking may lead to afterwards, when, probably, if the money thus wasted had been (as I told you), saved, and put out at interest until they were of age, it might have aided to put them into a snug business, and a respectable position in society."

My young auditors listened with the most respectful attention, but looked quizzically at each other occasionally, as if they thought it very singular for a stranger to be thus conversing with them. Probably they had never been reasoned with on the subject before, and were pleased to be considered thinking beings. The idea was entirely new that smoking a segar might lead to a life of dissipation, and perhaps a prison. They had never before been told that the use of tobacco destroyed the health, operated on the nervous system, unfitted them for business habits, and sometimes, was the means of impairing their happiness and usefulness. Doubtless, this was news to them, but they understood what was said, and appreciated it. They were addressed in kind and familiar language, and they saw *their* benefit was the object. After canvassing the subject thus, I said, "Boys, do you ever taste liquor?" The one who said he did not smoke, replied, that he was a Cadet of Temperance." "I am glad to hear that; but have you taken the pledge?" "No," said the Cadet, "but I am willing to." "Now, boys, will you all take a pledge that you will never drink spirituous liquors, nor smoke another segar?" The Cadet thought it useless for him to take a pledge not to use tobacco, for he was sure he never would do it. "But let thy intentions be ever so correct now, there are always temptations to get into wrong habits among young men, and many have not the moral courage, when in society, to refuse what they know to be wrong. To such the pledge may give strength; and if a young man or boy can say, 'I have taken the pledge to abstain both from liquor and tobacco,' it may prove a help to him, and when his companions find he is true and firm to his good resolves, they will soon respect him the more, and reverence the virtue in him, which they are conscious they have not in themselves. Boys, will you take it?" They looked hesitatingly at each other, and the novelty of the whole affair interested them, and I could see, as they stood silently, they were pondering upon it. At last, the boy I had first addressed, said, "I will take it!" "I will, too," added the Cadet. "And will you?" "Yes," said Bill; "I sometimes smoke three or four a day, but I can quit!" "And I will, too," responded the last one.

The four lads stood on the pavement before me, and I then explained to them the importance and solemnity of taking a pledge, and the responsibility of keeping it. I told them I had no written pledge, but we were in the presence of the Almighty, who knew our thoughts, words, and actions, and He was the witness to see this act, and record it. I then repeated: "I solemnly promise, that I will never drink spirituous liquors, nor use tobacco in any shape." One after another, clearly and calmly, the boys pronounced the words, and each, as he finished, gave me his hand, to seal the compact. I then told them my name, and where I lived, but forgot until after we parted, that I had not inquired their names.

We may never meet again. Probably they will not remember my name, but I hope the interview will be blest to them in its consequences, and be a lesson to me to obey those intimations that may lead without question, "to sow beside all waters" in faith, trusting implicitly to the Lord of the harvest.

ANNUAL REPORT OF THE MANAGERS OF THE ROSINE ASSOCIATION.

PHILADELPHIA, April 4th, 1850.

Within the past year, we have presented our members and contributors with our annual, semi-annual, and a quarterly Report, and were we to produce one monthly, we could scarcely then do justice to all the topics that are connected, directly or indirectly, with the important work in which we are engaged, and which ought to claim our attention. In pursuing our reformatory operations, we are necessarily led to investigate the causes of crime, and trace its progress; and some of us, who have visited most frequently the scenes of vice, and are most familiar with the prisoner's cell and the diseased sufferers in the almshouse, alone can tell how much ought to be done, and how great is the necessity (while we pray for the blessing to rest upon our own efforts) to ask, that the Father of mercies may send more laborers into the field, and awaken other minds, with more powerful energies, to combat in the moral warfare, which ought to be fought daily—not alone in what is considered the haunts of vice, but by our own firesides, and in the circles often directly around us.

Many persons have an indefinite idea that there is a great deal of libertinism among men; but, if the facts can only be kept private, no one feels it to be their business to investigate; and thus the man of dissolute habits is constantly received into what is called good society, while his victims (who are generally the sufferers, from poverty, ignorance, and neglected domestic government) are cast out by what appears to be destiny, but is in fact the operations of that same society that upholds the equally or more guilty man, and treads upon the weak and erring woman.

As a proof of the injustice constantly practised, we will refer to a circumstance that has occurred very lately. Two minors were discovered by their father to be in the habit of visiting a couple of young girls (one of them only seventeen), residing in an improper house. The father, instead of correcting and improving the morals of his sons, proceeded to the residence of the unfortunate girls, had them arrested and thrown into prison, where one of our managers found them, and saw there, at the same time, paying them a visit, one of the young men on whose account they had been incarcerated. The opportunity was embraced of conversing with the youth, and showing him (what his father evidently did not understand) that crime was the same in both sexes, and that, if either party deserved a prison, it was himself and brother, as circumstances had placed them in a position in which they had enjoyed the advantages of society and education, of which the unfortunate partners of their guilt had been deprived. There was at the same period another girl in the prison, who had been placed there on the same account by another parent, while his equally guilty son was pursuing, in unlimited liberty, his vicious propensities.

We ask not for more leniency towards crime, but we ask for more justice. We ask society to place the ban equally upon man and woman, while they indulge in habits that sap the morals of the community—habits that are destructive to health, domestic happiness, and to the well-being and doing of those who ought to be contributors to the general good, but who, by their corrupt practices, become the curse and demoralizers of those around them.

Here, then, is the work at the fireside—here is the every-day duty. We must purify the atmosphere around us. We must instil principles into our sons, that will make them abhor vice. Our husbands, our brothers, our friends, must see that we are pure in word and deed, and that only as they assimilate with our feelings can they be dear to us—and here we shall find is the place to plant the moral standard. It is upon the family hearthstone.

Viewing it thus, and we believe it to be the true philosophy, women have the morals of the community in their own hands. Napoleon said, "What France needs, is mothers!" and we can say, what the *world needs*, is mothers!

In the records we have collected of the unfortunate inmates of the Rosine House, we find very few who have had the continued care of judicious mothers. A large majority have lost or been separated from their parents in early childhood, and have been cast upon those whose circumstances, or their want of proper principles, prevented them from bestowing what they did not themselves possess,—that consciousness of the ever-presence of the Divine Being that can alone restrain the evil thought or deed, and give the desire at all times to walk and act purely and rightly. Mothers! in our reports we have appealed to you before; and we now solemnly call upon you to make every family a moral reform society, and every domicile, where you can exert an influence, an altar, sacred to virtue and purity.

We are told there are six thousand women in our city, who are living lives of sin and shame; but who can estimate the number of men who associate with them, or the amount of vice and misery arising from these depraving connections. In our missionary visits to the abodes of these unfortunates (of which we have now paid nearly three hundred), we have frequently met with men, with whom we have conversed, and have endeavored to convince them that, in our eyes and in the sight of the Almighty, sex made no distinction—crime in both was the same; and that they were equally as amenable to the Divine law, and ought to be to the legal one, as the poor outcast with whom they associated. We have had some letters printed, addressed to them, in which we have endeavored to awaken their moral sense and their religious obligations.

The attention of our Board has also been drawn

to the condition of the children, *particularly females*, who are employed, either by their parents or others, in peddling small articles through the city. We believe such a life to be highly demoralizing, producing habits of idleness, and causing such children to be surrounded by temptations which leads them into every species of vice, and almost prevents even the possibility of future integrity or usefulness. We have presented to the Councils of our city a Petition, asking, that if there be a law that will prohibit children from being thus employed, it may be brought into operation; but, if there be none, that a suitable Ordinance may be passed. Our petition was favorably received, and has been referred to the committee on police affairs.

We are aware that many objections may be raised, and the inquiry made, What is to be done with these children? We would answer, let there be a Temporary Home for such, where they can be placed under good influences until they can be apprenticed into suitable families. We emphatically say *apprenticed*, as we believe that the present plan of hiring children has a very injurious tendency, as housekeepers generally feel no responsibility resting on them to educate or instil principles into the child that is only hired; while, on the other hand, the child feels her independence, is difficult to govern, and prematurely becomes her own. mistress, without knowledge or wisdom to direct her, and too frequently falls a victim, not to her vices, but to the mismanagement of those who ought to know that childhood needs the steady, firm government and continued care of just principles and loving hearts.

While we recommend that these children should be apprenticed, that they may be judiciously cared for, we are aware that the prejudice against their being indentured has arisen in a great degree from the belief, that children are often cruelly treated who are thus situated. We would therefore plead with housekeepers to remember, that we are as accountable to society and to our Creator for these children (while under our care) as for our own, and that their future happiness and usefulness depend upon their proper training. The educational, the kind, the gentle influences which we may throw around them, may qualify them for respectable stations in life; and the coming years, with their abundant harvests of good fruits, may repay us fully for the patience and forbearance which the waywardness of youth may have occasioned us to exercise. Parental fondness often blinds us to the faults of our own children, while the same errors committed by the foster-child excite in us only condemnation. Have we not reason to pray continually that in us, individually, the passage may be realized: "From her mouth proceedeth wisdom, and on her lip is the law of kindness."

In the late report of the chief officer of the New York Police, a most sad and frightful picture is drawn of the numbers and habits of the vagrant children in that city. In Boston, the chief marshal has made similar statements. We have not been able to obtain any statistics of such children in Philadelphia; but, our frequent riots, and the report that we have six thousand women living degraded lives, bring sufficient proofs that the childhood has been wrongly passed, that has led, in a more advanced age, to habits of crime, that shock every right feeling, and disgrace our city.

We have always been strongly impressed with the importance of education as a preventive of evil, and the statistics of the Rosine bring us additional evidence. In the whole number of inmates, one hundred and eight, who have been under our care, not one has been highly educated, and only three knew the multiplication table perfectly when admitted. The listless vacancy that is the result of ignorance, is a very productive source of vice, as the mind, if not properly trained and occupied, will crave unrestrained and improper indulgence, and the animal faculties will predominate over the mental. Great effort is now being made to increase the number of schools for young men, whose early education has been neglected. For these exertions too much praise cannot be awarded to Judge Kelley and his associates, but the subject ought not to rest here. The annals of our inmates show, that the same causes produce like effects in men and women; and the deficiency in mental, moral, and religious culture, which in the man produces intemperance, fighting, rioting, vicious associations, and finally leads to the prison and almshouse, operates with equal force upon the female mind, and thus our houses of immoral character are increased and filled with women, who, with very rare exceptions, exhibit a degree of ignorance which is disgraceful in this age to any community.

Of the one hundred and eight who have been under our care, twenty-nine did not know their letters; seventy-nine could read some at their entrance, but of that number very few sufficiently well to make reading a pleasure; forty-eight could not write, but had to make their mark.

In presenting this statement, we desire to call

attention to the subject, and ask those in whose hands the power lies, if something cannot be devised to introduce a more general degree of education among the poorer classes. Every child, male and female, ought to be considered the child of the state, and if the parents or guardians cannot, or will not give them a sufficient degree of education to qualify them for usefulness, and develope their faculties, the state ought to claim them for a certain period, and bestow upon their mental and moral culture, a large portion of the funds that are now appropriated to prisons and courts of justice. We believe a much smaller amount wisely employed, would train our youth for respectability and usefulness, than is now appropriated to support our police, the courts, the prisons and the almshouses. Pennsylvania should only need these institutions for emigrants, who have been placed under less favorable circumstances.

To remedy, as far as was in our power, the evils of ignorance, we have insisted on all our inmates attending the school, and the progress of many has been pleasing to themselves, and to us. A young girl, who six months since was brought from the prison, in her fifteenth year, who did not know her letters, and was quite ignorant of sewing, during that period has learned to read tolerably well, is improving in her writing, and can now cut, fit, and make a dress, in a manner that would be creditable to an experienced mantua-maker. Every girl who stays six months in the house, can (if she will) enjoy the same advantages, and make equal progress, while at the same time, she may be initiated in housewifery. A person in our employ, teaches *Ladies*, "*Fowler's System of Dress Cutting*, by measurement." Our inmates have also the advantage of her instructions, and of understanding the art scientifically, and let their situations in life be what they may, they can (if they choose), be competent to make dresses for themselves and others.

In the review of our operations during the past year, we have had, as we must ever have in this work, many occurrences to try us and prove our faith and patience; but while we see an increasing number circling around us, who have been in our Institution, and are now placed in respectable families, where they are a credit to themselves, and to us, we feel encouraged to make renewed exertion, and ask again and again for wisdom to act rightly, and for gratitude that our efforts in so many instances have been so successful.

Within a few weeks, one who was under our care fourteen months, has been respectably married. Her mind during that period appeared to be religiously affected, and when she returned to her relatives (from whom she had been separated several years), she became connected with the Methodist Church. The young man she has married was a member of the same class, and a connection thus formed, promises well for the future happiness of both parties.

The writer, ten days since, visited a friend in the country, who has one in her family who left the "Rosine" eighteen months since. Her bright and happy face spoke its own testimonial, as she welcomed her former friend, and the lady with whom she lived acknowledged she had never had a more kind and capable girl in her house. She feels she is to her a treasure, while by the general propriety of her conduct, she has won her way into the affections of every member of her family.

While writing this passage, a young woman called who was formerly an inmate, but who has been several months living with a widow lady. Her tears flowed freely as she spoke of her past life, and of her gratitude to those who she considered had saved her, and laying her hand on the Bible beside her, she said, "the Almighty knows in the future I only wish to do right—I wish to take that pledge." Solemnly then, upon the book she made her promise. May the Power she then invoked, enable her to keep the resolutions of that hour.

Another, to whom we referred in a former report, as having been six years mistress of a noted house, after spending seven months in the "Rosine," was placed with some friends in Jersey. In consequence of her continued good conduct, we have received from one of the family, twenty-five bushels of potatoes, and within a few days ten bushels more from a neighbor of the first donor, who had also become satisfied, that the benefits arising from the Society to such individuals, can only be estimated by Him who holds the balance. Through the kindness of other friends, we have been supplied with nearly all our vegetables during the winter.

In our various reports, we have spoken of the necessity of a "Temporary Home," where respectable women who are friendless, but who are able and willing to work, may be sheltered and protected, until employment can be procured for them. Our knowledge of this necessity has come gradually upon us. We discovered that some of the Intelligence Offices in our city were in the pay of persons who kept immoral houses, and that young and innocent girls, inquiring for situations, were sent to these houses, and thus led to ruin. In other cases, they have wandered from house to house, inquiring for employment, until faint, discouraged, and disheartened, they have entered the only doors that seemed open for them. Many women came to the Institution telling their friendless and homeless condition, and when we informed them our house was not the proper home for them, they have begged to be allowed even to lie upon the floor, as the watch-house, or a worse place must be their only resort, if we refused them. Under these circumstances, we have had to give them shelter until we could provide them with places, and in several instances, we have taken them to our own homes; but such individuals have never been considered as inmates, or subjects for the Institution.

With the knowledge of these facts, came the feeling of the necessity of a suitable Intelligence Office. We accordingly opened one, and have received applications for situations from nine hundred and ninety-seven women. Of these we have procured homes for five hundred and sixty-four. But there were still four-hundred and thirty-three, for whom we could not get employment. We knew there was work enough in the country for all of these, if we could give them a "Temporary Home," and establish a communication through the different sections of our own, and the neighboring states, by which both parties might become aware of the necessities of each other.

With this view, some of our members called a public meeting to consider the subject, and the result has been, the formation of the TEMPORARY HOME ASSOCIATION, for the benefit of friendless women and children. This society, though springing thus from the "Rosine," is entirely unconnected with it, and stands upon independent footing. Upwards of a hundred women have become members of it, and twenty-two hundred dollars have been collected towards the sum of five thousand, with which they propose to commence operations.

These facts prove, that the energies and labors of the "Rosine" members have not been confined to the inmates of our house. Our aims are both prevention and remedy! We entered into the work when and where Providence opened the way, and we have endeavored to be faithful, as the performance of other duties opened before us. We have not chosen our path, but humbly acknowledge we have been led along by that Hand, that saw fit to choose his own instruments for his work of mercy.

The reformation of women is particularly the province of women, and through their influence alone, can we expect those who have deviated from virtue, to be again restored to a respectable station. Men may shelter, feed, clothe, and give moral and religious instruction, but every woman knows she can only be upheld and supported by her own sex; the formation and operations of this society give the repentant wanderer the surest promise that she will be sustained in her upward and onward efforts. With pleasure we perceive, that those who have gone from the Institution into families to live, show by their conduct a continued affection, as they return to visit the family whenever circumstances will admit. They had felt perhaps for years, that they had no home, but the social affections had not died in their hearts, and the Rosine has been to them home, parents, and friends.

At our quarterly meeting in October, we received

letters from two who had been under our care, but who have been living in families, one a year, and the other two years. In these letters they expressed their gratitude, and asked permission to become members of the Society, that they might assist, by contributing to the funds, in doing for others, what had been done for them. The one who left us two years since, besides clothing herself comfortably, has placed forty dollars of her wages in the saving fund. Another, who has been living in one family nearly two years, and who has become a church member, is now a subscriber to the "Christian Advocate," and another religious journal. These are the right kind of evidences. When we see a desire to do good to others, and to cultivate a literary and religious feeling in themselves, instead of spending, as formerly, their ill-gotten means in gaudy ornaments and riotous living, we must feel that Providence has blest the work, and opened the eyes and minds of some who walked in sin, and made them see that the paths of virtue are the ways of peace and pleasantness.

Some persons imagine a house of reformation should be a species of prison, but we believe that the influences of a suitable private family, are more healthful than a continued seclusion, *after an individual is properly prepared to enter such a home*, and we therefore cannot name any particular period as necessary for them to continue in the Institution, but feel we must judge by the circumstances of each case.

The number of garments made in the house for the use of the family during the past year, is - - - -	297
For customers, 77 dresses; 15 vests; 43 pairs of pantaloons; 67 shirts; 50 chemises; 56 quilts; 43 sheets; 14 pillow cases; 108 sun bonnets; 25 pairs of drawers; 28 mantillas and sacks; 29 coats; sundries, numbering 73, making a total of - - - -	628
Whole number of articles made, - -	925

Our expenses have been, during the year, for rent, salaries, clothing, marketing, &c., - - - - - - - -	1,522 82
Loaned to Rosine Store, - - -	260 68
Cash on hand, - - - - - -	50 11
	$1,833 61

Our receipts have been, for work done in the house, - - - - - - -	$261 79
Annual subscriptions from members, -	365 00
Annual subscriptions from gentlemen, -	254 00
Donation from Fanny Kemble, - - -	200 00
Subscriptions collected by R. Wainwright,	54 25
Interest on loan, towards the purchase of the house, - - - - - - - -	168 00
Donations solicited or received by the Managers, - - - - - - -	530 57
	$1,833 61

This statement shows our income is still insufficient to meet our expenses, and we have been forced to solicit contributions in both goods and money. Those only who have been collectors for other societies, can realize the unpleasantness of the task, and understand the effort required to raise the amount of five hundred and thirty dollars, besides articles of merchandise, to meet the necessities of the family. Providence has opened the hearts of many to respond to our call, and we have received donations in coal, oil cloth, zinc, groceries, queensware, crackers, soap, starch, shoes, dry goods, drugs, and stationary. The printers' have also exhibited their usual kindness and generosity, and Drs. J. D. Griscom, H. S. Patterson, Henry T. Child, and George Truman, have bestowed their attendance gratuitously.

We have thus been enabled to support the house, and trust that the hand that placed us in this work will still open sources of revenue to maintain it. But we look not for miracles. We know that the industry of our inmates ought to pay a due proportion of our expenses, but many of them come to us very ignorant, and are mere learners while they are in the house. As soon as they become good work-women, *if we think they are otherwise prepared*, we place them in situations as suitable families present, that they may earn the bread of independence, and feel the responsibility of endeavoring by continued effort, to win that character that will enable them to find homes and means wherever they may be located.

Our annual subscription list might readily be increased, if every member would feel she was a collector for the society, and invite her friends, male and female, to become subscribers. The Managers would thus be relieved from the necessity to which they have been subjected, of soliciting funds.

If they fulfil their duties as they should, they will see far more to do than they can accomplish without being collectors. We have paid nearly three hundred visits to immoral houses, and this we feel to be the true missionary work. Here is the spot in which we should labor. The heathen at our doors are to be converted. Christian men and women, will you not help and sustain us? There are women in your city who think they would commit a sin to go to church; that a prayer from their lips would be a profanation and mockery; yet the name of their Maker is uttered hourly, not in prayer or praise, but in disgusting oaths, and awful blasphemies. The game of cards, and the drunkard's revel, are the daily opiates to drown thought. And where are the mothers laboring to prevent this evil? Where the missionaries to present the remedy? Have they gone to the banks of the Ganges? Sisters! this is our mission! Let us ask the Father, that he will qualify us to work in his vineyard. The field is truly white unto harvest! Both souls and bodies are to be gathered.

Father, give us strength and wisdom,
  To discern, and do thy will;
Purify us for thy mission,
  Self subdue, and love instil.
Father! we have had thy blessing—
  Still, thy blessing would we ask!
Make us better—truer—purer—
  Fit us for the Christian's task.
Thou hast opened here before us,
  Where the path of duty lies;
Where immortals may be gathered,
  Trained and cultured for the skies.
With thy arm beneath—around us,
  We have toiled and knew no fear!
Still we crave thy help, thy blessing;
  All is safe when thou art near.

Our members and subscribers are requested to pay their annual contributions, at the store of the Rosine House, as soon as convenient after the Annual Meeting.

REFLECTIONS BY MY MOTHER'S BEDSIDE.

Occasioned by hearing her say, a few days before her death, that she felt "as in the wilderness." These lines seemed to dispel the misty feelings that clouded her mind, and were succeeded by a state of peaceful quiet, and unwavering faith, that soared beyond the bounds of time, and brightened her dying eye, as she exclaimed, "Lord, let now thy servant depart in peace!"

The Wilderness—the Wilderness
  Is not a dreary place;
Amid its countless sands we still
  God's mercies ever trace!
The desert rock, the desert plain,
  May seem both bleak and bare,
The barren heath seem void of life,
  Yet God is even there!
The storm may come, the wind may howl,
  The lightning rend the sky,
The thunder roll from pole to pole,
  Yet God is ever nigh!
Where through creation can we turn,
  To what wild savage spot,
By sea or land, from clime to clime,
  And find where He is not?
In every leaf and flow'ret wild,
  In insect, beast, and bird,
In every pebble stone, and shell,
  His holy voice is heard!
Then why in human hearts alone,
  Is felt a dreary void,
And why, when all around is good,
  Is man alone alloyed?
Why, in the Temple, where *His* love
  Most wondrously is shown,

Is found the only taint of sin,
  The want of faith alone?
The bird that leaves the chilling clime,
  And seeks a warmer home,
Doubts not the Spring will bloom again,
  And brighter days will come—
Returning then, in trustful faith
  She builds her little nest,
Fulfils the duties of her kind,
  And leaves to God the rest.
But we (with reasoning powers endued,
  And favored far above
All nature round), yet sometimes doubt
  His wisdom—goodness—love.
We know that rain and storms but give
  To verdant beauty birth,
And streams that overflow their banks,
  Enrich the drinking earth.
Thus is it with our inward man,
  Yet feeble, weak, and frail,
We cannot see the hand of love,
  That guides each swelling gale.
When chilling winds, and wintry storms,
  Around our path prevail,
How oft the sinking spirit feels
  Its trustful courage fail.
Impatient nature ever longs
  To draw the veil aside,
Dispel the clouds that shroud the sun,
  And all his glories hide.
Oh! could our spirits always feel,
  Tho' darkness reigns around,
That God is with us through the night,
  And in the cloud is found.
Oh! could the heart, in trustful faith,
  Calmly await the day,
Nor think the night-dews linger long
  Upon our weary way.

Lord! give us patience, faith, and hope,
  And lead us as thou led
Thine Israel through the wilderness,
  And over Jordan's bed.
And make us feel, the Wilderness
  Is as a garden fair,
The desert, with Thy glory filled,
  Thy presence, everywhere.
The storm, the cloud, the barren heath,
  Alike thy wisdom show;
Thy finger rules the worlds above,
  Thy love, the world below.

ANNUAL REPORT OF THE MANAGERS OF THE ROSINE ASSOCIATION.

Managers:—President, Annis P. Furness, Pine, seven doors beyond Broad St.; Vice-President, Sarah Tyndale, 22 Prune St.; Treasurer, Mira Townsend, 101 Arch Street; Secretaries, Mary M. Hastings, 24 N. Schuylkill Eighth St., Lydia Gillingham, 54 N. Fifth St.

Ann S. Campion, 27 Branch St.; Susanna Lower, 253 N. Seventh St.; Mary R. Wetherald, Camden; Lydia Longstreth, 272 N. Third St.; Elizabeth Pugh, Germantown; Rachel Wright, 273 Green St.; Ellen Lord, West Penn Square; Esther Hancock, 100 Wallace St.; Anne M. Needles, Twelfth and Race Sts.; Sophia Lewis, 119 Wood St.; Elizabeth Hunt, Fifth below Green; Sarah J. Webb, 244 Green St.; Margaret Skillman, 94 Wallace St.

PHILADELPHIA, April, 1851.

In meeting again with our members and friends, we naturally revert to the subjects most likely to interest them, and the questions they would most probably be desirous to ask. What is your progress? Your actual success? Are you encouraged to persevere in your efforts? To these questions, some of us who have been the longest in the work can reply, we have met with some who had not strength to persevere in their good intentions, but this has not discouraged us. When this Association was formed, we were aware of our own weakness; we knew we made many good resolutions, which time, or even trifling circumstances, induced us to abandon; how then could we expect more firmness and stability, more perseverance in the path of rectitude, among those who had never known or felt the advantages and good influences that had surrounded us, and had been as supporting angels, whispering to us of love and kindness, of truth and purity? We knew well, that to many who would come under our care, these gentle voices were almost unknown; with them impulse had been the governing power, their reasoning faculties had been little cultivated, and religious influences were almost unknown. Yet with all these discouraging facts, after the experience of three years and a half, we can truly say, *we are not discouraged.* We consider this a great, a glorious work, and can only lament that we have not more time and energy to devote to it. When we consider the situation of many unfortunate young women, who have been brought up, as it were, in the bosom of iniquity from childhood, for in some of the streets of our city, the very atmosphere seems impregnated with drunkenness and debauchery, can we wonder at the lowness of the moral standard, and must we not rejoice in the knowledge, that even some of these can be elevated, that they can pass through the moral regeneration that will snatch them from this state of crime and degradation, and place them, where they may sit "clothed in their right mind," the good, the noble, the generous feelings of their natures developed, and their aspirations awakened after all that is high and holy. And this we believe has been verified in some instances. Some of our first inmates were those to whom the prison cells were familiar, who had passed through every degree of crime, who were truly nuisances in the community; and now these women are filling respectable stations in life, the stigma of reproach has passed from them, the Church has acknowledged them as Christians, and the approving voices of their own consciences bring them a happiness previously unknown. With some of these the language has repeatedly been, "The blessed Rosine!" One who had lived a number of years in violation of the moral laws, in speaking to one of our managers a few days since remarked, "Before I went to the Rosine, I felt as if I were living in a tomb; all that was good seemed dead within me; I had no hope; I believed there was no possibility of rising to a higher state. The first ray that dawned upon me, was from the words of one of the Managers of the Rosine, who visited the house where I was staying. I grasped the hope, and went to the Rosine. More than three years have passed since then. I am now housekeeper in a wealthy family, where I am respected and am happy. I have as good clothing as I desire, am a member of a church, and now expect to place part of my wages at interest, to provide for a future day." Another of our first inmates who had spent two years in a prison, and had returned to the same evil way that led to her incarceration there, was brought by one of our managers from a house of most notorious character, to the Rosine. Upon leaving there she was placed in a worthy family, where her good resolutions were strengthened, and her hope and faith encouraged. Thus sustained, she has won golden opinions from all around her, and a most affectionate interest endears her to those with whom she has been living. She, who in her years of dissipation never laid by a farthing, has now fifty dollars in the saving bank. Another, who was formerly under our care, has married very respectably within the past three months, and has gone to housekeeping with every prospect of doing well. She is the third of our children who has married worthy and respectable young men. The first one who entered, upon opening the Rosine House, staid with us fourteen months. She was then received by her family. Soon after she became a member of a church, and has since married a young man a member of the same church. Her history was known to some of the ladies of that congregation, and with her, they have entered into the work of visiting houses of immoral character. We have now in our institution a girl of seventeen, who was brought from a house of that kind through the missionary efforts of this woman, and who has been indentured to the managers by her mother, as the only means of saving her. Two others, who were formerly apprenticed to us when about seventeen years of age, under similar circumstances, staid their time, behaved exceedingly well, and are now acting in a manner entirely satisfactory to their friends. We mentioned in our report of last year, that we had received donations of thirty bushels of potatoes, in consequence of the good conduct of one who had been six years the mistress of a noted house. During the past winter, we have received five bushels more from the same source. One of the first objects of our care was placed in a worthy family in moderate circumstances. They thought they could not afford to give her more than seventy-five cents wages, but as the home was desirable in other respects, she went there. She has now been with them three years, has become a member of the Methodist church, and though she has been offered $1 25 per week in other situations, still stays with them. In speaking with one of us, she said, "They took me, when perhaps no one else would; they have always been kind to me; the lady is in delicate health, and might not get any one to suit her. I know they cannot afford to pay me more wages, but I owe them such a debt of gratitude that I cannot leave them." We might multiply sketches of such cases, which cheer us on to increased efforts, but we will only add, that *among our first inmates are seven who are now placed in respectable positions, where they are enabled to contribute to the funds of the Society, and having expressed a desire to become members, their names have been presented to the Board of Managers, and they have been unanimously elected members of the Association.* This fact is truly cheering when we consider, that all of these women, when they first came under our roof, had been living in open violation of the laws of both God and man, they had been without hope, banished from the society of the good and the virtuous, the influences of the Bible and the church were equally unknown, and the game of cards, the nauseous snuff, and the intoxicating draught, were the constant resorts to drown thought, and enable them to endure existence. Other associations can point to those whom they have benefited, and say, "See what we have done!" But the object of our Institution is not to blazen forth to the world that we have saved such or such a woman, but quietly and unobtrusively to throw good influences around her, convince her she has duties to perform in life, that the upward path is open to her, and qualify her as far as we are able to join in the world's work, and then send her forth, with the memory of the past buried in her heart, to start afresh, determined to win for herself the rewards of honest labor, and the approval of a good conscience.

We have had many proofs of the benefits arising from our visits among these unfortunate beings. A few days since, two of our managers were called upon by a fine-looking young woman, who they recognized as one they had visited eighteen months before, as the mistress of a house of bad character. She was of respectable family, had married foolishly in her fifteenth year, against the will of her friends, and was soon deserted and thrown upon her own resources. Thus situated, she became the prey of the spoiler; step by step she learned the iniquities and sorrows of a life of crime, and finally, as the mistress of an abode of infamy, was visited by two of our members. In her late call upon them, she said, "Until you conversed with me, I had not thought of the possibility of a return to respectable life; no one had ever spoken to me as you did; your words went to my heart; in one week after your visit I left the house, resumed my own name, and have since supported myself by my needle; I have met with great difficulties and deprivations, but nothing shall ever tempt me again to crime." We feel constantly the necessity of more laborers in this widely extended field, and regret extremely that the time of our managers, which ought to be spent in the Rosine House, in visiting the homes of these sadly erring ones, and in attending the many calls to the prison and almshouse (which appears to some of us to be a peculiar duty), should have to be devoted to going round to collect our subscriptions, and begging funds to maintain the Institution. It would be a particular kindness and relief to the managers, if those who are willing to contribute to this important institution would call upon one of them, or at the store of the Rosine House, and leave their subscriptions. The managers acknowledge with the truest feeling the sympathy and kindness they meet with in making their collections, and are assured there is in the community a sufficient appreciation of the necessity and benefits arising from this Society, to be willing to support the Institution nobly, and release the managers from the unpleasant necessity of begging from door to door.

In referring to the causes that keep these poor unfortunates from reforming, and sometimes draw them back into the sinks of iniquity, we find the most prominent, is the indulgence in liquor, which may truly be said to be the greatest curse in the community. Two of our members, in spending a day at the Moyamensing prison, visited fifty women, and upon inquiring into their cases, found only two of them who had not been committed, either from having been drinking themselves, from being with intemperate persons, or in houses where liquor in some way was the foundation of their difficulties. In spending another day in the prison, they visited about seventy women, and found only five of the number, who by their own confession, had not become inmates there from drinking themselves, or associating with inebriates. When will our legislators look at this subject in the proper light, and feel the necessity of a law which shall close every dram-shop, and only permit this bane of society to be sold, when prescribed by a respectable physician.

From a report just issued by the Managers of the House of Refuge, we find the committals there during the past year, have been 231 white children, and 148 colored. Could we investigate the histories of these children, we believe there would be few cases in which intemperance, or kindred evils in the parents, had not been the primary causes of their offspring becoming the tenants of the Refuge. Many young women who have been under our care have formerly been inmates of the Refuge.

During our visits at the prison, we have felt most forcibly the necessity of another institution. We find many women there (frequently the mothers of families), who are notorious drunkards, and who, even with a babe at the breast, are continually changing places from the dram-shop to the prison, and who, sometimes after being discharged, are again apprehended and returned to the prison, before they reach their miserable homes and deserted children. These women are not the proper subjects of a prison. They have committed no other crime than yielding to the temptations which our injudicious laws permit in every square to be laid before them. Ought we not then to labor for a change in these laws, and to make an effort to reclaim these inebriates, by promoting an association that will open a house of industry, where drunkards, both male and female, shall be taken when arrested, and employed usefully, instead of confining them in idleness, to be still more depreciated in their moral character by the depressing effect of inactive seclusion, and the disgrace of having been inmates of a prison. Such an institution properly conducted, where every man and woman should be placed when apprehended for intoxication, and there forced to labor, and the proceeds therefrom applied to the maintainance of their families, would be a blessing to the community. The expected vacation of the present House of Refuge, will present a suitable opportunity to try the experiment in that building, and leave our prison to be tenanted only by criminals. Of 155 women who have been inmates of the Rosine, 77 have been in the habit of drinking, and many others acknowledged they had occasionally resorted to the intoxicating glass. Indeed it is a common remark among them, that no woman can lead an immoral life without resorting to liquor. Another fruitful source of temptation to break the moral law, we feel bound to recall before our friends continually—*It is the low price of women's labor.* An excellent young woman who is industrious, and a well-qualified seamstress, but whose health will not permit her to engage in housework, has been making shirts for one of our stores all winter. She made the bodies and sleeves, for which she received 25 cents. They were required to be done neatly, and she has been forced to work in the evenings to make six per week, bringing her only $1 50. She could not procure respectable board for less than that sum, which left her without one cent for shoes or other necessaries. Her health has been much impaired by going to the shop without suitable clothing, no hour of rest or relaxation could be taken, and her whole physical and moral energies are consequently depressed. In this despairing condition, too many of our women are tempted to enter a course of life, from which under other circumstances they would recoil with horror. This is be no means a solitary case, for there are thousands of similar ones in our city. We are aware of the necessity of a change. The subject has been repeatedly brought before the public, but we see no probability of an improvement, *until the owners of our clothing stores shall, at a public meeting, resolve that they will raise the prices of labor.* There are very few purchasers who would not be willing (if they understood the object) to pay a few cents more for the articles they want, and those few cents may be the preservatives of the integrity and virtue, perhaps even the life of some of these oppressed operatives. We wish to impress upon the public, that true economy demands that the laborer shall be sufficiently paid. Let us remember, that the man or woman who is tempted to crime by the lowness of wages, must still be supported somewhere, *and we must furnish the means.* If we will not give them the opportunity to support themselves honestly by their labor, *we must maintain them, either as paupers or criminals.* When shall we awake from our apathy, and by the potency of our will, decree that labor shall have its proper reward?

We have in our reports, spoken of the necessity of honest intelligence offices, and the benefits resulting from that established at the Rosine. We desire to call the attention of our friends to this subject, as many excellent women come to our office, and feel they can apply there safely for situations. The necessity of care in these persons we have long known, as deception is often practised on unwary females, in many instances resulting in their ruin, from being sent from intelligence offices to houses of immoral character. We have also known of young women being entrapped by advertisements in the newspapers. The mistress of a celebrated house in this city told some of our members, she was in the habit of advertising, and asked if they did not remember seeing such notices. The last one, she said, ran thus—"Wanted by a widow lady in easy circumstances, who has no family but an invalid son, and one domestic, a young lady as companion, and assistant in sewing and chamber-work. One from the country would be preferred."

Thirty young women, she said, called in answer to this advertisement. We have also known of cases where girls looking for places from door to door, have been spoken to in the street by the keepers of such houses, and engaged to do any work they desired, and at any price they chose to ask. Need we wonder then when we see all around us the arts of the designing, and the many causes that lead to temptation, that so many fall; many, we believe, who wish to be good and virtuous girls, but the circumstances around them seem to lead to their ruin, often, with almost the swiftness of a dream.

During the past year, we have procured situations through our intelligence office for 468 women; 670 have applied for places. The most of these applicants are entire strangers to us, but among them are probably many, who may (through this medium) have been saved from a life of misery.

We hope our friends when needing domestics, will remember the *Intelligence Office of the Rosine.* Within the last year we have given a temporary shelter for a few days to 65 women, until we could procure places for them, but the opening of the Temporary Home now presents a more suitable place for the respectable but friendless female.

Our school, we believe, has been a great advantage to our inmates. Our family during the year has been larger than ever before, and it has been pleasing to see the interest evinced by some of them. An opportunity presented a few days since, for one who has been about a year in the house, to get a very desirable situation. Upon her hesitating, we inquired the cause, and found her objection to leave was her desire to gain instruction, and fearing she would lose the advantages of the school. For this purpose, she wished still longer to be permitted to continue in the institution. Many who came to us ignorant of a letter, are now reading and writing. We feel the school to be an important part of our plan, as every means of gaining useful knowledge, and every source of innocent enjoyment, may prevent that vacancy of mind that leads to the desire for company and unprofitable amusements. We have not been sufficiently aware of the importance of education as a preventive of crime, and the consciousness has been forced upon us by the examinations of our inmates. Of 155 who have been under our care, 55 could not read understandingly, and many did not know a letter; 95 could not write: but we may form some idea of their attainments from the knowledge, that *only three knew the multiplication table perfectly.* We are accustomed to plume ourselves on the educational advantages enjoyed in this country, and doubtless, those whose attention has not been called to the subject, can hardly believe the amount of ignorance, even in the free states. But of this we may form an idea, from a statement of an agent of the Bible Society. He says, that in Burlington County (one of the best counties in the state of New Jersey) he visited 150 families who were destitute of the Bible, and all knowledge of its contents. In the state of Indiana, there are 175,017 persons over 21 years of age who cannot read or write. On examining the records of our House of Refuge we find, that of 704 children received, 560 could not read intelligibly, and many did not know their letters. In the Eastern Penitentiary, of 2,300 convicts received, 594 could not read, and 517 could read, but not write. In the Moyamensing Prison, of 175 convicts sentenced in one year, 83 could not read, and 27 could read very imperfectly. These statements must induce us to believe that the promotion of education and habits of temperance will do far more for the suppression of crime, than all the prisons in the country.

We mentioned in our Semi-Annual Report, that Thomas & Martin had sent $50 to the Institution for the purchase of goods, to be made up by the Rosines, and distributed among the sufferers by the great fire in Front and Water Streets. Wm. D. Jones & Brothers, also contributed two pieces of muslin for the same purpose. The proceeds of these donations was 183 garments, which afforded relief to many who had escaped with only the clothing on their persons. Another advantage resulted from this beneficence—the kindly feelings of our inmates were called forth, and it was interesting to see the industry with which they applied themselves to the task of doing good. It gives us great pleasure to say, that after laboring for three years and a half among those who have been considered the most hardened, the most degraded, and certainly the most hopeless part of the community, that we have never yet met with one who was utterly abandoned to evil. However sunk and depraved they may be, however little consciousness they may possess of the original divinity of their natures, yet the Almighty still keeps one spark alive in their bosoms, which may be recognized even in their lowest condition, and if touched by the hand of sympathy and kindness, may, like the iron on the anvil of the blacksmith, send forth glowing emanations, and be shaped into forms of usefulness and beauty.

The number of garments made in the Rosine House during the past year, has been:

For the sufferers by the fire,	183
For the use of the Rosine family,	491
For the Temporary Home, 2 comfortables and 13 mattresses,	15
Sundry articles for customers,	1617
Total,	2306

Our expenses for the year have been:

For rent, salaries, clothing, marketing, etc., ...	$1676 65

Our receipts have been:

For work done in the House, . .	365 75
Interest on loan toward the purchase of the House, ...	168 00
Donations and annual contributions, .	1015 40
Total, ...	$1549 15

By this statement we find the Institution is in debt, and our treasurer has had to borrow $127 50 to meet expenses. This should not be so. If our members would individually exert themselves to get donations and annual subscriptions, the Institution might not only be supported, but our house be paid for, and the managers have leisure to perform their proper duties. In a little more than a year our lease will expire. Will not our friends enable us to pay for the House, and thus keep a shelter open for the returning penitent, where she may meet with kindness and encouragement from her own sex, and be trained to enter the paths of usefulness. $3,300 will be needed to effect the purchase.

Within a few days one of the originators, and most earnest laborers in the Rosine House, has passed away—

ELIZA PARKER.

Her name has been identified with the rise and progress of the Institution. No outward monument need be erected to her memory. She lives in our hearts, and we can entirely understand the emotions of one of our former inmates when she said—"I feel as if I had lost my own mother." Over the grave of the mother of Eliza Parker, is placed a stone with the inscription—

"Our Mother.—She taught us how to live and how to die."

Eliza sleeps upon the bosom of that mother, and we feel the only words to be added, are,

"She learned the lesson!"

Such a woman belongs not to a family, a church, a society. She belonged to the race. Her sympathies went forth everywhere, and, following the example of her Divine Master, it might emphatically be said—

"She went about doing good."

The soothing touch of her hand, the gentle tones of her voice, the quiet rapidity of her step, and the wisdom and kindness of her words and actions, are remembered by many, and they look around and ask, "By whom shall her place be filled?"

The Semi-Annual Meeting of the Society will take place on 5th day or Thursday, October 9th.

It is desirable that our Members should pay their subscriptions as soon after the Annual Meeting as possible.

THE FUNERALS.

We have laid in the ground another of our Rosine family. It was Alice. She had been an inmate nearly two years, and we had become much attached to her. She was an active, energetic Yankee girl, when she came to this city, and, had not the blight passed over her, would have probably made an exemplary Yankee matron, honored and esteemed in her neighborhood, and a long and useful life might have been crowned with the esteem and reverence of all who knew her. How, and when she lost her position in the home circle, where she had been the idol of her mother and the pride of her father's heart, it is not meet to tell; but she came to Philadelphia alone, and a stranger, and buried in a round of dissipation the harrowing thoughts that she dared not face, or dwell upon. In one of our visits to the house where she resided, we met, and conversed with her, but she was not then prepared to go with us. To drown the misery of the thoughts which hung like a cloud above her, she resorted to the cup of inebriation. She shrunk from her own reflections, and banished the thoughts of that dear old home in Connecticut, and the memories of former years, by drinking more madly and wildly as month after month passed away.

The newspapers spoke, in their local items, of a young girl who had fallen from the window of the third story of a house of bad character, had been very much hurt, and was taken to the hospital. It was Alice. As she laid on her bed of suffering, she could no longer banish the intruding thoughts that would come and drive her almost to desperation, and she resolved, if her life was spared, she would endeavor to walk more worthily. She had learned, that in the Rosine House she would meet the sympathy of the good and virtuous,—that an opportunity would be afforded to cultivate her better and higher faculties ; and, as her health approached restoration, she was strengthened to resolve to make an effort to regain a position in which she might fearlessly dare to meet *herself*. When she left the hospital, she came directly to the Rosine, and told the story of her temptations and trials, of her weaknesses and good resolves. Except a trifling lameness, her health appeared to be restored, and Alice seemed a happy girl, in the first real home she had found since she left dear old Connecticut. More than a year had passed away, when she began to complain of pulmonary symptoms, and gradually her face became more pale, except when brightened by the hectic flush, and Alice knew that her days were numbered. We often sat beside her, and read and talked with her, and watched her setting sun with feelings of deep interest. She was calm and collected ; she felt that her peace was made, and she, who formerly dared not to meet *herself*, feared not now to meet her Father in Heaven. Her dying words were, "Jesus, I come ! I come !"

One of the ministers, who had ofttimes talked with her, preached the funeral sermon at the Rosine House, but only the family and some of the managers went to the cemetery. It was a company of females alone. We assembled around the open grave, and stood in solemn silence. Alice had selected a hymn, which she had asked some of her companions to sing over her, and, after a pause of a few minutes, the mournful melody ascended from lips, that, until they entered the Rosine, had been unused to both prayer and praise. Again we stood in silence, and again harmonious voices breathed the sacred chant. Moore's beautiful lines were borne upon the breeze, and responded to by every heart present:

"Were not the sinful Mary's tears
An off'ring worthy Heav'n,
When o'er the sins of former years
She wept, and was forgiv'n?

"When, bringing every balmy sweet,
Her day of luxury stored,
She, o'er the Saviour's hallowed feet,
The precious perfume poured.

"And wiped them with those golden hairs,
Where once the diamond shone,
Although those gems of grief were there,
Which shone for God alone.

"O, thou who sleeps in error's sleep,
O would'st thou wake in Heav'n,
Like Mary kneel, like Mary weep,
Love much, and be forgiv'n!"

And Alice, too, was forgiven! We felt that her tears had washed away her stains, and her confidence in Divine mercy had smoothed her dying pillow, and placed before her mental sight that angelic band that seemed to be calling her away to the realms of eternal life. "Jesus, I come! I come!" was her response; and she, who had walked the earth an abandoned outcast, was numbered among the redeemed in the kingdom of her heavenly Father.

The first inmate we lost by death in the Rosine, was a young woman from the neighborhood of Cape

Island. Her father was a farmer, in moderate circumstances, and Amelia left her quiet home to gain a few dollars in one of the large hotels on the Island, during the busy season, by being employed as chambermaid. But temptations and evil ones seemed to be everywhere, and, when the time arrived for poor Amelia to return to her home, she sent her mother word she was going to the city, as she was promised a good situation there. And so Amelia came to this great vortex of good and evil, and many a time the heart of the old mother yearned to hear something of her daughter, and to know of her well doing. But she knew Milly (as they called her at home) had little practice in writing; and, therefore, though she longed for a letter, she hardly dared hope to receive one. Months passed away, and at last a letter came. It was to inform her of Milly's death. She had died among strangers, and who or what they were the mother knew not. She had been a gentle, good girl; and, though the anxious mother had ofttimes wondered why neither her daughter nor intelligence came to her, yet no thought crossed her mind, that Milly could be led into error, or bring sorrow upon her. The mother who has passed through a similar dispensation alone can understand how she felt, when the long-looked for letter came, and said her absent one had been sick some weeks, but not considered dangerously ill, when a sudden paralysis had deprived her of speech, and a few hours after of life. The letter simply said, she was at No. 204 North Eighth Street, and the mourning parent supposed it was the good situation she had spoken of to them.

The hour of interment had nearly arrived, but no intelligence was received from the friends of Amelia.

The funeral had been delayed as long as was deemed prudent, to give them time to reach the city, but no one came. The family and managers had assembled, the minister had delivered his sermon, and all present were standing singing the parting hymn, when the door opened, and the sorrowing mother hung over her pale and lifeless child. We pass over the natural manifestations of grief, and the ceremonies of interment. The mother returned with the family to the Rosine House; the managers departed, and she was alone with them. The inquiries relative to the illness and death of her daughter were all answered satisfactorily; but the number and circumstances of the inmates seemed to excite her wonder, until she ventured to inquire the meaning and character of the individuals around her. The matron had been instructed to evade, if possible (consistently with truth), the revelation of the object of the house, or the story of poor Amelia, but question after question was asked, until the whole was revealed to the astonished and heart-broken mother. "Her Milly, poor Milly, the babe she had nursed, the child she had loved and cherished, the pride of her heart, the gentle, the kind, the good Milly, whom she had hoped would be the stay and comfort of her old age, and who, when the angel of death called for her, would lay her gray hairs in the grave. My child! my child! betrayed, abandoned, dead. Oh, that the grave had closed over me, before I had seen this day, this sorrow."

In pursuing the varied duties connected with the Rosine, we have seen many a sorrowing mother and heard many a recital that has filled us with indescribable emotions. In several instances, they have brought their young daughters to us, and plead with us to take them under our care, as the only means by which they could be saved from a fate *far worse than death.* One of these girls, who was a year in the Rosine (while her friends, with the exception of her mother and sister, supposed her to be at boarding-school), is now a bright, happy-looking wife and mother, while several others are respectably situated, and bless the Rosine, as the instrument in the hand of the Almighty, that has saved them in the hour of temptation, and guided their steps into a higher and purer path. In our Reports, we have alluded to the cases of many of those who have been under our protection, but many others have claimed our care who have never entered the Rosine, but whose situations require quite as much effort, and faith, and patience; and of these we never speak. It is not our part to blazon the weakness, the folly, or the missteps of another, but it is our duty to aid, *as we may*, each separate individual, according to their necessity and our ability. We feel continually the need of Divine guidance, and to be endowed with that faith and hope that never flags or wearies. We know, that they who despair never accomplish their aims, however great or noble, and that confidence in the goodness of our cause, and our own unshrinking fidelity to it, can alone assure us of success.

SEMI-ANNUAL REPORT OF THE MANAGERS OF THE ROSINE ASSOCIATION.

President: Annis P. Furness, Pine, seven doors beyond Broad St. Vice-President: Sarah Tyndale, corner of Ninth and Sergeant Streets. Treasurer: Mira Townsend, 101 Arch Street. Secretaries: Mary M. Hastings, No. 24 Schuylkill Eighth St.; Lydia Gillingham, 54 N. Fifth St.

Managers: Ann S. Campion, 27 Branch St.; Susanna Lower, 254 N. Seventh St.; Lydia Longstreth, 272 N. Third St.; Rachael Wright, 273 Green St.; Ellen Lord, West Penn Square; Esther Hancock, 100 Wallace St.; Anne M. Needles, Twelfth and Race Sts.; Sophia Lewis, 119 Wood St.; Elizabeth Hunt, Fifth below Green St.; Sarah J. Webb, 244 Green St.; Margaret Skillman, 94 Wallace St.; Rebecca C. Grim, S. E. corner of Sixth and Wager; Elizabeth Carr, 440 N. Fourth St.; Abigail Ellis, 246 N. Seventh St.; Elizabeth Hutter, 180 Race St.

PHILADELPHIA, Oct. 9th, 1851.

Another half year has passed away, and again, we are called to report our progress to the Society, and to our contributors. Again are we asked, what have you accomplished? what is your success? and again we must reply, We are sowing, sowing—sowing on all soils, and beside all waters. We have not turned from the hard and stony ground, because we saw little hope of reaping a luxuriant harvest, for we have seen even the strong tree standing upon the almost earthless rock, and sending its roots in a wonderful manner in search of sustenance, and the tree thus supported, has given its fruit and its shade; therefore, we know that He who put us into the vineyard, and bade us labor, has a higher knowledge than ours, and that the seed cast upon the rock, or by the wayside, may be watered by the showers and the dews; the bright sun may warm it into life, and the Lord of the harvest may bless it, and cause it to bring forth fruit even a hundred fold. Feeling thus, there can be no cessation of labor, but ever hoping and trusting, we dare not consider any soil too barren, or any rock too bare, for the creative hand to fertilize, and crown with uses and beauty. And when the homeless, friendless outcast comes, weighed down with griefs and iniquities, apparently so degraded and hardened, that we feel there is little soil to receive the seed, who can say that this despised one may not be elevated to the condition of an angel? Who of us can read in the book of destiny the mercies in reserve for this individual? We believe such have been received into this Institution. Three are now laid silently in the earth who came to us thus. Two of them had long been familiar with crime, and they had drank to its very dregs, the cup of iniquity. But the hand of disease rested upon them, and they lingered upon the bed of suffering, until the Father said, "It is enough." Kind and virtuous women bent over their pillows, read to them the words of inspiration, and pointed them to the home where the weary rest, and the heavy laden may enter through the gate of prayer. The medical attendant who prescribed the physical palliatives, also spoke of the healing power of the Physician of Souls, and the words of exhortation, of prayer, and of praise, were breathed beside them, by those who preach glad tidings. Thus surrounded by good influences, the profane and reckless woman became the humble, patient child, brought through Divine mercy into a new phase of existence, preparatory to the translation to that state where temptation may no longer assail. We had the consolation to believe that in each of the three cases, an evidence was given of the acceptance of their prayers! One believed she experienced a foresight of Paradise, and the dying words of the one last buried, were, "Jesus, I come! I come!" Need we make other comment than to say, if the Rosine had not opened its doors to these women, they would all probably have passed out of existence in houses of immoral character, and under the care and influence of those whose steps lead down to destruction. We cannot limit the power of the Almighty, and we believe even in such abodes of wickedness His voice is heard and known, but can we suppose in such circumstances, their minds would have been led to seek through prayer the door of hope? Surrounded by all the horrors that congregate in such scenes of infamy, their last words would probably have been imprecations, and their last sighs groans of agonized remorse. If the Rosine House has been the agent of no other good than thus to cast its blessed influences over these unfortunate wanderers, it had done a good work, but we believe many other minds have been awakened to a sense of their condition, and brought to the footstool of mercy, some of whom have continued walking consistently from the time they first came under our care, nearly four years since. In our last Report, we mentioned that one of our former inmates had $50 placed at interest, the savings from her wages since she left the Institution. Since that period, we have received $30 more from her, which has been added to the $50, making $80 now at interest. She is also a contributing member of the Society, one of the seven former inmates who have been elected members by the Managers.

A few days since, one of our Board visited a woman in the Penitentiary, who kept the house where this young woman lived in her days of infamy. She was taken exceedingly ill while there, and the mistress of the house fearing she would die, came to one of the Managers of the Rosine, requesting her to come and see the girl, saying, "I could not bear that she should die without some good person seeing her." Providence blessed the deed! the girl was restored and taken by her new friend to the Rosine House. After remaining some months at the Institution, she was placed at service, and the $80 alluded to, have been the savings from her wages since that period. These facts were related to the convict in the Penitentiary, and a ray of pure feeling illumined her face as she said, "I have never heard from her since she left my house; you make me so happy! I am so glad I could cry." Here was a treble benefit conferred, on the fallen one who had been raised to usefulness and respectability; on this unfortunate woman, who in the seclusion of her cell had thus unexpectedly had one of her good deeds brought before her, in such a manner that her heart was filled with rejoicing, and she felt, that in the true balance of the Almighty, this one redeeming act which had been thus blest, might outweigh a multitude of sins. And she who had been the instrument of Providence, to give the hand to one, and now to speak the word to the other, felt her heart filled with gratitude, and her faith strengthened to persevere without yielding to discouragements, but to continue to *sow* in all soils, and beside all waters.

190 women of this unfortunate class, have been received as inmates since the opening of the Rosine House, and to a great number of friendless and destitute women, of *respectable character*, a shelter was given, previous to the opening of the Temporary Home, which Institution was founded and brought into existence by the Managers of the Rosine Association. Of the necessity of both these societies, it is now needless to speak. A preventive and remedial institution are equally needed: the one to save and protect the innocent and friendless; the other, to snatch the erring from the grasp of iniquity; to raise the fallen; to place within their reach the means of honorable existence, and to point them upward and onward to that higher and better state, where they may glide imperceptibly into the social and holy relations of life.

507 women and children have been provided with homes and employment, from the Temporary Home, since the house was opened, one year since, and 1195 from the Rosine, since this Institution and Intelligence Office came into existence. Total from the two Associations, 1702. These facts reply to the queries, "What have you done?" "What are you doing?" And we may add further, that in one or the other of these Homes, every woman who is able and willing to work, and whose object is to maintain herself honestly by the labor of her own

hands, may be sheltered and protected; and whatever may have been the errors of the past, if a disposition is shown for amendment and future rectitude, she need no longer say, "I have no home, no friends!" for both home and friends are offered to the deserving, as well as to those who evince a disposition to become the deserving.

Upwards of 50,000 copies of our various Reports have been circulated—18,000 of them in pamphlet form. They have been our missionaries, speaking for those who could not speak for themselves, awakening sympathy, telling the reader his duties and responsibilities, for verily we are guilty in this matter concerning our sister, if we can aid her cause, and withhold our hand. She is our sister, even if she be covered with rags and iniquities; and from the fact, that the Almighty has opened hearts and hands to provide for these, we know that their cries have ascended to Heaven, and the Angel of Mercy has been sent with his dispensation of love, to overshadow those to whom the blessings of this life have been granted, and give them a new heart and a new sight, that they may read afresh, and understand the doctrine that was given to the world long ago, but which was read apparently without understanding; for when the people read, "Do as you would be done by"—"Go and sin no more"—"There is more joy in heaven over one sinner that repenteth than over ninety and nine just persons," and, "Inasmuch as ye have done it to the least of these, ye have done it unto me;" they professed to believe it, and to be the followers of Him who preached these doctrines, yet still the prisons were unvisited, the detected violator of the laws, and the weak and erring woman have been cast aside (perhaps by those equally guilty), with "Stand off, I am more holy than thou." But this angel of mercy has awakened heart after heart, and made them interpret these passages, and see they were meant to be the every-day experience of men and women, and a Howard, a Fry, a Dix, and others, were inspired to show the people that the dead can still be raised—the dead in sin—that the lost may be found, and that the fatted calf may still be killed, in rejoicing over the repentant prodigal.

The miracles and parables were full of meaning. They were not intended solely for that time, but for all time; not only for that people, but for us and all coming generations; and as we show in our lives the manifestations of our faith, we prove in the only way our discipleship, for it is now as of old, "By their fruits ye shall know them." Reading thus anew these doctrines, we have sent our missionary pamphlets to say, our eyes have been in a degree enlightened, and we are trying to live these doctrines in our own experience, and already we can say, in a degree, we understand them, for we have said to the erring woman, "Go, and sin no more;" and behold, we have seen her clothed in the white robe, and in the peace and harmony of our own spirits, some of us can testify, that we have known something of the joy of heaven, over the sinner that repenteth.

But with all our efforts, we feel oppressed with the magnitude of the work that ought to be accomplished, and with the knowledge that we are surrounded by sources of evil, that in every square poison the atmosphere, and generate vices of every description. The injudicious system which our law-makers have adopted, of increasing our revenue from licenses to sell liquor, is producing the most alarming effects in our community, and our statistics show, that the expenses of supporting our prisoners and paupers are increased, in consequence of the indulgence in liquor in a far greater ratio than the receipts from the sale of licenses. Prior to the change in the License Law, in April, 1849, the licensed houses for the sale of spirituous liquors were 750, and they now number 2432. Thus we see 2432 proprietors are making a living for themselves and families, by the sale of intoxicating drinks, to pervert the manners and morals of our citizens; bring disease, poverty, wretchedness, and disgrace into their families, and produce, not only in themselves, but in their offspring, those downward tendencies that unfit them for the uses and virtuous enjoyments of life. In examining the cases of our inmates, we find many of them are the children of parents addicted to this vice, and as we believe that scrofula, consumption, and insanity may be transmitted from parent to child, we must believe that the disease of intemperance may descend in a similar manner. Dr. Howe says, in his Report to the Legislature of Massachusetts, that the parents of 306 idiots under his care, were habitual drunkards. We know children partake of the tempers, disposition, and appearance of their parents, and that the drunkard not only enfeebles his own system but frequently entails mental disease upon his family; and, when this intemperance becomes a fixed habit, a disease, it brings with it an irresistible impulse, which draws its unhappy victim into practices and positions equally disgusting and degrading, and his offspring must, by their very organization, be predisposed to vice and unhealthy stimulants. Within the past week a young girl was received into the Rosine, whose parents were both drunkards, and her whole narrative proved, that she had imbibed the poison at the breast, been subjected to its deadening, debasing influences, and finally was brought to ruin by a comrade of her father's, in the presence of her mother, who was lying drunk upon the floor. Did our limits permit we could give other startling facts, at which humanity revolts; but, to bring the subject fully before our citizens, we must refer to statistics, which affect the pecuniary interests of every one.

The money now paid into the Treasury of the Commonwealth, for licenses for taverns, distilleries, breweries, beer and eating-houses, amounts to about $60,000 per annum, while the annual expenditures to support our Prisons, Almshouse, Houses of Refuge, Court of Quarter Sessions, City and Marshal's Police, are about $550,000. To every reflecting mind it will not be necessary to state, that these expenses are caused mainly, either directly or indirectly, in consequence of the use of stimulating liquors.

Of 5000 cases admitted in one year into our Almshouse, 2323 were intoxicated when received, 281 were cases of mania potu, thus showing that more than one half of the number admitted were the direct victims of this injudicious system, and we may safely draw the inference, that a large proportion of the other half were indirectly paupers, from the same cause. When we refer to the Report of Marshal Keyser, of July, 1851, we find the number of arrests, by his police, to be 7131; of these, 73 were for vagrancy, 636 assault and battery, 135 fighting, 625 intoxication, and 3622 for breaches of the peace. During last year 5987 persons were brought before the Mayor for drunken and disorderly conduct. The great majority of these individuals have families, into which they carry poverty, disease, and degradation, and the professed benefits derived from it, are, the reception of $60,000 into the treasury, and the support of 2432 rum-sellers.

Some of our Members may perhaps inquire, why these statements are made in a Report of the Rosine Association, and what particular connection they can have with our inmates. We believe a knowledge of these circumstances, and of their effects, is of vital importance in our reformatory movement. When case after case comes before us, of women, whose minds appear to be weak, where we find little or no principle, and scarcely a perception between right and wrong, we must look for the causes of this imbecility, this absence of principle, these deviations from correct conduct. We find the solution in many cases to be intemperance, in one or both parents, the consequent deterioration of the mental faculties of the child, the degrading scenes it witnesses, and the debased associations into which children are brought from the dissolute habits of their parents. Thus vice and recklessness become familiar, and they are predisposed by their organization and position to enter at an early period into the soul-deadening career. At almost every house of immoral character liquor is sold, and to enhance the profits of the keeper the unfortunate inmates are tempted to drink constantly, to benumb their own sensibilities, so as to enable them to endure their wretched existence, and prompt them to induce their visitors to enter also this fearful road to ruin. Thus the fondness for stimulants is cultivated, until the whole being is debased.

When an inmate is received into the Rosine House the Temperance Pledge is usually administered, and when they depart, we have reason to believe they generally intend and desire to aim at a higher, better life. But the dram shop under its varied names is in every square, the temptation on every hand, and in almost every case, when those who have been under our care abandon the situations in which they have been placed, and return to their former haunts, we find the first temptation has been the fatal cup, in some professedly respectable drinking-house. Have we not reason then to investigate this subject, and urge our friends to assume their duties, in endeavoring to remove this fruitful source of evil, which is pervading with its poisoning influences our whole city, demoralizing our community, rendering nugatory in a great degree the efforts of our benevolent institutions, and draining our pockets in the form of taxes, to support our Courts, our Police, our Almshouse and Prisons. Two-thirds of our charitable institutions might close their doors if the sale of intoxicating liquors was prohibited.

But, amid the regrets and disappointments to which we are thus subjected, we have much to cheer us. During the past 18 months, our family has been larger than ever before, and the continued good conduct of many of those who came under our care nearly four years since, gives us the best evidence that we have not labored in vain. The tokens of affection we are constantly receiving from some of these poor friendless children is highly gratifying. Occasionally a note bespeaking their feelings is quietly slipped into our hands. On last Valentine's Day, one of our managers received seven of these pledges of love and gratitude. Some of them were with difficulty deciphered, as the authors probably were ignorant of a letter, when they entered the house, but they all breathed a consciousness that they were better women than they had been, and that the Rosine had been the instrument of making them so.

We will refer to a circumstance illustrative of the kind and generous feelings which is sometimes evinced by our inmates. A woman from Ireland deserted her husband and two children, and came to this city. Here she sank herself down step by step, until one of our Managers found her in the prison, and brought her from there to the Rosine. After a course of good conduct for several months she wrote to her husband, informing him of her situation and expressing her penitence. He replied immediately and invited her to return, assuring her of his forgiveness. Her anxiety to be reinstated in her home and in the hearts of her husband and children was now so great, that her companions became deeply interested, and called a meeting among themselves, at which they addressed a petition to the Managers for work, by which they might in their leisure moments earn something towards defraying her expenses back to Ireland. Their petition was granted, and about ten dollars was thus earned by over-work.

During the past six months the number of garments made for customers has been - - - - -	533,	bringing	$202 06
By inmates for their own emolument, - - - -	57,	"	11 62
To pay for the Irish woman's passage, - - - - -	24,	"	10 00
For the use of the inmates and Institution, - - - -	170		
Total, - - - -	784		

190 Women have been received *as Inmates* since the opening of the house, besides a great number of respectable women, to whom a temporary home has been given, until they could be placed in permanent houses. Of the 190 inmates, 79 have been placed at service in respectable families, 2 have been sent to their friends in New York, 1 has returned to her relations in Scotland, 5 have married—one marriage took place in the Institution, 5 have been restored to their parents, 3 have died, 11 were sent to the almshouse, 3 were received, and went to housekeeping again with their husbands, 58 have been dismissed as unsuitable cases, or left, with, or without permission, and 28 are now in the Rosine House. Our family is sometimes increased for a few days, by the return of some who have been at service, when they have occasion to change their places. At such periods we always encourage them to come back, as to a parent's house, and other situations are then procured for them.

Our expenses within the six months have been,

For rent, salaries, clothing, marketing, &c.,	$868 81
Cash returned, borrowed previously to our last report, - - - - - - -	127 50
Total, - - - - - -	$996 31

Our receipts have been,

For work done in the House, - - -	$202 06
Interest on loan, - - - - - -	86 91
Annual subscriptions paid and donations solicited, - - - - - - -	587 50
From the committee to celebrate the arrival of the Steamship City of Glasgow,	70 00
Board of inmates working on their own account, - - - - - - -	23 00
Total, - - - - - -	$969 47
Deficiency in income, - - - - -	26 84

CERTIFICATE BY AUDITORS.

The undersigned having been appointed by the Board of Managers of the Rosine Association to examine the Accounts of the Treasurer, Mira Townsend, have attended to the duty assigned them, and find the Books have been accurately kept, and are correct in every particular.

MARY M. HASTINGS,
ANNE M. NEEDLES.

9th Month, 19, 1851.

It is exceedingly unpleasant to have to refer in our Reports to our pecuniary necessities, and to be forced to solicit from door to door the means of supporting our Rosine family. We have still hoped that amid our wealthy citizens some hearts would be opened towards these poor outcast children, who would feel the necessity of endowing such a Home, where they could be sheltered, protected, taught "to support themselves honestly by the labor of their own hands," their minds cultivated by educational, moral, and religious influences, and where finally they might be placed in positions to be good and useful members of the community.

The Rosine is no longer merely an experiment; it is an *Incorporated Society*, taking its place amid other benevolent associations, and second to no one in its necessity and usefulness, in the earnestness of some of its laborers, or their devotion to the interests of these unfortunates. We feel that our purpose is a high, a holy one, and that we have a claim upon the sympathies and purses of our citizens, to aid us in effecting our object.

Our duties are numerous, and highly responsible. To receive, examine, and judge of every case that presents for admission; to administer to the various necessities of our household, and cause our inmates to be mentally and physically instructed; to provide homes for those who are prepared to leave; to visit houses of immoral character, the almshouse and prison; to receive numberless calls from persons on business, connected with, or relative to the Institution; to receive and reply to numberless letters; attend to the numerous outdoor interests of our inmates, and lastly, to raise funds to support the Rosine House and family.

Our friends will perceive that these varied duties consume a great amount of time, and some of us feel, when we are required to go out day after day soliciting funds, that this is not our *proper sphere.* Some of our other duties must be neglected, that we may have time to solicit contributions; for our family must be fed and clothed, and our other expenses paid, or we must say to these friendless ones, We have no longer a home for you.

And now, in less than another year, on the 31st day of next July, our lease will expire, and by an agreement with our landlord, we may then become owners of the property, by the payment of $5,000.

The price of the house is $6,333, $1,300 of which sum is now invested in a mortgage on the house. $1,750 we have out at interest. Will not our friends aid us in raising the $3,000, that an open door may be secured to these, "the poorest of the poor." We acknowledge the kindness of our friends in their contributions, both in goods and money, but the cause is not our cause alone, it is their cause also; it is the cause of purity, virtue, morality, charity, justice, and religion.

ROSA GOVONA.

We are frequently asked by those who were not present at the formation of the Rosine Association of Philadelphia, the meaning of the name. To such we may reply—Rosa Govona, a young Italian girl, was left in poverty, and earned her living by honest industry. A young and destitute orphan claiming her sympathy, she said, "Come and live with me; you shall earn your living honestly, by the work of your own hands." The two labored together; and soon other poor girls presenting, she took them also under her charge, and they engaged in lace-making, and other similar employments. The number of girls increasing gradually to seventy, they entered into the silk and woollen manufacturing, under the care of the priests, who provided for them in an old convent the necessary accommodations.

The business increasing, they were enabled to add to their family, until they numbered three hundred women. The government encouraged them, by giving them contracts to supply the army with clothing, and the manufacturing of gold lace, and other fancy military trimmings, increased their profits, and gave them great opportunity to exercise their industry and ingenuity to the best advantage. Rosa was the mainspring of the whole, and her genius and virtue regulated everything in such a manner, that the propriety of their conduct and their prosperity was equally remarkable. The fame of this institution spread over Italy, and Rosa was invited by the authorities of other places to found similar establishments, which she did in seven cities. Leaving Mondovi (the place of her nativity), after making arrangements for the future prosperity of the Rosines there, she took some of the experienced hands with her, and, with the aid of the government and the priests, established the other institutions. In these, poor and unfortunate girls were received, and taught to labor; and over the door of each of these houses was inscribed, "You shall support yourself honestly by the labor of your hands."

The story of Rosa Govona being published in Chambers' Miscellany, and copied in the Advocate and Guardian, met the eye of an individual, whose mind had been drawn to commiserate the condition of many of the unfortunate women living in vice and degradation in Philadelphia. She had often asked, "Can nothing be done for them?" She could not suppose that all were hopelessly depraved who appeared so. She believed the Almighty had implanted good feelings and right desires in every mind; and that, though circumstances might have prevented their development, and evil associations cultivated the lower propensities, yet the germs of a better, higher, nobler nature were there, and only needed to be awakened and encouraged by influences that might be cast around them, to elevate them to the enjoyment of rational pleasures, and give a desire for a life of useful and respectable industry. With these impressions, the story of Rosa Govona came before her, and a light dawned upon her mind. She exclaimed, "If Rosa could do so much, surely *we* can do something!" The subject was laid before some of her friends, a meeting was held, and the Rosine Association formed, which now numbers upwards of five hundred women as members. Ninety-six females have been inmates of the Institution, many of whom, after living several years in the indulgence of criminal habits, have been received there, retained under instruction some months, and are now placed in respectable families, where they give evidence by their conduct and conversation, that, however erring and unfortunate the past may have been, the right opportunity and influences alone were wanting to elevate them, give them a sense of propriety, and animate them to aim at the fulfilment of the high and sacred duties of woman. These facts prove, that, though the unequal verdict of society had taken from them every hope of the possibility of restoration to happiness or usefulness, yet, as soon as they felt they were under the protection, and were sustained and encouraged, by their own sex, those passions which disgraced and degraded them became softened, hope again sprang into life within them, and once more they felt they had an object to struggle and live for. They were down—society had placed its heel upon them. The Rosine Association was formed. The hand of woman was extended—the probe, the wine, and the oil were used. The age of miracles was not passed. The dead were raised, and women, who had truly been dead in sin and without hope, are now clothed in their right minds, and sitting at the feet of their Heavenly Father.

The name of Rosine Association was given in honor of Rosa Govona. Her story proved how much could be accomplished by energy and industry; and no name could be more appropriate than that of the one who had been so great a benefactor of her sex in her own country, and whose example inspired others on a distant shore to enter also into these "walks of usefulness."

The Temporary Home Association, formed in June last, has come into existence from the many applications from virtuous women in destitute circumstances, who applied to be received into the care of the managers of the Rosine House. Another Institution was felt to be needed, and, after due deliberation, the Temporary Home Association comes before the public, for the purpose of preparing and sustaining an asylum which shall be a cheap, safe, and respectable boarding-house for women seeking employment—where the stranger, with or without funds, shall be received and sheltered, until homes or business can be procured for them, and where also children, who are cast unprotected upon the street to beg, to steal, or to starve, may find a temporary home, until a permanent one may be open for them.

Eight institutions have been the result of the labors of Rosa Govona in Italy, and the Rosine and Temporary Home Associations in Philadelphia (though differing in their plans from those established by her) have been in a degree fostered into existence by the emanations from her genius and goodness, and prove, that however humble the individual, every one may have influence, and effect great good, if they choose to exercise the faculties Providence has given them.

The situation of manufactures in this country, and the habits of our people, prevent such institutions here as exist in Catholic populations, where the influence of the priests leads females to lives of seclusion and devotion, in accordance with the precepts inculcated by them.

The managers of the Rosine, believing that the cultivation of the higher faculties and the social qualities leads to the greatest usefulness in life, and that American habits were too changeful for women to be permanently benefited by manufactures, resolved to endeavor to prepare the inmates of the Institution for entering into all the family relations, by educating them, mentally and morally, and teaching the various branches of sewing and domestic housewifery. The object of this Society, is not to keep those it seeks to benefit cloistered for life, but to prepare them for usefulness, and send them forth to take their portion of the world's work, that they may redeem the past misspent time, and become a blessing instead of a curse to society.

A letter has lately been received from the sister of the individual who has brought the name of Rosa before the Philadelphia public. This lady and her brother have been travelling the past two years in Europe; and, knowing the circumstances here related, paid their first visit after they arrived in Turin to the Rosine Manufactory. She writes thus:

"We have just returned from the Institution founded by Rosa Govona. We have stood upon her grave, and copied the inscription on the marble slab inserted in the wall above, which we will send for the benefit of your establishment.

"The Rosine is a large house, occupying two sides of a square, the balance of which is devoted to a vegetable garden for the family, which consists at present of 220 women. On one side of the house are ranges of balconies, supported by immense columns, affording, in each story, a fine covered promenade. We regretted exceedingly, the only one in the house who could talk with us, spoke French so imperfectly, that it was almost impossible to gain information from her (though she was very obliging), but, in the store, we found a man, who in good French gave us their history. He said, they had no school—none were admitted under 15, nor over 22 years. The Institution is under the care of the government, and, in case of deficiency in the funds, the Queen balanced the accounts. They work from seven to twelve, and from two till dusk, working for themselves only in other hours. They require little while living, and are buried respectably. On Sundays and *fête* days they are allowed to walk out with the permission of the Superior. Our lady cicerone led us into a number of rooms, where the women were employed in picking wool, spinning, reeling, etc.; and from there into the weaving room, where they manufactured not only for themselves, but for the regiments. They wear a brown woollen mixture for their bodices and sleeves, but their skirts are green. In the silk rooms, from the cocoon to the most splendid silks, and ribbons, all passes through their hands. In the tailor's rooms, the entire clothing of the troops is made, and, in the embroidery departments, laces are netted and ornamented for the robes of the priests, and for the chapels. Comforts are quilted in another division. The kitchen, eating rooms, and chambers are large, and well lighted, and very much on the plan of some of our own institutions. They have brick floors, blue woollen coverlets, and images of the Madonna in each dormitory, and countless pictures of the saints everywhere.

"The Rosines rise, according to the season, from 4 to half-past 5. They eat a simple breakfast, dine at 12, and take supper at 7, at which periods they have reading, from a person seated in a high chair. They publish no reports, so we could not learn much of their financial arrangements. The Rosines can remain in the house while they live, but, if they leave, they take only their wardrobe. We saw among them several quite aged women. The house is called the Retira della Rosina, and is built on the spot where Rosa was established, in 1749, by Carlo Emmanuel. The notary told us, there were four institutions dependent on this, in Savillon, Saluce, St. Damiena, and Chierri.

"In the church attached to the house, is the tomb of Rosa, and her portrait, in oil colors, hangs in a little room attached to the oratory. An engraving, half-sheet size, is in another room. We have endeavored, but in vain, to get a picture of her to send you, as a shrine for your poor unfortunates.

"A little fancy cap, which is very becoming, was introduced by the foundress, and is still worn by the Rosines. Our cicerone offered to dress a doll for us, in the full costume, but, on account of the carriage, we had to be satisfied with the cap, like her own, made of the silk and ribbon manufactured in the establishment. She blushingly refused our money, when pressed to accept it. The Superior is a venerable-looking lady. We regretted much we could not understand each other.

"The inscription on the tomb of Rosa has been translated. It tells her worth.

"Here lies ROSA GOVONA, of Mondovi; who, in her early youth, dedicated herself to God, that, to His glory, should be raised Institutions in her own country (Italy), in which abandoned girls should find a retreat, and be made to serve God, giving them for their government, the best rules for employment in piety and labor."

ANNUAL REPORT OF THE MANAGERS OF THE ROSINE ASSOCIATION.

Managers:—President: Annis P. Furness, Pine, seven doors beyond Broad St. Vice-President: Sarah Tyndale, corner Ninth and Sergeant Sts. Treasurer: Mira Townsend, 101 Arch Street. Secretaries: Mary M. Hastings, 24 N. Schuylkill Eighth Street; Lydia Gillingham, 54 N. Fifth Street.

Ann S. Campion, 27 Branch Street; Sophia Lewis, 119 Wood Street; Elizabeth Hunt, Fifth below Green Street; Sarah J. Webb, 244 Green Street; Rebecca C. Grim, S.E. Corner of Sixth and Wager Streets; Elizabeth Carr, 440 N. Fourth Street; Cynthia Collins, Chestnut above Seventh Street; Mary H. Middleton, New below Second Street; Mary Murphy, corner of Twelfth and Arch

Streets; Eliza Yard, corner of Walnut and Eighth Streets; Susan Kimber, Franklin above Green Street; Susanna Lower, 254 N. Seventh Street; Ellen Lord, Washington above Tenth Street; Anne M. Needles, corner Twelfth and Race Streets; Lydia Longstreth, 272 N. Third Street.

PHILADELPHIA, April 1st, 1852.

Years come and go, and leave no impression upon the mind, save by the events that marked their progress. Some of these we have noted down, and presented their record to our members and subscribers, during the five years of our existence as a society. At each annual gathering we are led to review the past, and trace the feelings, as well as the events of the circling periods, and with some of us, the memory is still fresh of the calling and circumstances of our first meeting. We have been told that the love of sin was more natural to us than the love of the good and the right, but when we looked into our own hearts we could not believe it; for though we acknowledged we were weak, and sometimes erring, yet our souls were filled with the love of the good and the beautiful, and if we occasionally stept aside from the perfect image of goodness pictured in our minds, it was not owing to the sinful deformity of our natures, but simply, that we were not perfect, not God-like altogether, though made in his image. These were the thoughts that were living in our minds, though many of us had never uttered them, and when the invitation was given to assemble ourselves together, to consider what could be done for those, who having been placed in unfavorable circumstances, had been in a degree corrupted by them, and thus yielded to the temptations with which these circumstances had surrounded them, our hearts sprang at the suggestion that something could be done for these, and with trembling emotion we entered the meeting, full of faith that something *could* be done, and yet we knew not what course *should* be adopted. The longing in our natures after the high and the holy, convinced us that God had not merely made us in his image, but that he had also endowed us with a portion of his spirit, and that these, our unfortunate sisters, were also formed in his image, and gifted with the same aspirations; but poverty, ignorance, or corrupting associations, had sunk them into vicious habits, and dimmed the light in their souls, but we could not believe these emanations from the Deity himself could be put out, and therefore we hoped the hour had come when the Father of mercy would guide us in some path, where we might become the instruments to help open the eyes of these blind ones, and rekindle faith and hope upon the altars of some of their hearts. We had been accustomed to consider these unfortunates as irreclaimable, because so few had been reformed, but a little reflection showed us the reason why the number was so small. It was not the fault of the individuals, so much as that of society—of ourselves. What had been done to educate these women, and provide them with remunerating employment? What influences had been cast around them to train them in principles of rectitude; and then, when temptations clustered about them, and they were drawn into the whirlpool of vice, where was the hand outstretched to save them? Where was woman's ministry of love to pour in the oil, and the wine to strengthen the weak, to encourage the desponding, to stimulate them to return to the paths of virtue, and give them the means of honest, respectable employment? Some few men have given efforts of this kind, but with poor success, because they could not inspire hope that any degree of perseverance in the right, would gain them the favor of their own sex, and without that, they knew little could be accomplished. And woman, with all her kindness and benevolence, with all the religious fervor with which she labored for the heathen in foreign lands, remembered not that the heathen were beside her own door-stone; that the neighbor, the sister in her own land, had grown up in ignorance of the Scriptures she was sending to a foreign shore; that thousands of her own countrywomen needed her efforts, even to learn the letters that were the steps that might reveal those blessed pages to them; and with all the zeal with which she traversed sea and land to make converts, she had not the moral courage to enter the abodes of sin in her own city, and draw from thence the unfortunate victims of licentiousness. And what now could or would be done, was yet hidden in the shadows of futurity; but the very assemblage of several hundred women to consider the subject, was ominous "of the good time coming." It spoke of advancement, of progress in our appreciation of what duty and benevolence required, and with the acknowledgment of our past omissions, came the willingness to give our time, our money, and our zeal, to this, the most important of Home Missions.

Five years have elapsed since that period, and some of us who that day put our hand to the work, have never flinched from it since, but have breasted the difficulties in our path, relying on that Power who we believed had opened a way in which we could speak of glad tidings to the hopeless, and give them that aid that might enable them to believe that there was yet a possibility of returning to respectable and useful life. Those only whose hands have been constantly to the oar can tell the amount of time, labor, thought, and feeling, that have been expended; but when we look around and see what has been accomplished, and observe the bright happy family in the Rosine, our hearts are raised with gratitude, that we have been selected as the instruments to awaken the hearts of the people to help us in this cause, and that we have been enabled to open a house that has been truly not only the home of the friendless, but the beacon light that has shed its beneficent influence to illumine the weary and benighted, and to show them there was a way to escape from the horrors and degradation of their condition, and be elevated to the position of a useful Christian character. And that position we believe some of our inmates have attained. Three who have gone down to the tomb, died with prayers and blessings upon their lips; others have mingled in the family circles of other homes, and proved by their actions and usefulness that we have not labored for nought. Daughters have been restored to parents, from whom they have been separated for years, and sorrowing hearts have been gladdened by the lost being found. One girl, who was the widowed mother's only child, had been lured from her, the mother knew not whither, until she was traced by one of our earliest inmates, who was then laboring as a missionary, to save those who like herself had gone astray, and who she hoped might become able, as she had, to assume the position of a respectable married woman, and a professor of religion. This girl, then only 17 years of age, she heard was in prison, whence one of us brought her, and she remained under our care more than a year. Last autumn her mother sent a request for her to return home, as she was sick and needed care. Some of us have visited them occasionally during the winter, and it has been more than gratifying to observe her tender devotion to that once deserted parent, and heard her speak with tearful eyes of the change the Rosine had wrought in that daughter.

Four years since, a mother came to us, begging us to receive her child, a girl of 17. She was bound to the Managers, and remained under our care until she was of age. She was then received by her friends, and supported herself by tailoring, which she learned while with us. She has been married two years, and was visited within a few days by one of our members, who found her comfortably settled in a well-furnished house, with a beautiful bright child playing beside her, and her own face radiant with smiles, as she welcomed her old friend to her home. Those only who have seen a beloved one snatched from destruction and restored to their own esteem, and to that of others, can appreciate the feelings of the friends of such individuals; and those only who have risen to self-esteem from the miseries of a life of infamy, can place a value on the benefits that may be derived, from being for a period an inmate of the Rosine. In our last report we spoke of one for whom we had deposited $80 in the Saving Fund, earned since she left us, in another home, where she had been receiving the reward of honest labor. $102 are now placed to her account in that Institution, thus proving, that even the reckless carelessness of habits of dissipation may be conquered, when a sufficient stimulus is presented. Some time since, Judge Kelley requested us to visit a girl of fifteen years of age in the prison. We brought her from there, and found she was the child of a respectable mechanic in the upper part of the city. She had been enticed from her father's house, and for three months (being afraid to return), had wandered from one scene of infamy to another, feeling herself truly homeless and friendless. Some nights she had slept in out-houses, into which she had crept for shelter, and at last was put in prison for taking an article of clothing which had previously been lent to her. She is now indentured to us, and we hope her residence in the Rosine will prove as great a blessing to her as it has to several others who have been placed with us by their friends, under a similar engagement.

One, of whom we have spoken as having been led to ruin in her 12th year, and from that period until she came under our roof, in her 25th year, had been leading a life of the lowest degradation, who, by her own acknowledgment, had been in prison over fifty times, is now earning her living by vest-making, which she learned in the Rosine. We had seen this woman so often in the prison, and in worse places, that even to us she appeared altogether a hopeless case, and when we received her under our roof, it was not that we expected to benefit her, but that we could not refuse her application. Those who knew her formerly, a disgusting bloated object, could now hardly recognize her in the respectable-looking tailoress. Her feelings appear to have been awakened to a proper sense of her condition, and in the deep humility of her spirit, she has been led to cry earnestly, "Lord, be merciful to me a sinner!"

During the past year we have been indebted to several gentlemen of religious character, whose hearts have been touched with sympathy for these poor wanderers, and their prayers have ascended to heaven for and with them. Providence has thus raised friends around them, who are willing to add their efforts to ours to train their minds, so that they may be able to appreciate their advantages, and be inspired with gratitude towards the Giver of all good gifts.

Many of our inmates have been under the religious influence that brings peace, and to some we believe the words of peace have been spoken, and they can truly say, I rejoice in the Lord, for he has been my Saviour, my deliverer! I will praise him! Let all his works praise him!

Our Sabbath afternoon, evening, and mid-week meetings have been regularly kept up, and on the Sabbath morning some of our ladies collect the family, and have Bible and other suitable reading and conversation. These Sabbath opportunities are usually very interesting, and some of us have felt that it was good for us that we were there. A sense of the Divine presence has rested upon our minds, and a portion of it seemed to pervade the whole assembly. With the exception of the summer months, our school has been in operation, and considerable progress has been made by some, while all had the liberty to continue their studies to the higher branches, if their industry and application might lead them onward. Some lectures have been delivered on Anatomy, Physiology, Chemistry, etc., and we have now, through the aid of kind friends, lectures once a week, on scientific, or moral subjects.

Five evenings in a week are devoted to their religious and mental improvement, and the other two to mending their clothing, and attending to their own particular concerns. Of the necessity of devoting a great portion of time to mental improvement our friends may judge, by a statement taken from our Book of Record.

Of 223 individuals who have been inmates, 71 could not read understandingly when they entered, 124 could not write, 105 had been intemperate, 65 were foreigners, 47 Philadelphians, 22 from other parts of Pennsylvania, the balance from different parts of America, 59 professed to be Catholics, 52 Methodists, 24 Episcopalians, 28 Presbyterians. The others scattering, or no religion.

Our subscribers sometimes ask, Can they not by their labor support the establishment? Our reply must be, that we do not expect they ever will. Our Institution is a *school*, in the fullest meaning. We do not receive these women for what can be made out of their labor, but that they may be benefited, physically, mentally, and morally, by being under our care. That their organic powers both of body and mind may be improved, their knowledge increased by the cultivation of their faculties, and while every effort is made to inspire habits of industry, so much of their time is devoted to educational and moral improvement, that with the necessary periods of relaxation, the hours must be limited that are given to the pecuniary profit of the Institution. Another reason for the small amount accruing from their labor is, that we have to get a great deal of our work from the shirt and tailor stores, and the prices given are so low, that for a great amount of work little is obtained. Another reason is, that owing to their defective educations, few of them can be placed on customer work for months after they are received, and some not at all, and those who do progress, and become able to take work on their own account, are permitted to be considered boarders in the family, and are charged $1 50 per week for board and washing, and whatever they can earn over that amount is passed to their credit. The object of this is to stimulate them to industry, to accustom them to habits of application, and to inspire them with the knowledge that they can support themselves honestly by the labor of their own hands. This system of course places the best workers on an independent footing, and deprives the house of the surplus profits from their work; but we feel bound to do all in our power for the benefit of the inmates, even if it should be a pecuniary loss to the establishment.

The depressing and degrading lives which many of them have led, with the constant use of stimulants, causes them to feel sensibly the change from scenes of revelry to the quiet of a well-ordered family. We therefore deem it important that every hour should be occupied in such a manner that they may feel that their whole time is devoted for their own benefit. We might possibly procure more lucrative work than tailoring, dress or shirt making, but we do not wish our girls to learn trades that might lead them to depend on shop work, as we have had sorrowful proofs of the temptations that surround those who depend on that kind of employment, owing to the precariousness of their getting work, and the improper associations into which they might be thrown. We consider the family relation as much more advantageous for them, and our aim is, to qualify them to enter into such situations as they may be calculated to fill, with pleasure and profit to their employers, as well as themselves.

One of our first inmates has now been nearly four years in the family where she was placed from the Institution. Three others have been living about two years in the same families, and at this time one of our members has three in her employment, filling the stations of seamstress and chambermaid, child nurse, and cook. One has been there over a year, the second seven months, and the third three or four months. Some time since, we sent two into families in one neighborhood in the country. We have since received applications from the same locality for five more, in consequence of their good conduct. Eighteen months since, a woman came to the house of one of our managers, about 9 o'clock at night, asking permission to go to the Rosine. She had passed down step by step the path of ruin, until in a state of inebriation she entered one of the dreadful dens of wickedness in Baker Street. While in a state of insensibility there, she was stripped of her clothing, and when sense returned was lying entirely naked on some straw in one corner. A poor creature, not much better than herself, threw an old spread over her, and when evening came, with bare head and feet, and no article on her person but an old calico wrapper, she came up to beg the shelter of the Rosine. Could a more disheartening object appear than this woman presented? The member to whom she came would probably have turned from her hopelessly, but she had received others before in a similar condition, whom she had seen restored to respectable life, and the affections of a husband and children, therefore a hope sprang in her heart, that perhaps this too might be a returning prodigal. The woman was sent to the Rosine, and after a season was placed with some friends in Jersey, where she has since been living, a valued member of the family. We hear frequently of her, and know they would part with her very unwillingly. Several young women have come to us from New York and Baltimore. One from the former place was sent by her friends. She came to the house of one of the managers, who finding she had not been very much exposed, thought under the circumstances she would not place her in the Institution, but kept her in her own house, until a suitable home was provided for her. She has since married respectably, and is doing well. A very pretty German girl of fourteen years of age was sent to us by the mayor of Baltimore. Her mother had died three weeks after her arrival in this country, and the father took this child somewhere towards Pittsburg, where he died, leaving the girl among strangers. She went on board a canal boat, intending to come to Philadelphia, where she had two uncles residing. The captain of the boat finding she had no company, invited her to go with him to Baltimore, offering to take her gratuitously, and bring her back to Harrisburg, where she could pursue her route to Philadelphia. Childlike, she was pleased with the prospect of going, and went with him; soon she discovered his object was her ruin. She resolutely opposed him, and when they arrived in Baltimore he refused to take her back (fearing she would expose his conduct), and took her down to one of the lowest sinks of sin in Baltimore, where he left her. It was heartrending to hear her describe the iniquities she witnessed while in this house, where she remained a week, when, one of the policemen hearing of a child being there, reported the case to the mayor, who rescued her, and sent her here, in charge of one of his officers. Our sympathies and indignation were both excited by the story of this poor girl. She told her uncles' names, but knew not where they lived. Fortunately we soon discovered the abode of one of them, a respectable mechanic, and the young traveller was placed in her uncle's house, who promised she should never again want a home.

A young man, an entire stranger, called on one of our members, four years since, to say he had seen a young girl in a house of bad character, who had been there but one week. Her youth and beauty interested him, and when he found she was from the country, had come to the city in search of employment, and had been lured to the house by one with whom she became acquainted at her boarding place, while seeking a situation, his sympathies were awakened, and he was willing to expose himself in order to save her. Two of our ladies proceeded to the house, found her, and one of them took her home with her, and kept her there, until she succeeded in placing her with a married sister. Afterwards she called several times to see the two friends who had rescued her, but for the last three years they had known nothing of her, as the sister with whom she lived had moved, our members knew not where. A few days since, one of them had been out of town, and was returning in a public conveyance, when she was attracted towards a lady who sat opposite her, and said, "Have I not seen you somewhere?" "Yes," said the lady, "my name is ——. I am the sister of Emma." The whole story flashed upon her mind, and with great interest she inquired what had become of her protegee?—The story was soon told. They had moved to another neighborhood. Emma was married, and at housekeeping. "Do go and see her," said the sister, she will be so glad to have you come.

We might fill a volume with such histories, but a few only can be told. These show, that our duties are far from being confined to the inmates of our house. Almost always we have some outdoor cases which require attention, and occupy considerable time, yet it may not be advisable to place them in the Institution.

We frequently receive communications requesting us to go to houses of bad character, to endeavor to save individuals there. We always attend to such missions. Within a few days an anonymous letter requested us to visit a young girl, apparently not more than fifteen, who in consequence of an advertisement in a newspaper, had been engaged in such a house, as a domestic. We found her there, but our visit was unavailing. She had breathed the malaria of the atmosphere, and had become blinded. She saw not the precipice on which she stood. Reluctantly we left her to her fate, urging her to come when her eyes should be opened.

The subject of intemperance, year after year, has claimed our attention, and we have referred to it in our reports, as, in nearly every case, where those who have been under our care long enough to appreciate their advantages, have returned to bad habits, *liquor has been the cause of their downfall.* The opportunities for indulgence in nearly every square, present constant temptations, by which even the best resolutions are overcome, and they are thus induced to become once more the disgrace of humanity. Impressed with the importance of a change in our laws, in the early part of this session the managers of the Rosine addressed a memorial to the Legislature, stating the evils arising from our liquor laws, and petitioning the restriction of the sale of malt and spirituous liquors, to medical and scientific purposes. The statements we have made in our reports, of the amount of crime and pauperism produced by liquor, has caused many reflecting minds to consider the subject, and created a healthful excitement.

William J. Mullen has laid before the public an excellent article giving unanswerable statistics, and the general demand for the liquor law of Maine, proves that our people are awaking to the vice and misery around them, and are becoming sensible that the greater part of it is caused by indulgence in intoxicating drinks.

Our friends are generally aware, that the Temporary Home for respectable females, who are out of employment, was brought into existence through the efforts of some of the managers of the Rosine, who felt the necessity of another institution, to prevent young women who were friendless and out of employment, from becoming the prey of the tempter, through the necessities of their circumstances. A number of other minds were influenced to give their efforts to this object, and the Home was opened 18 months since. Within that period a temporary home has been given to 395 women and children, until they could be provided with situations, and 1250 individuals have been placed at service through the Intelligence Office of the Home. It gives us great pleasure to see the successful operation of this association, and we believe the two societies are doing, and will do, an immense amount of good. Preventive and remedial efforts are both needed, but if we can procure the proper restrictions upon the vending of liquors, in a few years there will be far less occasion for them.

The Intelligence Office of the Rosine has continued its work of usefulness. Since it has been in operation we have procured situations for about 1400 women and children. These with the 1250 who have gone to places from the Temporary Home, make 2650 individuals, many of whom, probably, have been saved from ruin, and placed in positions to earn their living honestly and respectably.

Is not this truly the work of humanity? Giving alms is oft times well, but furnishing productive labor, homes, and respectable associations, is far better. For this object we claim the sympathy and assistance of our friends, and the friends of mankind.

The work-room of the Rosine has never been conducted more satisfactorily than at present. If our friends would more generally bring us their family sewing, we should not be forced to resort to the stores for employment. If a fair remuneration was given for all the work done in the house, our circumstances would be far more independent than they are at this time.

The number of garments made in the Rosine House within the past year, for the use of the family, has been - - - - - -	593
Made for the stores and customers, including 85 shirts, 217 vests, 36 pairs of pantaloons, 29 dresses, with sundry other articles, numbering altogether, - - - - -	1284
Total, - -	1877

Bringing to the Institution, - - - -	$491 33
And to Inmates, working on their own account, - - - - - - -	100 00

Our receipts have been,

From the work-room, - - - - -	491 33
Interest on money collected towards the payment for the House, - - -	180 00
Donations and annual subscriptions, -	1554 50
	$2,225 83

Our expenses have been,

For rent, salaries, clothing, marketing, fuel, &c., including the funeral expenses of two inmates, - - - - -	$2,098 15
Cash on hand, - - - - - -	127 68

CERTIFICATE BY AUDITORS.

The undersigned having been appointed by the Board of Managers of the Rosine Association to examine the Accounts of the Treasurer, Mira Townsend, have attended to the duty assigned them, and find the books have been accurately kept, and are correct in every particular.

MARY M. HASTINGS,
ANNE M. NEEDLES.

9th Month, 19, 1851.

Through the benevolence of our friends, our accommodations have been greatly increased the past winter. Messrs. Archer & Warner put in the gas pipes gratuitously, and Cornelius & Co. presented us with the fixtures. The Gas Company of Spring Garden put the gas for the year at a nominal price. To these gentlemen we present our sincere thanks, and could they be made sensible of the advantages of our inmates resulting from the difference in the light, we know they would feel fully paid. To our physicians, whose services have always been gratuitous, our thanks are also due; also, to our contributors, both in money and goods.

We have had to be beggars from the formation of the Society; and while Providence continues to awaken repentance in the erring, with desires for a better, higher life, we must continue to plead for them, unless some person, or persons, whose means and sympathies are co-operative, should relieve us of this most unpleasant part of our work, by endowing the Institution. Our friends may recollect we rented the Rosine House on a lease for five years, with the privilege of becoming the owners at the end of the time, if we could pay for it. The price is to be $6,333 33. We have succeeded in obtaining $3,000, and a friend, well known to the public for his liberality and benevolence, has promised $500 more toward it. We may truly say we are ashamed to beg—but how can we cease to ask, while the existence of the Rosine depends upon our efforts. We look back with wonder and gratitude at our past success, and dare not now lose our hope and faith. Our family has numbered over forty much of the past year; and, owing to the severity of the season, and the uncommon demands upon the purses of our friends, we have not been able to collect as much as would meet our current expenses, and have had to encroach on part of the fund contributed especially for the purchase of the House.

Need we say more than thus to lay our necessities before our friends, and invite them to send their contributions to our treasurer or either of the managers. The lease will expire in July, and we feel the necessity of exertion *at once*, that we may secure a permanent shelter for the most unfortunate class of our fellow-beings.

We have thus presented you with the history of the Society and of our progress. Two hundred and twenty-three individuals have been considered inmates of the Institution, but we have given a temporary shelter to many others of respectable character, but homeless and friendless, until we could procure other homes for them. Our family is also occasionally enlarged by the return of those who have formerly been inmates, but who have been in situations. We desire them always to consider the Rosine as a parent's house, to which they can return for safety and with pleasure.

Believing that the Divine power that has hitherto upheld us will still be extended, and that we shall continue to receive the aid of the benevolent, we desire to continue our missionary work, and invite all ladies who are interested in the cause of Missions, of Temperance, or of other good works, to become members of the Society, and thus pledge themselves to the cause of humanity and virtue.

The Annual Meeting of the Society is held on the first Thursday in April. The Semi-annual in October.

Our members and subscribers are requested to pay their annual contributions at the Store of the Rosine House, as early as convenient after each *annual meeting.*

PRISON VISITS.

We have often spent days in the Prison, going from cell to cell, and, when particularly attracted, entering and conversing with the inmates in their narrow abodes, querying why they were there, and, in many instances, taking down their names, the charge against them, and other circumstances of interest. Sometimes the investigation of these cases brings some labor upon us, as many are committed on petty charges, that only require the interference of a respectable person to procure their release. I knew a poor but respectable woman, who was returning from her day's work, when, seeing some persons collected on the pavement to witness a quarrel between two women, who had been drinking, she stopped, and tried to separate them. Just then a policeman came along, and, in spite of her protestations of innocence, she was arrested as a party concerned in the fight, and the alderman, who only heard the policeman's statement, committed her.

In another instance, a young woman, who lived with a friend of ours in Jersey, came on a visit to the city, and, staying longer than she expected, required some clothing washed, and was directed to a colored washerwoman in Bedford Street. Upon paying for the washing an altercation ensued between them, the country-girl supposing she was imposed on by the washerwoman. Both became angry, and probably spoke louder than politeness warranted. In the meantime a colored lad, about nineteen years' of age, came in, with his bundle of soiled garments, and finding the women disputing, stood silently listening to their debate. It was summer time—the door happened to be open, and a policeman, in passing, heard the angry tones of the raised voices, and entering, arrested the whole party on a charge of disorderly conduct. After they were committed to prison, the country-girl, who knew we were acquainted with the family with whom she lived in Trenton, induced one of the inspectors to send a note, requesting our presence in the prison. We immediately went down, recognized the young woman, and, upon going to the alderman, procured the release of both the women, and, at our request, the innocent young man was also liberated.

In some of these prison visits I have conversed with about 70 women during the day, and from their own stories have found that, with few exceptions, their offences have arisen either from drinking themselves, or from being in company with others with whom the poisonous beverage had been doing its work. Many unfortunate girls are incarcerated there, whose offences it were hard to define; but the word "disorderly" on the slate by the cell-door, covers a multitude of transgressions or misfortunes, and means almost anything, or nothing. In former days it very often meant merely the cupidity of the policeman and alderman, who hoped each to get a dollar from the unfortunate one, or through some sympathizing friend, for their release. There have been scores of such committals to the Moyamensing Prison, when the officers who arrested the unfortunate ones merited the dreary cell far more than the accused one. We know an instance where a poor girl was sent to the prison, who had no dollars to pay for her freedom; but the officer, on questioning her, found she had a trunk, filled with good clothing, at her boarding-house. He went there, and requested the landlady to break open her trunk, and pawn some of her clothing, to pay the costs to himself and the alderman. The woman refused, and he then took out his own keys, unlocked the trunk, and gave four good dresses to a colored woman to pawn, directing her to bring him the money at the alderman's office. Upon receiving it, he went down to the prison with a release, and brought her out, pretending to pity her, and saying to her, "Mary Ann, I feared you would die, shut up in the cell, this hot weather, so I had to go to your boarding-house, and get some of your clothing, to pay your costs, and then I came immediately down to release you." With this show of compassion he salved over his own larceny, and made the unfortunate one believe he was really entitled to her gratitude.

A lively young widow of the name of A., who was engaged putting up medicines for the celebrated Dr. T., on her way one morning to her work, saw an old man, of whom she had some knowledge, sitting on a cellar door, counting over his money. She stopped and spoke to him, and picking up his porte monnaie, said, jestingly, "If money is plenty, share it with me." It happened to be near an alderman's office, and a policeman, who was lounging there, saw the transaction, and arrested the frightened girl, who had only thought of a jest. We found her in the prison, committed on the charge of larceny. The next day after our visit there, we called on Dr. T., and received excellent credentials as to her character, and then proceeded to the alderman's office, who said he had rendered her case on his list of committals to the attorney-general, for the examination of the Grand Jury, but he would write me a note to Mr. Mann, and endeavor to withdraw the case. He remarked, that when he committed Mrs. A., he did not think she ought to go to prison, but when the officer swore that he had seen her take the porte monnaie, he had no other course to pursue. . . Having received the exculpatory note from the alderman, we then went to Mr. Mann with our story and document, who kindly relieved the Grand Jury from the examination of one case, by giving us an order for the relief of the jocose but mortified widow. From there we returned to the prison, to set the captive at liberty. None of her friends know of the circumstance, as she could not bear they should know she was in prison on a charge of larceny, and she appeared exceedingly embarrassed about accounting to them for her absence during the week she had been in painful durance. We could relate many other interesting cases, among those whom it has been our good fortune to assist, by procuring their release from the Moyamensing Castle. They come up as we write, one after another, in our memory, until we feel as if we could narrate a whole volume of prison histories. We have procured the liberation of over fifty women. Of some of these we have known little, but that they were more sinned against than sinning. We will relate one more history.

MARGARET.

When we went down to the prison with the release of Mrs. A., and that of another woman who had been committed by her landlady, on a charge of assault, on account of a little difficulty occurring between them about some domestic arrangements, we met the officer there who had the charge of the Black Maria, or prison van, and inquired for whom he had come. He said for Miss Margaret S., to go before the Grand Jury. We had seen Margaret when we were down at the prison before, and had been employed in investigating her case. She was tall and genteel in her appearance, with a face remarkably interesting and lady-like, and only seventeen years of age. Her parents were deceased, and she lived with her old grandmother, in the lower part of the city. Margaret had fallen in love with a young man of whom she knew little, but that he was good-looking, and professed to love her. He had said they would be married as soon as he could get into business to support her, and with all a woman's faith she placed implicit confidence in whatever he told her. She had an uncle, a seafaring man, who came home just then to her grandmother's, with the fruits of his voyage. In conversation with her lover, she mentioned that her uncle had a bag full of money, she knew not how much, in his chest. This seemed wonderfully to increase his affection, and desire to be married, and with a lover's logic, he managed to convince Margaret that there would be very little impropriety in transferring the said bag of money from her uncle's chest into his possession. With this unknown capital they would get married, and he could at once go into business. The heart of a young girl at seventeen is generally easily swayed by her lover, and her old grandmother had probably not implanted very strong or clear principles of justice in her mind. Suffice it to say, Margaret made the transfer without having the least idea of the amount of money the bag contained. He also induced her to go with him to a boarding-house, while he made the necessary preparations for the marriage. She left her grandmother, and went with him. Before the evening of the same day, her suspicions were strongly excited as to the character of the house. Among other visitors there were a couple of men, who inquired if she knew G. F. She replied she did. "Then," said they, "do you know anything about his being concerned in a robbery?" The alarmed girl instantly replied, "I took the money—he did not take it!" It appeared that George, with all his charms and attractions to a young girl of seventeen, was a married man, and had been for some time under the surveillance of the police, and at that period was an object of suspicion of being concerned in the robbery of a jeweller's shop; and the officers, having discovered that he had taken Margaret to this house, which was one of noted bad character, they had gone there, hoping to ascertain through her something about the jewelry, and proposed the questions which led to the development of a circumstance of which they knew nothing, but with consummate address they obtained from her the history with which she had been connected. Poor Margaret! The ride to the Mayor's office was not as she expected, to pledge her vows to the man she loved. Her preparations for the bridal hour were suddenly arrested, and she and her betrothed both consigned to the cells of Moyamensing Prison. Her reflections that night were not the anticipations of the wedded happiness she had expected. Her lover, in whom she had so much faith, was a married man, and all those dreams of bliss were blasted. He had, without doubt, intended to add her to the unfortunate nameless ones of our city. He had induced her to commit an act which had brought sin and disgrace upon her, and ere life had much more than dawned, he had crowned her brow with dishonor. And who were the companions that mentally stood by her in that long night of sorrow? There was her aged grandmother, who had nursed and loved and toiled for her, and there was her uncle, who had been so proud of his beautiful niece, and whom she had wronged so basely. In the bitterness of that hour of sorrow, she could have fallen at their feet, and asked their forgiveness; but the shadows of her own thoughts were her only companions, and the prisoner's blanket, on the bare floor, and the stool beside her, were the only witnesses to her misery.

A friend of ours, who is willing to labor for the erring and unfortunate, providentially was at the prison when Margaret arrived there, and was interested at once in her appearance, and after making inquiries into her case, resolved to do what he could to extricate her from the consequences of her imprudence and crime. We also, in our prison visit, found her there, and heard that our friend had the case in hand. We saw him, learned what he had done, and promised him to accompany her to Court. We found arrangements had been made for the trial of George for the larceny, and as Margaret had merely been the "cat's-paw" for him, she was to be admitted as state's evidence against him.

It was at our subsequent visit to the prison that we met the officer, who had come to take poor Margaret before the Grand Jury. If our friends feel as we feel when we see that dismal carriage, called the Black Maria, which conveys so much misery to and from the prison, they can understand why we begged that officer most earnestly to let us escort her to the Court House in the omnibus. He consented, with that kindness and politeness which we have received from all the police officers with whom our position has made us acquainted, and we accompanied Margaret to the door of the Jury Room, and back again to the prison.

The day of trial came. We sat beside her in the Court room. We could not bear that one so young and so lovely should be exposed to the gaze and remarks of rude persons without the protection of a friend to shield and guard her from the probable consequences of her folly and error, and we felt that our proper position in that Court room was by her side.

George F. was a young man, of respectable appearance, with an attractive countenance, and as we saw him in the Court room we could readily understand how a girl of seventeen could give her love and her faith to such a man, and be swayed by his influence, even against her own convictions of the right; and a world of thought passed over us, as we sat there, of the importance of the proper training of youth, to fit them, by the instillation of principles, to meet the varied temptations that might come in their path to lead them astray. And we thought of the effort that was made, and the funds that were raised to send missionaries to the far-off heathen, while here were the heathen at our doors, and but little effort made to save them. Here were a young man and woman to whom the voice of warning and exhortation had probably never been particularly addressed. True, they lived in what is called a Christian community, but their perceptions were dim of that higher light and intelligence that separates man from the instinctive animals, and prompts the feelings of that love and reverence that desires to bring every action to the footstool of Divine justice, and would humbly ask from day to day, "Father, am I right? Give me thy wisdom to illumine my path! Show me the right, and give me strength to obey thy law in my heart, and thy teachings from day to day, as thou seest fit to enlighten my understanding."

The trial progressed. In due season Margaret was called to the witness stand. The color had faded from her face, but as she rose from her seat the rushing blood betokened the inward emotion. The attorney, Wm. B. Mann, with the perceptive delicacy of the gentleman, noticed the embarrassment of the unfortunate girl, and ordering a chair immediately before him, invited her to take the seat, and thus avoid the painful exposure on the witness stand. We shall always owe him a debt of gratitude for that act of kindness, and so will poor Margaret. When the trial was over, we brought her home with us, and kept her under our care three months, because we hoped we might do her good, and strengthen her for the future combat of life; and that kind friend who had by his interference saved her from being tried as a criminal, and in all probability convicted, labored with us to engraft upon her mind principles, that might arm her against the temptations and trials that might lie in her path. When she left us she went to live with her grandmother, and before a year elapsed we were told Margaret was the bride of a young man who had lived in the neighborhood, and they had gone to take life's journey together, in New York. Since then we have had no farther knowledge of her history. May that Providence who raised up friends to shield and save her from the consequences of that transgression, give her strength and wisdom to resist every other temptation that may lead to evil.

REPORT OF THE MANAGERS OF THE ROSINE ASSOCIATION.

President: Annis P. Furness, Pine seven doors beyond Broad Street; Vice-President: Sophia Lewis, 119 Wood Street. Treasurer: Mira Townsend, 43 Arch Street; Secretaries: Mary M. Hastings, 24 N. Schuylkill Eighth Street; Lydia Gillingham, 54 N. Fifth Street.

Managers: Ann S. Campion, 27 Branch Street; Elizabeth Hunt, Fifth below Green Street; Sarah J. Webb, 244 Green Street; Rebecca C. Grim, S. E. corner Sixth and Wagner Street; Elizabeth Carr, 440 N. Fourth Street; Cynthia Collins,

Chestnut above Seventh Street; Mary H. Middleton, New below Second Street; Mary Murphy, corner of Twelfth and Arch Streets; Eliza Yard, corner of Walnut and Eighth Street; Susan Kimber, Franklin above Green Street; Ellen Lord, Washington above Tenth Street; Emily Taylor, 272 Walnut Street.

PHILADELPHIA, October 21st, 1852.

The return of each period of making our report to our members and contributors, always induces the mental inquiry of, What have we done? What have we to tell? We see the marks of our progress constantly accumulating around us, but ours is a work that we can see, and feel, yet cannot expose to the world. We cannot say, There is a woman we have saved! Here is a young creature just budding into life that we have snatched from the hands of the spoiler and placed in a position where she may become good and useful; or, here is one who we found in the depths of misery, degraded and despised, an outcast from all the charities and decencies of life, an object of loathing even to herself; and now behold her, "clothed, and in her right mind" sitting at the feet of her Heavenly Father, and endeavoring to walk according to the manifestations of "the right" in her own soul. These are facts we see, but we cannot uphold the individual to the public gaze, but rather endeavor to bury the memory of the past, and blot out (if possible), even from their own minds, that they were ever otherwise than they are. Would that we could cast a lethean oblivion over the temptations, the iniquities, and the horrors of that one sad period of life, that all could be forgotten, and that once more in the innocency of childhood those harrowing recollections might sleep forever. But alas!

Though life may more brightness and happiness bring,
No Lethe can o'er it forgetfulness fling.
Though God may speak peace to the penitent soul,
Yet, Man's unforgiveness each thought will control,
And still, like a cloud in its wind-wafted way,
Bring gloom o'er the sunlight of each blissful day.

The youthful mind, to whom the pangs of remorse are unknown, on whom the look of scorn has never alighted, can hardly understand the feelings of these unfortunates in their efforts to rise into the higher life. Constantly mingled with these undying memories, comes the consciousness, that for them society has no place, no position; that while the destroyer who wrought their ruin (or was at least the partner in their guilt), may still be the friend and escort of the fashionable, the young, and the innocent, sometimes the sought and the admired in the polished circle they (the victim, or at most the companion in the crime), are turned from with contempt and aversion as though they were an accursed thing. Thus the injustice of society upholds the male profligate, while from the erring woman it takes every incentive to reformation. Hope itself dies within their hearts, and with each taunt, each rebuff, the spirit of despondency revives, and the consciousness of their inability to regain the foothold they have lost. This is the especial period for us to exercise our mission. When the weary, drooping penitent feels she is friendless, hopeless, the Pariah of her race, without God in this world, banishing even him in her thoughts, and endeavoring in the disgusting revel to forget her own responsibility, then is the moment when our charities and sympathies are doubly claimed, when woman's hand alone has power to raise and give vitality to the virtue and hope that lie buried in her heart. 'Tis ours to lead her from temptation's path, convince her there is a higher, better way, that she can attain it, and that we will uphold and support her in her efforts to rise from the slough in which she was sinking; but in this work we as well as she have need of enduring patience and prayerful energy; often must the tearful eye be turned heavenward, and the silent supplication be breathed, "Father, help us!" ere we can feel she has attained the desired eminence, and with strong integrity of purpose, can fill and occupy a station of responsibility and usefulness. Yet such has been many times our experience, and when we have believed that the heartfelt prayer and orison of praise ascended from truly penitent and grateful lips to the Father of mercies, our sympathies have mingled with theirs, and the purest, deepest feelings of our natures have awakened. The giddy flatterer in the whirl of fashion, calls the object his imagination has robed, "an angel," but, if our natures can ever know the angel living in us, it is when we are endeavoring to raise the lowly, and place them in the elevated position, Providence (through us) has opened for them.

In referring to the record of the history of our inmates, we find the following statement is made of the last 12 admitted, and this may be considered as a fair specimen of the situation of these unfortunates, and from this account we may partly trace the causes of their subsequent misfortunes. No. 1. Lost her mother at 3 days old—her father died before she was born. No. 2. Her mother died when she was 4 months old. No. 3. Both parents died before she was 9 years old. No. 4. Her father died when she was a babe—her mother a drunkard. No. 5. Cannot remember seeing either parent. No. 6. Her father died when she was 5 months old. No. 7. Illegitimate—cast upon strangers. No. 8. Mother long since dead, and father married again. No. 9. Both living. No. 10. Father died before she was born—mother when she was 12 years. No. 11. Mother died when she was 8 years of age. No. 12. Both living, but very poor and thriftless. Yet early orphanage is not always the greatest evil. The crowded condition of many poor families, a number of both sexes sleeping in the same room, drinking, profanity, and other immoralities familiarly before them from childhood, ever will produce a degree of early corruption that prepares for every vice in after life.

253 women have been inmates of the Rosine House, 10 of whom have been married since they left us, and are living with their husbands. More of them may have been settled in the same manner, but as they go to all parts of the country, we have not always the opportunity of hearing from them, and cannot report their histories. A number have been restored to their families, from whom they had long been separated. Many are living in situations where they are earning their living honestly and creditably. One has lately left us, a girl of sixteen, who has won friends who are willing to give her a good education, and all the advantages that money and kindness can bestow. Another, who a few weeks since passed away to the spirit-land, was among the earliest objects of our care—one of our managers found her in the Almshouse.

She had been reared in the bosom of affluence, but the blight had fallen upon her. Her brothers and sisters were among the princes of the land, but she was the alien, the outcast from their homes and their affections; no hand was stretched forth to elevate or sustain her, and in the bitterness of her heart she was ready to curse her kindred and her existence. She became after a period an inmate in the home of her new friend, and lived with her three years. The touch of humanity softened her feelings, and the kindly influences around her awakened her better nature. She saw she had not passed the boundary of sympathy, but that down as low as she had gone the eye of Providence had followed her, and inspired hearts to draw her to themselves, and infuse into her being the faith and the hope that was living in them. As years passed away, she became a member of one of our churches, and mingled with those to whom her early history was unknown. She was esteemed and respected, and when, within the past year, her health declined, and she knew she was bound to the unknown bourne, calmly, peacefully, and joyfully she awaited the messenger, and to her former friend, and to others, frequently expressed her gratitude and praise. As some of us stood beside her coffin, and reviewed her past life, we retraced our first meeting in the Alms-house, a lonely, friendless wreck, and followed her on in her upward progress, until now, when we believed she had passed to that better land to which our hopes are bending. Her day's work was done, she had received the penny—kind and sympathizing hands smoothed her dying pillow, and "Good Samaritans" administered the oil and the wine. Gratitude and praise was the aspiration of our spirits as we leaned over the white-robed form before us.

Another who came to us from the Almshouse soon after we opened the Rosine (who was of respectable parentage in the South), but who had wandered from her home when only seventeen, was also abandoned by her relatives, and lived several years in violation of conscience. Soon after coming under our care, her quiet deportment and unaffected penitence won our esteem, and after leaving the Institution, she too became a church member, and, we believe, desired to be a consistent one; integrity and industry marked her conduct, and has secured her a home among highly respected friends. A few weeks since, a brother of hers, who had been watching her upward progress, came to the city to take her back to her relatives. Ofttimes, when speaking of the Rosine, her eyes have filled with tears, and her trembling lips have pronounced blessings upon the Institution and its supporters. She feels that through it all that is worth living for has been restored to her, and the pathway opened to a bright and happy future.

But it is our task not only to reclaim those who have been long in the path of error, but also to arrest the young just passing the boundaries of virtue, and avert the intended evil from the innocent and unsuspecting. In consequence of our connection with the Society, cases frequently come under our care, and require considerable time and attention, that we never place in our Rosine family, and many of them have been attended with the happiest consequences. To one of these we may refer. A young woman called upon one of our managers, looking exceedingly poor and in ill health; she was an orphan, from New Jersey, and had come, as is frequently the case, for better wages and the enjoyment of city life from the quiet of her country home. She lived some months in a family, conducting herself with perfect propriety, when, in an unfortunate hour, she formed an acquaintance with one who, under a marriage engagement, planned and effected her ruin, and then absconded. Resolving to hide her shame, she took boarding with a poor family, and having saved some money previously, managed with the sewing she could get to pay her board. But after a time her money was expended, and her endeavors were vain to procure a situation in a family with her child. In this condition, her clothes, piece by piece, were pawned; the winter came, and she had no garments suitable to meet its blasts; her feet were nearly shoeless, she had no resources to pay her board, and her landlady was herself struggling to keep her little family together; destitution and desperation sat side by side in her chamber; evening came, she laid her babe in the bed, and went to the street. Those only who have passed through the same can know her feelings that night; she had erred, but the love of virtue was yet in her heart, and she had hoped that her future life might atone for the past, but in the struggles of misery and starvation, she had not the courage to lie down beside her babe and die; she returned that night with a deeper load of sin upon her soul, but the money she procured brought her bread and some clothing. "I never went to the street," she said, "but when work failed, and I had no other resource." Thus she passed some months of wretchedness, when providentially she heard of the Rosine. Let the base, heartless profligate who plans the ruin of an innocent girl, look upon this picture—it is no romance, but one of numberless histories, which, if they were brought to the light, would shock every heart containing one atom of humanity. But the villain who would thus leave his victim in the misery of her circumstances, we meet in the circles of society, politely waiting upon the gay and the young, lavishing his attentions that the air may not blow too rudely on some fair lady, or bending gracefully to pick up her fan or her bouquet.

We could not receive the babe in the Rosine, nor could we separate it from its mother, but another home was procured, and in a few weeks the words of consolation and of hope brightened her eye, and brought the hue of health to her cheek. A situation was then procured for her, where she continued for about a year, during which time she became acquainted with a dress-maker in the neighborhood, who introduced her to a gentleman, a respectable merchant, to whom she has been married some months.

A few days since she called upon our manager, whom she first sought, to invite her to visit her. She was then elegantly dressed, and with deep emotion referred to her first visit, and her situation at that period. "Now," said she, "I am comfortably settled, and my husband is as fond of my boy as if he were his own—I owe all this to you!"

The recital of a very few such histories is sufficient to show the importance of such an association as the Rosine, and, were the number of active managers quadrupled, they could not attend properly to all the cases that present, that require time, effort, and investigation. In our visits to the Moyamensing Prison we always feel the necessity of a committee possessing time, energy, and feeling, to take an interest in the cases of many individuals that are enclosed within its walls. Such a committee should visit there every week, but our numerous engagements preclude our attending to this duty as we should. Some of our members have, by their interference, rescued a number of women from this tomb of the living. When women of the more respectable class are arrested, they naturally shrink from exposure, and those who could aid them know little or nothing of their circumstances, or what to do for them. The day of trial comes. The poor woman has probably no witnesses on her behalf, and the judge must sentence according to the evidence. Thus, an error committed in a moment of temptation or indiscretion, blasts the character, and stamps with the infamy of a convict those who perhaps desire to be good, and who might have been saved from even appearing in court, if they had been properly befriended at the right period.

Within a few days, a young woman of estimable character was rescued from probably months or years of confinement, on a charge of larceny, when we have every reason to believe the act was committed only as a jest. But she had no proofs of her intention, and could not bear to let her friends know of her incarceration. By our efforts the case was arrested just as it was going before the grand jury.

An interesting, attractive-looking girl of seventeen was lately found in the prison by two of our members. She was there on a charge of larceny. A friend of our Institution, a gentleman, also became interested for her, and through his efforts she was saved. Our members who found her, attended court, and sat beside her, and when she was released, took her with them. She was a motherless child, cast upon the world to earn her bread as best she might. Like many another unfriended girl, sometimes she had work and sometimes not. At a period when the work had failed, and she was penniless, she became acquainted with a young man of very prepossessing appearance, who won her affections. His arts surrounded her, and she became his victim, and, still farther to sink her into sin, at his instigation, and through his persuasion, he induced her to commit a larceny, with the promise that he would then marry her. Discovery immediately ensued, and both were arrested. Her artless truthfulness interested those who saw her, and she has been rescued, while the unprincipled seducer (who has been discovered to be already married), is suffering the penalty of crime in the prison. Through the influence of our friends she has been placed in a respectable family, where she will be guarded, protected, and encouraged to strive to regain a respectable position in life.

Our reports would be enlarged to volumes did we narrate half of the cases that claim our time and attention. We regret that the cause of humanity should suffer, owing to our pecuniary circumstances, but while the time and energies of our managers have to be so constantly employed in the various duties of the Association, and collecting the funds to support it, these cases must consequently be neglected. From year to year we hope that Providence will open the hearts of some of those who have the means to endow the Institution, that we may be relieved from the necessity of being beggars, and can appropriate the time now spent in that manner to the performance of other duties.

We have mentioned in our reports that we had taken the Rosine House on a lease for five years, with the condition that (if we could raise the funds), we should become the purchasers at any time within that period. The lease expired July 31st, and two weeks previously, the Society became the owner of the property. But we had not the means to pay for it entirely. A ground-rent of $1,333 still remains upon it, and we were forced to borrow $1,500 from a friend to enable us to make the arrangement—thus we still owe $2,833 upon the property. We started the Society with a large capital of faith, and that faith has not decreased, and we now believe that He who has prompted hearts to aid us thus far will not desert us in the future, but as we aim to act according to the light that is given us, our Association will be, as it has been, a blessing to many. The price of our house was $6,333 33. When we consider that $3,300 of this sum has been collected within five years, besides supporting a family, sometimes numbering over forty, we feel we have cause for gratitude, and when we see how extended our field of labor has become, we truly desire that our time, our strength, and the number of laborers may be increased. If we fulfil our duty we dare not sit with folded hands, and shrink from the sacrifices that must be made. But they are not really sacrifices. We must of course frequently resign our enjoyment of ease, and social pleasures—we cannot feel our time is our own, or at our command; but the consciousness of having benefited some of our fellow-beings, of saving some of those unfortunates from the sink of perdition, and placing them in a right position in life, opens to us that millennium state that we shall never see outwardly, and that only good works and praiseful hearts can enable us to experience—thus we do not really make sacrifices, but resign a lower enjoyment for a higher; the millennium comes to us in our spirits, and here we can feel the lion and the lamb lie down together, and know a peace that far surpasses the personal gratifications we have resigned.

An esteemed friend, who lent us the $1,500, in addition to his annual contribution presented us with $500 towards the payment for our House. Sixty-one dollars were sent anonymously for the same purpose, and a number of other persons aided us in raising the amount paid. To these friends, and to our other contributors, we would present our thanks; but we know they gave because they believed it to be right, and they look only to their consciences for their reward or praise.

But even the possession of our House does not entirely satisfy us. Within the past year a number of women have been refused admission into the Institution, in consequence of our crowded condition—we have frequently had several beds upon the floor, and then had to refuse applicants. In this situation, we have looked wistfully at the lots beside us, which could be procured had we the means, so as to enlarge our accommodations—but our poverty and our debt rise before us; yet have we faith and hope—and when we turn the weary wanderer from our door, we cannot but think of the hoarded wealth in our city, and believe that Providence will open an additional stream of charity, to enable us to pay what we owe, and increase our means of extending aid, protection, and encouragement, to those degraded daughters of misery.

Our visits to the prison continually impress us with the importance of having yet another institution. It is a House of Industry for drunkards and disorderly persons. Such individuals are nuisances in the community; and, instead of being allowed to disgrace their families by being continually arrested and sent to prison upon short sentences, to spend their time idly and be a tax upon honest, industrious citizens, they should be placed, with longer sentences, in a House of Industry, where they should be made to work, not only to support themselves, but also contribute to the maintenance of their families.

In examining the cases of the young women who come under our care, we find the generality of them have been orphans at an early age, or have been the children of inebriates: should it not become a question whether drunkards should have the right, not only to tax the community with their support, but with that of a race of beings predisposed by their organization to the same vice and its concomitant evils.

Investigations have been made in New York, which have resulted in the revelation of facts revolting to humanity, in regard to the outcast children in that city. The Warden of the City Prison says, "that nearly one-half of the persons arrested for petty offences have not attained the age of 21 years; and, that out of 16,000 criminals committed to the Tombs, 4,000 were under 21, and of these, 800 were between the ages of 9 and 15— of the 2,400 thieves confined there, 1100 were under 21." Mr. Matsell, the Chief of the Police, says, "from the reports of eleven districts it appears, that 2,955 children are engaged in these wards alone, in pilfering, begging, prostitution, and immoralities, of the most loathsome description, and of these, two-thirds are females, between eight and sixteen years of age." If similar investigations were made in this city, we hope the result might not present such fearful facts; yet, can we expect anything better, when we are surrounded by more than 3,000 taverns and beer-houses, and 800 houses of immoral character are open every night, and in some of these children may be found of from nine to twelve years of age. We have girls now in the Rosine who entered this course of life at that early period.

We have always been doubtful of the benefits to be derived from the action of the police in regard to houses of this character. Some months since, the keepers of twenty-five houses, in the neighborhood of Fourth and Plum Streets, were indicted. Many of our citizens rejoiced, supposing by this course the evil would be suppressed; but, arrangements were made, that, if they would remove, nothing farther should be done. And what is the consequence? If those persons removed, others of no better character occupy their places, and these dislodged keepers opened houses in other parts of the city that had been comparatively pure, and carried into these twenty-five neighborhoods the ruinous and seductive influences that had made Plum Street a perfect nuisance—a moral miasma, teeming with misery, degradation, and death.

Two or three years since, the same course was pursued in Elizabeth Street and Portland Lane.

The houses were indicted, the police absorbed all the money that could be drained from the unfortunate women, and they were then released to open houses of the same character in other parts of the city, thus spreading the moral and physical corruption. This state of affairs calls loudly for a suitable House of Correction and Industry, where all persons indicted for keeping improper houses should be placed, where they could be surrounded by reformatory influences, and where, with the drunkard, they should be forced to labor for their own support, and for the maintenance of their families. Very many of these women have children, some of whom have sufficient principle to support them away from themselves, and in ignorance of their habits of life; but the downward course of these persons is generally so rapid, that the children are usually subjected to the evils of orphanage, or are surrounded by such examples and circumstances, that they may be said to be living without God in the world, and all the knowledge they have of him is learned from the oaths they are taught to lisp in babyhood. These are truly the heathen! Need we wonder at the number of profligate and immoral women who crowd our city, when we are able thus to trace whence they come, and see year after year the unfortunate race increasing, and causing the necessity of the great police force, which, with all its efforts, cannot suppress the disorders in our midst.

But were our city filled with police, and in every street a prison, like the one in Moyamensing, still nothing would be done for the reformation of these persons. Too long have we considered punishment as reformation. The visitors of the County Prison do not expect reforms to be effected there, and they never can be under its present organization; but in an Industrial Institution, aiming expressly to benefit the inmates, much good might be effected and great evils prevented. An obstacle may present itself to some minds in regard to the difficulty of procuring work, but our army and navy contracts, which now serve to enrich only a few individuals, might be obtained, and thus a great supply of employment be thrown into this channel for both men and women. Caps, shoes, shirts, coats, pantaloons, &c., might all be manufactured there; and why should the vast shoe trade of the country be absorbed by the Eastern States, when our own citizens should be thus employed?

The many unfortunates who require our care, under their various circumstances, awaken new fields of thought, and bring to our minds new necessities.

The importance of a temporary home for friendless women and children first presented itself, and that has been brought into operation, and is at present in the full tide of usefulness. Now we feel the necessity of another institution, and desire to bring the subject, for consideration, before the community. We believe it to be of vital importance, and urge our friends to demand it of the proper authorities.

The number of women who have been provided with situations from our Institution and Intelligence Office amount to 1595. From the Temporary Home, 1791—making, from the two Associations, 3,386 women and children. Had the Rosine done nothing else but thus be the means of aiding and procuring employment for 3,386 persons, it would have effected a great work; but no one can estimate the amount of evil that may have been prevented, or the number of women that may have been saved from sin and misery.

The garments made within the past year for the Rosine family, number - - -	535
Made for customers, including 161 shirts, 392 vests, 97 pairs of pantaloons, 104 dresses, 48 pairs of drawers, 55 sun-bonnets, and sundry other articles, amounting to - -	1302
Total, for family and customers, -	1837

The receipts from the work-room have been, from October 1st, 1851, to October 1st, 1852, $557. Of this amount, $204 29 have been credited to girls who have learned trades in the Institution, and are now considered boarders, and who pay $1 50 per week for their board and washing. All they can earn over that amount is at their own disposal. The amount of board received is $146 50. In another year, should the same individuals continue with us, we hope the surplus over their board will be greater, as from practice they will acquire increased rapidity, and can accomplish more, and the excellence of their work will produce a more profitable custom.

Treasurer's Account from Oct. 1*st*, 1851, *to Oct.* 1*st*, 1852.

The receipts from the work-room have been, - - - -		$557 00
Deducting $204 29, earned by girls who are boarders, the remainder is - -	$352 71	
Per board of inmates working for themselves, - -	146 50	
Per subscriptions and donations, - - - -	2,287 41	

Interest on donations towards the purchase of the house,	192 10—	2,978 72

EXPENSES.

For rent, salaries, fuel, clothing, marketing, &c., - - - - - - -	2,583 81
Balance, - -	$394 91

HOUSE ACCOUNT.

Paid for Rosine House, by donations received at various dates for that purpose, - - - - - - -	$2,200 00
By mortgage on the House held by the Association, - - - - - -	1,300 00
By cash borrowed from a friend, - -	1,500 00
	$5,000 00
The ground-rent remaining on the property, of - - - - - -	1,333 33
Makes the full amount - - - -	$6,333 33
Debt remaining on Rosine House, by cash borrowed, - - - - - -	1,500 00
By ground-rent, - - - - - -	1,333 33
	$2,833 33

We have thus made a statement to our members and contributors of our pecuniary affairs, and some few facts connected with our operations; but, to the public, we can never reveal the heart-rending stories of those who claim our care and demand our sympathies, nor, as they enter again into the business and responsibilities of life, can we point them out as having been the recipients of your bounty, and the objects of the ministrations and blessings of the Rosine House. But, in that coming future, when all things are known, and they and ourselves must be judged, not by our deeds, but by our motives, and the circumstances that surrounded and operated upon us, perhaps some of these despised ones may precede us to the throne of mercy, and meet us, as we enter the spirit-land, with the joyful message, "Inasmuch as ye did it unto the least of these, ye did it unto me."

Our members and contributors will please pay their subscriptions to the Store-keeper, at the Rosine House; or to the Treasurer, Mira Townsend, No. 43 Arch Street—by so doing, it will prevent the necessity of being called on.

The Annual Meeting is held on the first Thursday in April.

A VALENTINE

TO MY DAUGHTER IN THE COUNTRY.

My Daughter dear, dost thou incline
To greet once more a rhyming line?
And, can thy Mother's rhymes impart,
A glow of pleasure to thy heart?
I know they can, for I have been
  Blest by a Mother's love,
And I have known, and felt, and seen,
  Ere she went home,—above—
That, in the holy name of Mother,
There was a charm owned by no other.
Years passed away, and she passed too,
  Translated into glory,
Time's phonographic hand revealed
  Of eighty years the story;

His tale was told, in hoary hairs,
And wrinkles, brought by pains and cares.
And yet, our Mother never seemed
  To us beyond her prime;
There was a freshness in her heart,
That took in every age a part,
  Still unimpressed by time.
Whene'er I think of her, there comes
  A dimness in my sight;
A starting tear springs from its well,
That does not grief or sadness tell,
But simply says, that she was not
  A Friend, Companion, Sister, Brother.
One word reveals that she was *all,*—
  In life's young days, she was *our Mother!*

I ask not for thee, Daughter, wealth,
  But common sense I crave,
And moral sense to act the right,
  And be no fashion's slave.
I ask for thee a consciousness,
  Of what *may be the right*—
A mental strength, that will not fail
  In following that light.
I ask not for thee happiness:
  The good are ever blest;
If they pursue where duty calls,
  The Father gives the rest.
It may be o'er a troubled sea,
  May be a Martyr's life;
A scene of combat and of toil,
  Of trial, pain, and strife.
Yet, still, 'mid these, what glorious thoughts,
  What angel whispers cheer,
When, through each scene, in humble faith,
  They feel the Father near.
And still, as toils or trials come,
  The childlike state is won;

Love, reverence, and faith have voice—
  Father! Thy will be done.

Year after year, my spirit strove
  To be *in truth resigned*,
To feel myself the plastic clay,
To yield resistless to the sway
  That governs matter,—mind.
I had, in my imaginings,
  My future dressed in flowers;
The toil of life I thought was o'er,
  Ease spoke of leisure hours;
Books offered what was dearer still,
The treasures that their pages fill;
  But yet, I saw it clearly,
Plainly as words could tell,
  There was a work before me,
Which, like a magic spell,
  Was ever in my vision;
It was my thought by day,
  It dwelt upon my pillow,
And, with unyielding sway,
  Became my one idea.
  I saw, with prophet's eye,
Shape after shape assuming
  Forms of reality.
I felt, and I believe it,
  That, up to Heaven's throne,
The wail of crime and wretchedness,
  In tears and prayers had flown;
And I believed the sinner's prayer
Was heard, and had acceptance there.
Then, then I felt my pleasure, ease,
  My time, my strength were claimed,
For those whom crime and woe had sunk,
  Whom foul dishonor named.
And then I felt, first truly felt,
  Submission's point was won,

And I could say in word, and deed,
  Father! thy will be done!
I laid upon the altar, then,
  The hopes of many a year,
The promised leisure, books, and ease,
  When fruitage time seemed near.
The joys and charms of social life,
  That round my heart entwined,
Amusements, lectures, pleasures, all,
  Were one by one resigned.
Not with resisting spirit, but
  With faith, time cannot move,
Resolved to follow what might seem
  The pointings from above.
And now, with faith unchanged, undimmed,
  My mission I pursue,
And only ask that I may cleave,
  Still, to the right and true.
But think not, Daughter dear, my days
  Are days of toil alone;
That happiness and leisure hours
  Are equally unknown.
'Tis true, I lead a vagrant life,
  And beg from door to door,
And sue for those I truly deem
  The poorest of the poor;
The homeless outcast is my theme,
  The child of sin and shame:
For her I plead, yet dare not speak,
  Her sad, dishonored name.
The guilty dome, the haunt of vice,
  Where profligates repair,
I ofttimes seek, in hopes to draw
  Some victim lambs from there.
The pris'ners small and gloomy cell
  Familiar now has grown,
And, in its silence, some have learned,
  To know my step and tone.

When there, sometimes my name is called,
From some far-distant spot;
For misery treasures mercy's tones,
Her step is ne'er forgot.
My Daughter! should'st thou ever be
Prepared to act my part,
Then, only, canst thou realize
The joy that lights my heart,
When at each door I turn the key,
And know a blessing waits for me.

Before me, on the table, now
Six Valentines are laid;
Tokens of love and gratitude,
In humble guise arrayed,
All from Rosines. And these, my child,
More pleasure can impart
Than costly gifts, or gems, or gold,—
For these bespeak the heart.
In some degree, I now can know,
The joy that is in Heaven,
When one repentant sinner turns,
And asks to be forgiven.
Thus occupied, my thoughts and hours
Are ever fleeting now,
The days too short—the midnight oil
Oft lights my thoughtful brow.
But cheerful, bright, my days, my eves,
Elastic nerve and mind,
For inward peace gives outward strength
To bear, and be resigned:
And oft I think my peace is like
Some gently-flowing stream,
That springs in mountain heights above
From the unfailing fount of love,
And joyful, in the beam
Of day and light, still wends its way,
Receives the dew, and gives its spray.

This letter, Darling, I had thought
  To send thee, at the time
When lovers are allowed to tell
  Their fondest hopes in rhyme.
Not that, to thee, I could not speak
  My feelings every day,
But that each season may be passed
  In some instructive way.
And I would wish, that throughout time
  We each may act a part,
That every thought and deed may find
  Response in either heart;
That love may not be breathed alone,
  As seasons come and go,
But, like the gentle stream, roll on
  In one perpetual flow,
Until the golden gate of life
  May ope—the goal be won—
And angel voices welcome both,
  With, "All is well! well done!"

THY MOTHER.

A CHRISTMAS AT THE ROSINE—1852.

"Christmas! a bright, happy Christmas to you! A merry Christmas!" was the cry resounding through the Rosine House, on the morning of the joyful anniversary. True, the sky was unpropitious, and the rain descended on the bespattered pedestrian as he wended his way churchward, or in search of pleasure. But no sky lowered in the Rosine—bright smiles were on every face, and a busy air of importance, as if each one felt that the enjoyment of the whole rested upon her shoulders. The workrooms, divided by large folding doors, were thrown into one, and wreaths of evergreen, intermixed with artificial flowers of domestic manufacture, were twined around the door casings, the framed rules, the looking glass, the gas fixtures, some scripture pictures, and the portrait of "*Our Mother*," that graced the wall over the mantel—"*Our Mother*" was the mother of two of the founders of the Institution, and the words upon her tombstone, "*Our Mother! she taught us how to live, and how to die*," seemed to have been an accepted lesson, so far, that some of her children felt bound to labor for the lowly and the outcast, and the feeling in the Rosine, is, "Had it not been for the teachings of that mother, the Rosine might not have come into existence, and we would have had no home, no friends, no character, no hope; therefore we must look upon her as *our mother!*"

I have seen a Rosine who was given to somnambulism, rise from her bed and kneel before that portrait, and cross her arms with a devotional air, then rise and touch the picture, and kiss the hand that had been placed upon it, and kneel again exclaiming, "It is a saint!"

The reverence of the Rosine was thus beautifully mingled with the feelings of gratitude, that unconsciously displayed themselves, even in sleep, thus proving the truth of the sentiment, "The good that is in us never dies." The good that had animated the mind of that mother, lived in the heart of the grateful Rosine, and to her, even in sleep, she was a saint.

But "Christmas! Merry Christmas!" rang from lip to lip, as the tables were arranged, and the thousand and one little fixings prepared for the day and the dinner. The busy needles and scissors, and all the paraphernalia of every-day industry, were hidden out of sight, and each lent their aid as it was called for, in the busy preparations. Several friends of the Institution had contributed towards providing the feasts for the day, and the Superintendent had made her arrangements, so that all moved in beautiful harmony. The industrial group of other days was the industrial group of the holiday, and light feet, and light hearts, and active hands proved the advantages of associated labor. The table extended the length of the two rooms, and places and seats were arranged for upwards of forty persons. Four fine turkeys and as many chickens, with sundry vegetables and sauces, sent forth their inviting odor, and the family took their positions at the cheerful Christmas board.

To many of the inmates such a table was a novelty. Though accustomed in the Institution to good and wholesome fare, yet smoking turkeys emitted an inviting perfume that was perfectly irresistible; and while the utmost decorum reigned, and each appeared to be sitting quietly, yet the whole party were such travellers, and so well versed in geography, that American politics were soon deserted for a free and familiar discussion upon Turkey and grease, of both of which they seemed fully to understand the attractive philosophy, and showed as little conscience in appropriating to themselves, as if they had been Russian or Austrian despots. No toasts were drank or speeches made, to be recorded by news reporters, but the incense from grateful hearts arose to Heaven, and bore the record of that Christmas dinner there.

Again the table was a blank! Active hands and

feet soon changed the scene, and in pleasant discourse and hymns of praise, the afternoon passed away. Some of the Managers and some friends came in to say "How do?" and give the civilities of the season, and a part remained to conclude the day with them. Some of the younger members of the family had asked permission to go to church, and others to take a walk to see Christmas; but they had been induced to consent to be happy at home, and a brighter, happier family than that at the Rosine, Kriskingle has rarely seen, even though loaded with gifts as he passed over his wide domain on the merry anniversary.

Evening came. Again the board was spread, and fruit, and nuts, and cakes displayed their temptations. Again the seats were filled, and solemn silence reigned. It was an affecting sight, every head was bowed—every eye bent downward, but tears glistened upon some cheeks there, and orisons of thanks and praise were the outpourings of grateful hearts. Had those who contributed to create this happiness been present, they would have experienced a mental enjoyment far higher than the possession of the golden dollars could have given, and the words of Him, whose birth the day celebrated, would have glided into their souls as though they were then first uttered, "Inasmuch as ye have done it to the least of these, ye have done it unto me." Many of those present were orphans, who had never known parental care. One, whose mother died when she was three days old, and whose father's path had been upon the rolling waves, while stranger hands had ministered to the necessities of nature. Several could not recollect either parent, and some only one, and connected with that one, was the enduring struggle for bread. To these, Christmas brought not the hallowed associations of blessed childhood, that cluster and bud from year to year in the unending wreath of family affection. To many, cultivation of mind was unknown, some scarcely knew a letter in the alphabet, and to some, previously to entering the Rosine, the history of Him whose birth they were commemorating, was as little understood as the changes of the seasons, and the reverence for his character was as indistinct as their belief in ghosts and fairies.

Some there were to whom the higher light had been given, and to whom the sacred texts were familiar, but in every heart there was a witness that revealed the inspeaking impressions of Deity, giving them, in all the depravity through which they had passed, a consciousness of right and wrong, and bringing them peace or remorse, as they attended to its manifestations and promptings. True, like Samuel, they did not recognize the voice that spake to them. Many of them, in recounting their history, have said, "Something seemed to tell me it was wrong;" but their perceptions had not been cultivated or attended to, and they understood not that the revelation from the Divine mind to our minds,

Is like the trembling of a leaf, the murmur of a rill,
Scarcely perceptible at first it seems so calm and still;
Yet, heeded once, it comes again—perhaps with louder tone,
And seems a thought which nature prompts, an impulse of our own;
But, when obeyed and understood, it louder tones imparts,
Than outward sounds—the Father speaks, within our minds and hearts.

But to many of the forty women who sat around

that Christmas table, new lights had been gleaming, and while from day to day they were imbibing the lore in the sacred pages, there was a language that to them had no mysteries. It was that of love and gratitude.

But the feast is over. One of the managers who remained, then produced a roll, saying, "Here is an article of dress for each one, if she will make it to-night." Hands and voices were both raised in reply, as "I will! I will!" resounded through the room. Scissors, thimbles, and needles were soon in requisition, and a few minutes of preparation presented as busy a scene in the manufacturing department, as the table had shown in the discussion of nuts, cakes, and apples.

In the meantime the evening hymn was raised, and the full hearts in melodious tones gave utterance to thoughts they knew not otherwise how to express. To some of them it had been not merely a holiday, but a holy-day. Their best feelings had been developed, and the memory of the Christmas of 1852, will be as a blessed memorial forever.

The busy hands have accomplished the work, and each girl's name has been written with indelible ink on the article she has made. Again the anthem is raised—the friends depart—one by one the inmates retire, and the Rosine House is hushed in silence.

REPORT OF THE MANAGERS OF THE ROSINE ASSOCIATION.

PHILADELPHIA, April 1st, 1853.

In presenting the Annual Report of the Rosine Association, to April, 1853, the Managers feel that the Members and Contributors to the Society, look for a progress corresponding with the advance of the age, in moral, mental, and mechanical developments. But in our work, from year to year, the progress is marked by the number we are able to receive under our care, and then, when the fitting period comes, to send them forth to labor in the world's work, not with the stamp of infamy upon their brows, but bright and hopeful, feeling their destiny lies in a great degree in their own hands; that now they have a home to which they can turn as to a parent's house, and friends to whom their progress is cheering, who will gladly counsel and befriend them in any exigency that may occur, and a shelter always open to receive them while their conduct merits approval. We cannot make good women, but we can throw good influences around the erring that may kindle the spark of good that was slumbering in them, and give them a consciousness that it is there, that it may be developed and cultivated, and bring forth good fruit; and this is a great work, and the grand secret of our success, lies in convincing these degraded ones, that they can become good, and do good, and that we believe it. If the doubt of their capacity lives in our own minds, it is communicated to theirs as with magnetic influence, therefore it is only those whose hearts are enlarged by the truest charity, and the largest hope, who can become efficient workers in the cause of humanity. The faith that is in ourselves must be transferred into them, as the virtue went out of Jesus, even by the touch of the garment. Much effort has been wasted, and means employed by reformers to little avail, because they, themselves, were deficient in the great elements of success, the want of faith in God and man. Prisons have arisen, and been crowded everywhere, and the Inquisition opened its doors of misery, because man has doubted his brother, and wanted to reform him in his own way, and in his blindness could not see, that the reformer must begin in his own life, and show by his own purity and goodness, and love and mercy, that these principles existed in himself, and that he had faith that they lived also in his brother's heart, though they might be covered up and hidden by the circumstances that had caused his condemnation. But punishment and contempt have never been the pathway into the inner man, and there lies the only spot to labor effectually. We must not only take him by the hand, but we must creep into his heart, and make him feel there is good there, and we know it, and that we will help him to cultivate it, and clear away the weeds and the thorns that have covered it up, and we will aid him to bring it out in the clear sunlight, and convince him, that he too may become a worker, not only for himself, but for humanity. This is our duty. Here our pathway lies; and just so far as we are prepared to enter into this mission, can we be suitable agents to labor in the Rosine. There is no Association that awakens deeper interest; there is none that calls for more sympathy, patience, mercy, love, industry, and energy. The two last qualities are mentioned, because we have had to keep them constantly in remembrance, from our necessities, our family claiming support, without having a sufficient fund to meet expenses. Our house had also to be paid for at a certain period, or we should lose our claim to its possession. To effect these purposes, and perform the other necessary duties, some of us have felt, that there was little time to lay off the harness; but we have never faltered, or turned aside from the opened duty, and still full of faith in our mission being blessed, not only to the recipients of our care, but to ourselves, we pursue our vocation, as time reveals it to us. Difficulties and discouragements have often surrounded us, and some have given way to these, and left our Board; but Providence has opened other hearts to become laborers with us, and we are strengthened and encouraged by the knowledge, that many of those who were formerly doubtful of our success, are now prepared to say "God speed the good work," and have become our annual contributors.

In our Report of last October, we mentioned, that we had partly paid for the Rosine House, but that twenty-eight hundred dollars still remained due on it, also, that our Rosine family had been so large, that our chambers were crowded to excess, and that many applicants had been refused admission. This has continued to be the case, and we must appeal to those who have the means to help us, so that we may be able to purchase the lot next to the one we now occupy, and put up a building that may enable us, not only to receive those who apply, but introduce increased facilities for the profitable employment of our inmates, that they may contribute more effectually towards the support of the Institution, than they can at present, with our limited room, and means. We have now but two rooms (and they thrown into one by a folding door), that can be appropriated for work, meetings, school, and hours of recreation, and our family for the last eighteen months has usually numbered over 40, sometimes 48. In the bed-rooms eight or ten women frequently sleep, when there are actually comfortable accommodations for only 5 or 6. It must be remembered, that some of these women never go out into the street; they are therefore constantly subjected, both day and night, to the depressing effects and disadvantages of an atmosphere, vitiated by the breaths of so many persons. Those of our friends who have attended our Sabbath meetings must be aware of this fact, and many of them have spoken of it as an evil that ought to be remedied. But we must either close our doors, and refuse to admit more than we can comfortably accommodate, or be subjected to our present inconveniences, without we can awaken that interest in our friends, that will provide the means to give a healthful, proper home to those who come to us, claiming from us all the charities and comforts of life, all in fact that is worth living for. It has often been the subject of our admiration, to see the kindness of our inmates towards one another in this crowded condition, and how willingly they make sacrifices for each other, and on entering our work-room, where quilting, tailoring, dress, and shirt-making, with all the branches of plain sewing are in progress, more than admiration has been excited, at the judicious management of our seamstress, who superintends all, and preserves through all the utmost decorum, propriety, and industry. It gives us great pleasure to be able to recommend the work done in the Institution, for customers, and invite our friends to give our inmates the opportunity of working for them. Some of those who have been under our care a considerable time, and whose propriety of conduct sanctions it, go occasionally as seamstresses into families, by the week, and appear to give entire satisfaction. The best evidence of this, that we can give, is, that in the past year, three ladies have become Managers in the Institution, in consequence of the pleasure and interest awakened by having sewing done for them by our inmates.

It is truly an affecting and interesting sight, to visit our work-room, and reflect on the change wrought on many of the individuals there; and yet it is only those who are familiar with their separate histories, that can fully feel or appreciate the change. It is a trite remark that reality is sometimes stranger than fiction. Of the truth of this, some of us, who most frequently examine them, and note their histories, are constantly reminded. Our Reports must necessarily be brief, therefore, when we refer to incidents connected with our inmates, we can only give a few outline facts, which need the filling up to give our friends an idea of the interest the whole story would awaken. In very many cases, early orphanage, and destitution of proper friends and care-takers, appear to be the foundation of the evil of the after life. In others, a worse evil than orphanage is presented, in the drunkenness and depraved habits of parents. Another cause lies in the prejudice in the minds of parents against indenturing children, and the custom of hiring them from family to family for the petty wages they obtain, and the children consequently grow up without education, or fixed habits or principles. Again, the idea, which unfortunately is too prevalent, that cooking and housework is degrading, and our girls at the period of life when they should be employed in domestic avocations, are found in factories, or struggling for bread as needle-women.

Of the temptations arising from the half paid labor of seamstresses, those only can tell who have them to endure, and though the "Song of the Shirt," and the occasional paragraphs in a newspaper have given an impulsive momentary thrill to the reader, nothing has been done to add one cent to the starvation prices frequently given by employers. Some gentlemen who are really benevolent, but are nevertheless governed by the advantages of trade, without remembering that souls and bodies, reputation and happiness, are involved in the prices of women's work, offèred, as a kindness, to give the Rosine a lot of shirts to make, at ten cents apiece. We had not much work at the time, and hesitated for a moment when the proposition was made, about accepting it, when we were informed we should be expected to find cotton and buttons. We declined the offer, and the shirts were given out to individuals. How many women were tempted to their ruin, how many eyes were blinded by their dim lights, at the midnight hour, over those shirts, we cannot tell, but we do know that those gentlemen on the Sabbath sit in their elegantly furnished pews in the temple devoted to the meek and the lowly one, and respond "Amen," and "Glory to God," as the preacher enjoins upon them, "to do unto others as they would have others do unto them."

Under these circumstances we conceive it to be our duty, to impress upon those parents whose children cannot consistently remain with them, the importance of indenturing them in families, where they may have a settled home, and judicious care extended over them, until they are of age, and endeavor to convince both parents and children, that domestic employments are not degrading, and that those ideas are mistaken which leave our families no alternative, but to employ emigrants, or negroes, and are constantly filling the avenues to shame and misery with our own American girls. It is deeply mortifying that it should be so, but it is a fact, that our dwellings are the abodes of enterprising foreigners, and the daughters of our own shores are clustered in those sinks of iniquity, where undying remorse drives them into habits of intoxication, and the maddening mental fever urges to a reckless indifference of character, propriety, and everything that once formed the happiness and holiness of life. Let us then feel it as an imperative duty, to impress on those to whom it may be needful, that honest labor is as respectable in the family as in the shop, and in the end far more profitable in a pecuniary way, as the changeful seasons of trade produce such fluctuations in the employment of shop hands, that the busy periods, with even the best remuneration, fall short of supplying the demands that must arise, and be met, when the work is deficient. Oh the pang that falls upon the heart of the young girl who has struggled to learn a trade, which she has hardly accomplished when the sound strikes her reluctant ear, that the season is over, and there is no work, and the board, and the clothing bills rise before her, and the half shodden feet almost refuse to bear her away. Could the employer look into the mental recesses where thought is buried, what a world of misery would he see, as one after another passes from his counter, and are lost to his sight. But if *he* does not read these thoughts, that well up till they find vent in tears, the libertine has marked them, and he knows the hour is coming, when necessity will tempt his victim, and she will become his prey. Thus it is, one by one, the houses of iniquity are peopled, and in an incredibly brief period, those who were among the fairest and loveliest of the land, are numbered among the outcasts, despised, and nameless. The hand of time passes heavily over these. Disease, and the gnawing worm in the heart, bear them on rapidly. The prison receives them in its cells, and amid the cold charities of the almshouse, they pass into the presence of the Almighty, perhaps without one glimmering hope, or daring to offer one petition for pardon. Ought we then with feelings of unwise delicacy to shrink from extending the warning voice, while year after year, as though borne on a resistless tide, victim after victim is swept away, and no hand is stretched forth to shield or save? The pulpit and the parental tones are equally silent. We know the vortex that ingulfs innocence, ignorance, and misfortune is all around us. Our city, with its 800 houses of prostitution, is becoming another Sodom, and who is laboring to stay the flood?

With this knowledge, and these convictions resting upon us, seeing "great is the field, and few the laborers," and how difficult it is in many cases to sustain these unfortunates in the path of right, even after they have resolved to aim at the better life, yet we are encouraged to persevere amid our discouragements, by the consciousness that our house and our efforts have rescued many who in all probability would have been utterly lost, and have been the means of restoring them to society, to usefulness, and to their own self-esteem.

In our reports we can only allude to a few cases as illustrations of the nature of our work. Some of these bring proof of how low humanity may sink, and yet be elevated. They show that even when it appeared as if they were deserted by both God and man, yet the Almighty eye followed them into the haunts of depravity, and inspired some of his more favored children to seek them out, to lead them as into a father's house, and give them the opportunity to endeavor to redeem the past, even if it be at the eleventh hour.

In one of our visits to Baker Street, we went up some steps outside of one of those dens of misery, which are hidden up alleys from the public gaze, and in one of the apartments found three young women. One, an Irish girl, had taken off her dress and was washing it in a bucket, which was the only article of furniture, except about two yards of rag carpeting, which laid upon the floor. It was a winter's day, but there was no fire, and no appearance of there having been one. The other women stood with folded arms, leaning against the wall. They appeared about five-and-twenty, and both were good-looking Americans. The face of one was bruised and purple, and all had evidently been drunken and degraded. In answer to a series of questions, we learned they paid 75 cents per week rent. Their bed and bed clothing, chairs, tables, and other conveniencies, were all comprised in the two yards of carpet. Upon opening a closet door, to look for cooking utensils, we found only a bottle and a candlestick. The bucket had been borrowed of a neighbor, and these were the comforts, and this was the place these women called *home*. Upon investigating their stories, the Irish girl said she came from New York, and was going back. The one with a bruised face had a mother, a respectable woman, who she thought would receive her if we would plead for her. A gang of rowdies had burst in upon them the night before, and in the attempt to defend herself from their brutality, she had received the bruises. We had heard of such instances before, therefore we entirely believed the story. The third, who we will call Mary, was the daughter of parents whose names were formerly familiar to us, though personally unknown. They had lived comfortably, were members of a religious society, and Mary had been brought up with all the privileges and enjoyments of respectable life. When about 16 she contracted an attachment to a young man, which not meeting the approbation of her parents, in the folly and inexperience of youth, she was persuaded to leave her home, and marry him. But the dream of love was a short one. Her husband was tempted to commit a larceny on his employer, and became a convict. Again she entered her father's door, but the light step and joyous eye were gone. She had brought sorrow and disgrace to the hearthstone, and bitter words were her greetings. Years passed. Her husband left the city when released from prison, and she has never spoken to him since. Her parents died, and there was little left for her. Then commenced the struggle for bread. It would be a long story, and a sad one to mark her progress, with all youth's promises blighted thus, and shame upon her brow, till we found her in her wretched home in Baker Street. When we spoke of the Rosine, and told her there was yet a possibility of gaining a position where virtue, respectability, and happiness might be her portion, she pointed to her bare feet, and said, I cannot go! But Mary did come, and a few days at the Rosine presented an altered woman. Her conduct while there met with entire approbation, until she left for a place of service in a respectable family. In our report of last April, we referred to the case of a woman who had been stripped in one of those wretched places, in Baker or Bedford Streets, and under the cover of the night came to the Rosine, with only one garment on her person. She was the picture of misery and depravity, an object of loathing to the beholder. But a few months wrought a change in her, and she was transferred into a respectable family in New Jersey, where she remained a year, gaining the respect and affection of those around her. At the close of that period she was married to a worthy young man, who had lived as foreman three years in the same family? At the period of our last intelligence from them, they were preparing to remove to the West. Who of us can tell, what the future destiny of this couple may be. The western world opens a home, independence, wealth and honor to the adventurer that can grasp them, and the integrity and industry that recommended these individuals to each other, may be the means of placing them in an elevated position, when they may be numbered among the princes of the land. But had there been no Rosine, no open door to receive this friendless outcast in the hour of her extremity, and shield her from the bitter consequences of her destitution and depravity, the prison would doubtless have welcomed her within its dreary cells, from whence she would probably have issued more hardened and degraded, and the seal of infamy perpetuated on her brow. These are extreme cases, but they are not the only ones of the same character that have been recorded among our memorials. Vainly indeed to such as these comes the voice of the preacher. The hearts and purses of the pious have bade their missionaries seek the habitations of the poor, to tell them of the riches of the kingdom to come, but to these unclothed and hungry ones, steeped in habits of inebriation and vice, what can it avail to speak of the bread of life.

The only doctrine they are prepared for in this condition, is that breathed forth by human sympathy, which grasps the soiled and trembling hand of the sunken one, draws her from the vile associations that cluster around her, places her in a decent home and cleanly garments, convinces her she can earn the bread of honest industry, and, that though the cloud has rested upon her, producing almost Egyptian darkness, yet, there are hearts that acknowledge her womanhood, and believe in her capacity to conquer her dissolute tendencies, and achieve a victory over herself, and what appeared to be her destiny. Burns, in his undying verses, evinced his knowledge of the philosophy of humanity, when he wrote "A man's a man for a' that," and this inner manhood must be appreciated, while attention is bestowed upon the physical comforts. Then, and not till then, can we hope to find an understanding of "the bread that comes down from heaven." An acknowledgment of the mercies and blessings received, must be awakened before the tears of penitence can be shed, and in the gates of praise and deliverance alone, can the spirit be clothed in the garment of humility. We would not underrate the Gospel Missionary, but we have seen that the only effective gospel is that which feeds, clothes, and provides remunerative employment with one hand, while with the other it points to the source from which patient endurance of affliction can be gained, and whence comfort and consolation can be received. But amid the variety of cases that appeal to our sympathies and protection, many are yet in the spring of life. We have one in the Institution of only 14 summers, another of 15, and many have come to us of 16, 17, and 18 years. One of these, a girl of 16, who lost her father in early childhood, and whose mother is a confirmed inebriate, was placed in a family, from which she was unsuspectingly enticed into a house of bad character, and there detained. Providence raised friends to draw her from there, and place her in the Rosine. When she came to us, about one year since, she could only read the first lessons in the spelling-book understandingly. Of writing, of course, she knew little. She continued under our care six months, during which time, she availed herself of every opportunity of improvement, and, at the end of that period became an inmate of the family of one of our friends, and through the bounty of those who first snatched her from ruin, she is now receiving all the advantages of moral, religious, and educational instruction. The following commencement of a letter received from her by one of our Board, within a few days, speaks for her more than our words can tell.

"DEAR FRIEND—I received your letter on Monday, and I wish I could express to you my pleasure on receiving so kind and affectionate a letter. So far from considering myself neglected by your silence, I feel it a great privilege to be permitted to write to you, and know that I ought not to expect a regular answer to every letter, even while I was longing, day after day, to receive this gratifying token of your remembrance, and unless you had witnessed it, I fear you would hardly believe my extravagant delight on reading the dear little folded paper so expressive of your kind recollections. I positively danced for joy, bestowed a thousand caresses upon everybody I loved; dreamed of you all night, and arose next morning with a heart full to answer your letter, but was prevented by having a lesson more than I anticipated, and have not been able until now, to fulfil this most pleasing duty."

This is the natural outburst of feeling, from one who knows her new friends are the only ones to whom she can look for that affection and sympathy that every heart craves. A few of the words were not spelled correctly, but the whole letter is a creditable specimen of improvement. It is the intention of those friends to give her an education that may qualify her to support herself in any occupation that may open for her, and we are empowered to act in all things as if she were our own child.

One, of whom we have spoken, in a past report, as having drank of misery's most bitter cup from her 14th year, and who came to us soon after the Rosine was opened, has now $106, in the saving fund, earned honestly, since she left the Institution, besides clothing herself in a very respectable manner. She is now residing in a wealthy family in the city, and fulfilling the duties of active, useful life.

A very interesting girl of 16, came to us four years since, and after remaining several weeks became dissatisfied, and left the Rosine. Time passed. Through the intervening period, she has been living with a merchant in New York, as his mistress, enjoying all the pleasures his affection and money could bestow. But the canker was under all. The elegant robe could not hide it from herself. At length conscience became omnipotent, and in a letter breathing the spirit of the prodigal, though not outwardly in his circumstances, she asked to be permitted to return. "I have never been happy, (said she,) for I could never forget." She left him, after reflecting long upon the subject, and sacraficed her affection to her sense of duty. About six months have elapsed since her return, and she is still with us.

Very many are the sad reflections awakened, as we learn from day to day the unfoldings of the histories of our inmates, and find how few have been their opportunities of mental or moral improvement. Of the 271 women who have been inmates of the Rosine, not one has received a good education. Only three knew the multiplication table perfectly, upon admission, and these had made little progress in arithmetic. 93 could not read understandingly. 148 could not write. Only 2 had ever been in the public schools. 117 had been more or less intemperate. Many were orphans at a very early age, and cast upon the charities of persons, whose minds, or situations, were not favorable to the production of educated, virtuous womanhood, and even with the majority of those who had known maternal care, the circumstances and influences around them had been generally such as would be calculated (under temptation) to make them what they have been. In two instances, two sisters have been in the Rosine at the same time. We have also had a mother and daughter, and both came to us from the prison.

While these sorrowful revelations come to us from year to year, we are necessarily forced to inquire, what are the causes of this great amount of vice and misery? The reply that came to us six years since, has been echoed and re-echoed from year to year, and the words, intemperance, illy-paid labor, ignorance of moral or physical principles, and the absence of physical cleanliness and comforts, come with unvarying tones, and tell us, here is the groundwork of the evils of licentiousness. But the grand demon that desolates home, character, and happiness—that promotes idleness, ignorance, vice, and wretchedness, is intemperance. Through this, individual morality is lowered, the weak become vicious, the passions excited, and the evils engendered by this dreadful indulgence, taint the blood of generation after generation, and a race of weak and vitiated beings are filling our prisons, almshouses, and asylums. Are we willing these things should continue to exist, and increase in the same fearful ratio that the records of crime and poverty report in the past? As women, we stand under the law, but are not the framers of the law. Our property is taxed to support these institutions, but we have no voice in the appropriation of the funds. We see and feel the evils arising from injudicious legislation—we see the drunkard, and the son of the drunkard, in their debasement, and ignorance, giving their votes, to elevate the men who uphold the laws that sanction and license the source of so many evils, and we feel our voices are powerless, at the polls, and in the legislative halls. It is true they are so! The voices of the three millions of mothers in the United States are not recognized, in our judicial tribunals, except in cases of offences, but if our influence is not felt, and shown there, and throughout all the transactions of life, we have been unfaithful mothers, wives, and sisters. The mind of the child is developed under our care. The principles implanted in the nursery display their fruit in manhood. Has not the time then come for us to feel the responsibility of our position, and examine whether we have been faithful stewards? Have we sown the seeds of which we now wish to gather the harvest? To this point of self-examination we must come, and while we lament that there is no law to prevent these poor inebriates from sinking themselves and families in ruin; let us conscientiously ask ourselves, have we done all that we could? Are our own skirts clear? While we ask the Maine Law for the poor, how often in the private room at our social parties, is the wine and brandy circulated to sap the morals and pervert the principles of the young men, to prepare them to become inebriates, and excite the lawless passions, that induce them to people, and frequent our houses of infamy. These are subjects that demand a grave and sincere inquiry, and we ought to meet it honestly, and while we are laboring for the unfortunate women whom we hope to elevate, let us not confine our thoughts and efforts to this point, but feel that our duties lie, not only as remedial agents, but with double force in the preventive field. It is impossible to prescribe to any one what their duties may be, or in what part of the vineyard they may be called to labor, but as we endeavor to follow those intimations that are the pointers to the path of right, we shall all find there is work for us, and as we are faithful, more will be intrusted to our hands. We would fain believe the sin of intemperance a masculine vice alone, but fearful facts prove the contrary. From a table of statistics presented to us a few days since, we find that persons were employed to note the number entering certain dram shops in London, in one evening.

They stand thus:

MALES.	FEMALES.	YOUTHS.
173	365	38
109	247	41
96	105	17
60	103	17
116	149	14
75	111	13
629	1080	140

We rejoice that this record was not taken in Philadelphia, and would fain disbelieve the possibility of so many of these persons being women, but some of us who visit certain neighborhoods in our city, have to testify that a large proportion of our degraded population are women. We have visited, on different occasions, about 70 women in one day, in the Moyamensing Prison, and found, in almost every instance, liquor was the cause of their being there, either directly, or indirectly.

In two of our reports, we have spoken of the necessity of a House of Employment and Reformation, for drunkards, and disorderly persons. We are pleased to find the suggestion meets the approval of other minds, and hope the coming winter, a law may be passed, authorizing such an institution.

In the month of January, the Rosine House was

visited by the Grand Jury, and in their presentment, they say, "At the Rosine Association, we were gratified to learn that so much good had been accomplished by an institution so little known. The benevolence and untiring devotion of the ladies, connected with it, in reclaiming a class of unfortunate females, who, before the establishment of this asylum, were, to a certain extent, friendless, deserves the highest praise. There are a number of inmates, actively employed in appropriate branches of female industry, all being in good health, and well provided for, and apparently desirous of returning, to the paths of virtue. This benevolence furnishes *a Home, and not a place of confinement*, to those who have been misled, and supported as it is, by private contributions only, it cannot be too highly recommended to the attention and liberality of Philadelphians. The amount of good that is annually accomplished in a quiet way, deserves, and should receive the support of our citizens."

Their visit and notice was gratifying to us, as a proof, that we have been able to place the Rosine upon a footing to be recognized among the most important reformatory institutions of our city.

In addition to the care-takers, and instructors in the Rosine, a school teacher is still employed, and the progress of many of the girls is very satisfactory. A friend of the Institution has also attended gratuitously, one evening in the week, to give the inmates instruction in singing. Being confined so constantly in the house (and some of them never out), with little to vary the routine of their daily employments, their minds crave something to interest and entertain them, and the privilege of these musical instructions is much prized by many of them. Each hour of the day and evening has its allotted occupation, except the noon hour, for recreation, which they are permitted to spend as they please, provided the rules are not infringed.

Christmas, in the Rosine, was a happy day. Some kind friends provided the means for a repast befitting the season, and the generosity that prepared the feast sank into the hearts of the inmates, as a token that they were recognized in the social circle, and considered worthy to be participants in that general feeling of rejoicing, that animates the Christian, and has prompted him on the return of each annual festival to realize the fact, that, "Unto us a child is born, a Son is given."

Amid the reflections that most constantly arise with our work of reform, is that of the injustice of society, in stamping infamy upon the erring women, while the companion of her crime (usually her seducer), suffers little, perhaps not at all, from what the world may pass over, as "a little indiscretion." We would ask in the name of justice and humanity, should this be so? Why is it so? Is it because our minds are so perverted, that we can only view virtue and vice as a matter of sex? Who of us are prepared to receive the fallen woman as our friend, in the social circle, and who of us turn from the equally criminal man, and deny him the seat by our firesides, and our daughters. We may speak of the injustice of society, but each of us are parts of that social compact, and it rests with each individual to confirm, or deny, our opinion of its rightfulness, by our own conduct, and the course we pursue.

Our friends are generally aware that the Temporary Home, an institution founded by some of the managers of the Rosine Association, to give a temporary shelter to respectable but friendless females, and to procure homes and employment for them, has been in operation about three years. During this period, 768 women and children have been received into the house, until situations were obtained for them, and an Intelligence Office was opened, which has introduced facilities for procuring places, not only for the friendless, but for others; and 2122 women and children have already received the benefits of this association.

271 women have been inmates of the Rosine House, and the Intelligence Office there has also presented a large field for usefulness.

1687 women have gone to respectable homes through its agency, this making from the two offices 3809 women and children. We may give statistics of the numbers thus introduced into employment, and the means of gaining an honest livelihood, but no one can ever tell how many may have been saved from ruin through the agency of these two associations. Had we accomplished no other good than merely to be means of furnishing 3809 women with homes, and the means of an honest living, we had not toiled in vain.

Our work-room presents a scene of busy industry. During the past year, from April 1st, 1852, to April 1st, 1853,

The garments made for the use of the Rosine family number - - - - - - -	460
Those made for customers, including 132 shirts, 45 coats, 99 vests, 24 pairs pantaloons, 56 dresses, 57 quilts, and sundry other articles, amount to - - - -	1330
Total, - - -	1790

In our Report of last October, we made a statement relative to the purchase of the Rosine House, but, as many of our friends did not receive that Report, it is important to insert it in this.

House Account.

Paid for Rosine House, by donations received at various dates, for that purpose, - - - - - - - -	$2,200 00
By mortgage on the house held by the Association, - - - - -	1,300 00
By cash borrowed from a friend, - -	1,500 00
	$5,000 00
The ground rent remaining on the property of, - - - - - - -	1,333 33
Makes the full amount, - - -	$6,333 33
Debt remaining on Rosine House, by cash borrowed, - - - - - -	1,500 00
By ground rent, - - - - - -	1,300 00
	$2,800 00

This statement shows that we still owe $2,800 on our house, which at present we see no means of paying. Our collections each year are absorbed by the expenses of our large family, which usually number over 40, and which might be very much increased could we receive all the applicants, but, in consequence of our crowded condition, we have had to refuse many who came to us, and who plead earnestly to be admitted, promising to lie contentedly upon the floor if we would receive them. We started the Rosine in the belief that Providence would raise friends to help us. From year to year we have worked on, seeing that belief realized, and now, when the poor friendless wanderer comes to us, asking a home and friends, and we cannot receive her, we remember our debt, but, at the same time, we look wistfully at the lot beside us, and many a hope presents, that the day may come that we may be able to purchase it, and thus increase our accommodations. Some of us have been beggars from the foundation of the Society, and we would now gladly retire from the business could our family be maintained without it, but, while we are in our present circumstances, we must ask our friends to bear with us, and remember the promise made years ago, "The poor, ye shall have always."

Treasurer's Account from April 1st, 1852, to April 1st, 1853.

The receipts from the work-room have been, - - - - - - -	$623 64
Interest on donations at various dates towards the payment for the Rosine House, - - - - - - -	100 60
Donations and subscriptions, - - -	2,279 77
	$3,004 01

Expenses from April 1st, 1852, to April 1st, 1853.

Appropriated to the payment of the house, - - - - - - - -	300 00
Family expenses, including rent, salaries, interest on ground-rent, fuel, clothing, marketing, &c., - - - - - -	2,617 07
Cash on hand, - - -	86 94
	$3,004 01

AUDITOR'S CERTIFICATE.

Having been appointed a Committee by the Board of Managers of the Rosine Association, to examine the accounts of the Treasurer, Mira Townsend, we have attended to the duty, and find them entirely correct.

M. M. WILSON,
MARY M. HASTINGS.

THE FIVE POINTS.

It seems hardly worth while when we have so much vice and misery in Philadelphia, to go to New York to seek it; and then Mr. Pease and the Ladies Mission, and the Hot Corn stories have all made such graphic delineations, that there seems nothing left to tell, but we have been several times to the Five Points, and like all orators who are going to tell a long story, "We want to say *one word.*"

Our first visit there, was when Mr. Pease had just commenced his labors in that neighborhood, and we solicited his guidance through the Old Brewery. We had heard dismal tales of the horrors enacted there, and that it was requisite to get a policeman as a guard, during the peregrinations of a stranger. But we had visited every house in Baker Street, and Bedford Street, and Small

Street, and Mary Street, and Elizabeth Street, and Portland Lane, and many another such place, just two simple women together, and we had always been protected, and had faith to believe we always would be, therefore when we went to the Old Brewery, we forgot to employ a guard, and felt fully satisfied to brave the terrors whatever they might be, under the guidance of a pale, and rather frail-looking clergyman. The Old Brewery then was in the zenith of its glory, as a nest of vagabonds, and sure enough we found them there in every variety. In each room we stopped and conversed with the inmates. At some doors Mr. Pease seemed to feel as if he did not like to enter, or, perhaps thought *we* would not have the courage, but he was not aware that we had seen misery and vice in every form in our own city, and were familiar visitors of Duffy's lime-boxes, as they might then be called, lighted only by a hole a few inches square, cut in the door, where black and white, old and young, male and female, congregated night after night, to sleep on the bare but crowded floors, amid riot, drunkenness, and debauchery; and we had seen the poor creatures, when they came to their senses, emerge from these scenes of indescribable horror, with scarcely a rag left upon them, as those more powerful or less inebriated, had dragged the clothing off them, to pawn for more rum. Mr. Pease was not aware of all this, but we were, and when he hesitated at a door, *we* fearlessly walked in. But the Old Brewery is not there now! In its stead is the Ladies' City Mission House, a fine building with clean, decent rooms, rented to about 20 families, under the watchful care of the ladies, with a fine school-room and church below. Things are changed there from the time of our first visit, and they are somewhat changed in *our* Five Points too, but we need a world of remedies yet before the work is thoroughly accomplished.

Some four or five years after this excursion with Mr. Pease, we escorted some of our Chester County friends to his Mission House. That is the true mission that provides labor, and generates a feeling of honest independence in the individual it seeks to aid, and for this has he been laboring. The site of his House of Industry was formerly occupied by notedly immoral characters; and Mr. Pease, like ourselves, believes in the efficacy of carrying the war into the enemy's quarters, and bearding the lion in his den, so by some means he gained possession of some four or five of these houses, and employs some of the former occupants as braid-sewers, tailoresses, etc. We found on this occasion, about fifty women employed on straw hats. Thirty were tailoring, and some were at plain work. Ninety children were in the school, all of whom can have soup for their dinner, if they choose to take it. Our friends desired to witness some of the scenes they had heard described, and we passed through a couple of the houses in Cow Bay, but the dirt and the smell, and the miserable objects we saw, was too much for the uninitiated, and they had to retreat from the second house violently sick, and unable to explore any farther. But L. B. and ourselves proceeded. We went up an alley to a house standing back of the front ones, and entered a door which, when closed, left us in perfect darkness. We groped our way up a pair of stairs, by feeling only, and found a door at which we entered. A hole in the wall about 12 by 18 inches, which had probably been meant for a window, but which contained no glass, was the only means of light or ventilation in this room. Here, sitting on the floor, were two men and two women, and upon a heap in the corner, which upon closer inspection appeared to be rags gathered from the street, laid a woman who told us she had the dropsy, and was suffering greatly. A charcoal furnace in full blast stood in the centre of the room, and this, with a stool or two, formed the only articles of furniture. The fumes of the charcoal, and rum, and tobacco were so blended and intolerable, that it seemed wonderful they could exist in such an atmosphere: yet here these people lived, and here this sick woman had to endure her misery day after day.

The front room was about as cheerless, but had a larger window, and on what appeared to be a bag of rags laid a man, who said he was sick, and, unwashed and unshaven, looked a pitiable object. Several men and women were sitting or standing idly about the room, and they were all the most perfect images of drunkenness, filth, and debauchery.

Proceeding thus from room to room, we found little variety in the apartments, except that in some the window seemed larger than in others, though it was so thickened by dirt, and stuffed by rags that it made little perceptible difference, and in some there was an appearance of a few articles of furniture, at least, we supposed if the crust of dirt could be removed, there might be an imitation of furniture beneath. On every floor were several rooms, but we could not guess at the number, only as we groped in the dark entry, and found our hands resting on the handles of the doors. There was not a window to give a ray of light from the top to the bottom of the stairs.

When we arrived at the upper apartments we knocked at one door which was opened by a yellow girl, apparently about seventeen years old. She was shabbily dressed, but looked more decent than any one we had seen in the building. We could only compare this room to a play house where a dozen children had been scattering their toys in wild confusion, so completely was the whole floor covered with litter. In the favorite spot, the centre of the room, was the charcoal furnace. Beside it stood an old-fashioned Dutch oven, containing something that looked like tar. There were no other articles of furniture in the room, and the compound on the floor was of rags, sticks, old iron, etc., but we had neither light, nor time to investigate. Over the furnace hovered a woman with her head covered with an apron, almost saturated with blood, which trickled down upon her shoulders. On the floor, stretched at full length on some rags, similar to those already described, laid a stout, large man. After the opening salutation, we inquired what was the matter. "He is blind, and he struck her with that board," whispered the girl, evidently afraid to speak aloud. The board looked like a piece of flooring, about two feet long, with a sharp point at one end. We took no notice of the girl's information, and asked again, what was the matter? The woman looked up sadly, but did not speak. The man then gruffly replied, "I have been beating her!" and he added, "she gets drunk, and lets her daughter run in the street, and she's sassy." "But is she not thy wife?" "Yes, but she's so sassy I have to do it!" "What good will it do thee to strike and abuse her in this manner?" "Why she's sassy, and I can't help it!" We then asked what business he followed? "None!" said he, "but I go round among the Friends, and collect some money to pay the rent, and get along." "And what does thy wife do?" "Nothing! she is lame!" "Is this the girl that runs in the street?" "No! she is a younger one, 15 years old." The young woman said she sometimes went out to work, but was out of employment at present. We advised her to go to work in that room, and make it look more decent and comfortable, and then try to get a steady place, and keep it, for surely no one would hire her from a room looking like that. We told her she ought to be worth $1 25 per week. She could clothe herself well on 75 cents, and then she could spare 50 cents a week to help make her parents more comfortable. We then turned to the man, and asked if he ever thought of trying to get to heaven? "Yes, sometimes! I want to go there!" "But does thee think, abusing thy wife in that manner will take thee there? She is almost covered with blood!" "Humph," said he, shaking his head, "she's so sassy! But I guess I can get in at the gate." "Indeed, we replied, "we fear it will take a larger key than Saint Peter ever had, to get thee in at that gate, if thee ever strikes her again. Besides, thy wife might strike back." "She darsent do that!" and his voice assumed a swaggering tone. "Ah, but thee cannot see, and she might trip thee down!" We must confess we felt rather uncomfortable as we turned to the woman's upraised face, and saw a nod, and an expression of, "I'll do it!" Our conscience smote us, as we thought, perhaps she will take the hint, and do it.

We then brought the woman to the hole that admitted the few rays of light, to examine the wound, and found a cut two inches long. We had supposed before this, that she was a negro, but now found she had long hair, which was separated with difficulty, and which it required some courage and humanity to touch. We requested the daughter to wash the mother, and the wound, and come over to the mission house to get a plaster. But what was to be done with the profusion of matted hair? They had no wash bowl, pan, pitcher, or towel, and no scissors to cut off the gory locks. There was a pause to think what could be done. A knife would not answer—ours was very dull. "Can you not borrow a pair of scissors?" "I don't know!" But no effort was made. We had now arrived at the end of the surgical ministration, and the Dutch oven again arrested our attention. "What is that?" said we; is it victuals?" "Wensun," said the woman. "What?" "Wensun," echoed the man. Still we were stupid, till our companion caught the idea, and pronounced the word, "Venison." We always liked venison, but somehow we were not tempted then.

All this time our curiosity was awakened to know whether this man, blind and impotent as he was, thus lording his brutal sovereignty even in darkness, filth, and wretchedness, was white or colored. At last we asked, as the dim light did not reveal it. He gave a bitter sneering laugh, as he answered, "Can't you see?—I'm Injun!" We did not see. After recommending cleanliness and harmony to all, and industry to the daughter, we turned to retrace our steps down the dark stairway, wondering if spiders, roaches, and other vermin were swarming round us.

We entered a room below, where we found a man and woman, and told them the woman above had been hurt, and asked the loan of a pair of scissors. "No, I will not lend them," said the woman. "Not lend a pair of scissors to assist in dressing a wound?" "No, we will not," rejoined the man. We felt disposed to give them a homily on Christian charity, but thought words would probably be wasted, as both had been drinking, and were too stupid to be benefited. "They are our enemies," said the man, "we will do nothing for them." Poor things, what had they to quarrel about? They had neither money, furniture, nor reputation. We felt they had cause to quarrel with society, which had allowed them to grow up in vice, ignorance, and idleness, and to live in filth and wretchedness in the very heart of the greatest and richest city in America; and with the landlord of that house, who, for the sake of a few more dollars, kept the poor, degraded wretches, who were forced by their vices and misery to be his tenants, to live in darkness, and without means of ventilation.

The philosopher in his tub felt the importance of sunshine, and we certainly felt it too, as we emerged from that building, from which both outward and inward light seemed banished. But if no sunshine takes its beams of glory, and beauty, and happiness into those dreary and prison-like apartments, and there is no development of the fruits of the higher light in the lives of the individuals clustered there, yet we are confident, that beneath the crust of dirt, and the ignorance and vices that envelope the outer man, there is hidden a capacity to understand and enjoy the pure and the beautiful, were they placed in circumstances that would develope and cultivate the sacred germ that is placed in every human being. We have just such people in Baker, Bedford, and Small Streets, but give us a purse to locate them elsewhere, and a chance to cast a few sunbeams upon them, and we will find a heart and kind feelings in the very worst of them. Circumstances made them what they are—circumstances made us what we are. Our heavenly Father alone knows why he gave us such different surroundings. Of how little have we to boast! Had we been changed in our cradles, they would probably be what we are, and we what they are, and have been.

We visited several other houses. In one we were in a room from which twelve dead bodies were carried in three weeks. Men, women, and children were crowded in, the most of them, in such numbers, that it seemed wonderful the powers of locomotion could be maintained without continued jostling. Among the inmates were several fine, bouncing girls, who told us they were straw-workers, and could earn from $1 75 to $3 00 per week, and yet the force of habit is so strong, and there was so little stimulant to exertion, that they seemed hardly to comprehend that they could get other homes, and surround themselves by the comforts produced by cleanliness and industry.

We left the Points with a renewed feeling of gratitude, that our lot had been cast in more pleasant places.

REPORT OF THE MANAGERS OF THE ROSINE ASSOCIATION.

October 20th, 1853.

Six years have passed, each marked with the lines of progress, since the opening of the Rosine House. The Society came into existence on the previous April, and the birth of the new enterprise for the temporal and eternal welfare of those whose condition had been considered by many as hopeless and irredeemable, was an era that ought to be recorded in enduring letters, as a period honorable to the justice and humanity of the women of Philadelphia. We had been accustomed to receive in our parlors, and treat with all the courtesies of social life, men of at least suspected profligacy, and considering that if they stood well in the pecuniary world, affairs of mere gallantry were not sufficient to cast a stigma upon them, or banish them from the society of the most refined and virtuous woman. Who, in the polished circle, frowned upon the most delicate lady who ventured the happiness of her life with a reformed rake, or even with one without professing reformation; and where would we find the fearless woman, with sufficient moral courage or benevolence that would dare stake her own reputation, by countenancing or even treating with common humanity the fallen woman?

It was not that we were deficient in the gentle impulses of nature, but, that custom sanctioned injustice, and women, with all their high aspirations after the good and the beautiful, suffered the most divine and holiest principles to sleep within them, because society had drawn its arbitrary line, and they had not learned to do the right, because it was the right. But the moral courage that dared in 1847 to found a Society for the reformation, employment, and instruction of women who had led immoral lives, proved that a better time was coming, and had come; that with the demand of other rights we were prepared to claim the right to stand on virtue's side—to hold up in the broad sunlight our appeal for suffering woman, and to place upon the same platform the erring man and woman, each unsuitable associates while in the wrong, but equally capable of reform, and re-entering into the duties and responsibilities of social and religious life.

Many women (whose minds were still in leading strings) were not prepared for this movement. They could not see in the beginning, the end—they knew not that the germ of moral sense awakened in the formation of the Rosine Association, would reach with its purifying influence the very circle in which they moved; that while it opened an avenue for the reformation of females, it would awaken in their own minds an appreciation of their duties to their children and to others, both male and female, and teach them, that virtue was as important and estimable in one sex as the other, and the lapse from it equally to be condemned.

They saw not in the heroism that dared to say, we will grapple with the lion in his den—we will enter the sinks of iniquity, and draw from thence the victim lambs, and shelter and protect them, and strive to awaken in their souls a desire and capacity to espouse the right, more than a futile struggle, a foolish hardiness, that with other ephemeral efforts would yield to disappointments and discouragements, and sink as the bubble upon the foamy waters. But six years have passed away, and many of those who doubted the utility or success of our efforts, are now our annual contributors, and cheer us from year to year, with "God speed you in the good work."

The Rosine House was opened in October, 1847, with one inmate. Since that period 306 women have been members of the family, besides a great number of respectable but friendless women, to whom a temporary home has been given until employment could be procured for them. Many who have never entered our house, have claimed our sympathy and attention, and have been aided and encouraged to try the better way, and through our efforts have risen into positions, towards which they previously had not dared to look. There are those who are married now, and we believe, living rightly, who we found in the path of ruin, who owe their present happiness and power of usefulness wholly to the influences extending from this Association, and who in their secret aspirations bless the Rosine as the active source of their present happiness, and their escape from the horrors which no pen can or dare fully describe.

Many women are so circumstanced that they cannot become members of our Rosine family, yet (from our connection with the Society), their cases are made known to us, and we are enabled to become useful to them; and it *is* a privilege, to be permitted even to hand the cup of water to suffering humanity. Who can measure the influence of a single word or look, as it sinks into a mind that feels itself an outcast from the charities of life, or the hopes that may animate a desponding spirit to struggle against the depressing tendencies that surround it, when it feels there is even one in this wide world, who can understand its unhappy condition, and while they sympathize, can have faith in the possibility of its redemption! Is it not a privilege to be thus awakened to the claims of our fellow-beings, and to be endowed with a faith, that

"In all there is an inner depth,
A hidden secret way,
Where, through the dimly lighted soul,
God sends his living ray.
In every human heart there is
A faithful, sounding cord,
That may be struck by touch or look,
Or some kind, gentle word.
And, though despised, and trodden down,
Stained with the shades of sin,
Deciphering not those holy lights
That God hath lit within,
Yet prompted by that touch, or tone,
To cast their chains aside,
Regenerate life is in them still—
They have their angel side!"

Yes! in the six years that we have been laboring for the unfortunate and degraded, though it has been our lot to struggle with evil in all its forms, yet we can truly say, we believe in all there is an angel side. Intemperance, profanity, and dissipation may smother the Divine principle; or the associations from childhood may have been such, that it has never been developed; yet,

"In all there is an inner depth,
A secret, hidden way,
Where, through the dimly lighted soul,
God sends his living ray."

Among many proofs (if proofs were needful) is one of a woman, who has been noted, for years, for keeping a house of immoral character, and yet is known among her neighbors as "the good Samaritan." Her hand is ever open for the deed of mercy, and the sick and afflicted rise up and bless her. The collectors for churches receive her donations, though she knows she would be unwelcome, and the lady-occupant would shrink from her, were she to enter one of the pews. She has offered to contribute towards the support of the Rosine, and when we refused her money, her tears attested her sincerity, and the painful emotions she experienced in not being allowed to become a donor.

In some cases we have been permitted to be the active agents in awakening vitality in this buried germ, when even the possessor thought they could exclaim, "there is no good in me!" and to inspire in hopeless hearts a faith, that this seed, though it might be small as a mustard-seed, yet, by proper exertion and cultivation, might become as a tree of the forest. In some of the cases that have come under our care, a large degree of patience, forbearance, and hope have been needed, before there was much outward manifestation of this inner life; and some of us, whose faith was not an enduring principle, have had our hearts sink within us, and discouragements have bowed us down; but, others have felt that there are periods, when

"They also serve, who only stand, and wait"—

and this, in our position, must sometimes occur, when by patient waiting alone can our work be accomplished. And is not this labor of love a glorious one? To be permitted to extend the hand to suffering humanity—to be able to inspire the sinking outcast with the belief, that she can not only be raised from her lowly condition, but become herself a worker for others. It is truly the ministry of angels; and, as we are prepared to devote our hearts and energies to the efforts and sacrifices required, and our daily prayer is for wisdom, the blessing of Him who rewardeth liberally changes sacrifice to enjoyment, and the rich treasures of a peaceful spirit are our recompense, and animate us to labor from day to day.

The Rosine family, during the last two years, has been larger, generally, than could be comfortably accommodated. When we first rented the house, the calculation was, that we could receive thirty women; and, from the experience of other Associations, it was supposed the house would contain all that would apply for reception. But we have been gratified to find, that, as our ideas and operations have been understood, many of those for whom it was intended have appreciated its advantages, and desired to place themselves under its influences. Within the last two years our family has usually numbered over forty, sometimes forty-eight, and many have been refused admission, owing to our crowded condition. One of the disadvantages resulting from this has been, that we have parted with some of the members of our family at an earlier period than perhaps was best for the individual, and thus make way for others who were pressing for admission. Part of our family always lie upon the floor, as we have not room to put up any more bedsteads. In this condition, we cast longing eyes on the lot next to the one we occupy, hoping that Providence will open hearts to aid us in a pecuniary way, that we may be able to purchase it, and enlarge our Institution. Our contributors are aware that we still owe $2800 on the Rosine House, and the necessary expenses of our large family can only be balanced by soliciting subscriptions. We have therefore no *prospect* of being able to liquidate our debt, or make a new purchase; yet, the faith and the hope that have buoyed us up from the formation of the Society still live with us, and we believe, that as woman understands her mission, and man appreciates it, helping hands and hearts and purses will be prepared to aid in the good work, until that period when virtue and justice shall be so incorporated into human hearts, that Rosines will be no longer needed.

Our school has been continued through a considerable part of the year, but is omitted usually during the very hot weather. Of the 306 women who have been inmates of the Rosine, 118 could not read understandingly when admitted; 160 could not write, and only four knew the multiplication table perfectly; 124 were marked intemperate, but many others drank occasionally; 78 were foreigners, 75 Catholics, 236 either professing Protestantism or no religion.

As in former years, we have found that ignorance, illy-paid labor, and the temptations consequent upon it, with evil examples and associations, have wrought the work of ruin. Parents and caretakers have not sown the good seed early in life; and, in the impetuous and rash period of youth, they have been deficient in the principles of virtue and morality, and thus fallen victims to the influences and circumstances surrounding them, while oftentimes their whole natures revolted from the crimes in which they were indulging, and their aspirations were daily for a better, truer life. Those only who have experienced it, or who have listened to the painful details of their sad stories, can comprehend the difficulties these unfortunates labor under, when they endeavor to ascend the upward path by honest industry. Until the formation of the Rosine Association, when women awakened in a degree to the duties of humanity, it was almost impossible for them to obtain situations in respectable or religious families. Even the high professor, who claimed to be governed by the principles of "Him who ate with sinners and publicans," shrank from giving shelter or employment to these poor penitents, and except by those whose degraded habits led them to seek such associations, they have been avoided as an accursed thing. And even now, when there is a better understanding of the claims of our suffering sisters, and some of us are prepared to give them a helping hand and make sacrifices for their sakes, it is not always an easy thing to extend that degree of encouragement and sympathy that may infuse into their minds a comprehension, that while we consider their future destiny lies in a great degree in their own hands, yet, if they will aim at the platform on which others stand around them, we believe they can attain it, and will aid them in their upward progress. As our own minds become more thoroughly imbued with the consciousness that,

"'Tis worth and virtue make the man,"

then can we labor more effectually, for the faith that is in our own hearts will be transferred to theirs, and we can animate them to struggle—to bear, and endeavor to conquer their own weaknesses, and the discouragements around them, and convince them a position can be attained of respectability and usefulness. Early orphanage and the consequent exposure resulting from not being under suitable parental care, is another predominant cause of the irregularity of their lives, and their homeless and friendless condition. An idea of this can be given by referring to the record of the 16 last admitted. No. 1, father living but intemperate. 2, cannot remember her father—mother also dead. 3, an orphan at 9 years. 4, both living. 5, mother died when she was 8 years old. 6, mother died when she was 8 years old; she has never lived with her father. 7, her father died when she was $2\frac{1}{2}$ years old. 8, mother died when she was 2 years of age. 9, father died when she was in her 9th year. 10, an exposed orphan at 17. 11, mother died when she was 6. 12, both parents living. 13, mother died when she was 11. 14, mother only living. 15, mother lost when she was 3 years, her father when she was 6. 16, father died when 2, mother, when she was 5 years of age.

We are frequently asked, "Do you succeed in your reformatory efforts?" Do the women continue to do well after they leave the Institution? We can only reply, that when we first entered into the work we were not so sanguine as to suppose all would do well, who might claim the shelter of our home, for we knew the curse of intemperance was upon many of the victims of licentiousness, and while the law sanctioned the sale of the liquid poison, a higher hand than ours, alone could stay the plague. We opened the Rosine House from a conviction *that it was right*, believing that Providence would bless the effort, but that if we did not succeed, still *the duty was ours—the results were not ours*. But we believe, in very many cases, our labor has been blest, as is evident to those who visit the Institution, as well as in the cases of a large number who have left, and are scattered in various families, both in the city and country. Over a dozen have married reputably since they left our care. Parents and relatives have rejoiced over the lost being found and restored to them, and society is benefited by so many abandoning an evil life, and becoming respectable and useful laborers and contributors, instead of being nuisances and burthens to the community. But who can estimate the advantages and blessings bestowed upon the individuals themselves!—Those only who can understand the depth of their degradation and hopelessness, and can compare it with the condition to which they are elevated when they feel they are living in accordance with the laws of God and man, and their present and future is gilded by a hopeful, trustful faith.

Three years since, a woman, who had been a Rosine, but who had been restored to her family, and afterwards married, came to request us to visit a girl of seventeen, who had been ungovernable under her widowed mother's care; had gone to live in a house of bad character, and from there had been cast into prison for the larceny of a watch. We visited the girl, procured her release from the prison, and took her to the Rosine. Her mother bound her to us, as she knew she could not control her. She remained a year with us, and learned the tailoring trade. Her mind became under religious influences while there, and when we returned her to the maternal roof, at the age of eighteen, it was with the belief that we resigned a treasure. That belief has been realized, as the grateful tears of her parent testify, whenever we see her. While she was at the Rosine, her mother married a second time. They were respectable, but not religious persons; but the good seed that was sown in the Rosine, in the heart of that young girl, was not lost upon stony ground, but has brought forth good fruit. While she sat at work, at her tailoring, the hymns she had learned came welling up, from her grateful feelings, in tones of melody, and sunk into her parents' hearts. Her prayers for them, and for herself were sanctified, and she has been the means of leading them both to the footstool of the Redeemer. Father, mother, and daughter are now members of a church. Had it not been for the Rosine, this girl (if living), would probably have been either a convict in the prison, or leading a life of sin and depravity.

Many other cases of deep and touching interest come constantly before us, and excite feelings of grateful emotion, while others are of a more painful and thrilling nature.

A few weeks since, we read in the papers, that a young woman had thrown herself into the Schuylkill, near Fairmount. A day or two afterwards, they said, the suicide was committed on the day that was to have been the bridal-day. Few knew who Mary Burk was, or were sufficiently interested to unravel the history of that unfortunate girl; and yet there are those whose names are recorded in deathless characters, and chronicled through all time, whose merits or whose integrity would not compare with those of Mary Burk. Three years since, Mary came to the Rosine and asked admission. She was a blooming girl, from the shores of Erin. Her tale was a sad one. She had come a stranger to our city, and had gone to a boarding-house to stay till she could obtain employment.

She became acquainted with one, who wooed and betrayed her, and then left her to shame and repentance. In her agony of mind, she walked the streets, one night, caring not whither she went. Her appearance attracted the attention of a good man, and he compassionately accosted her. His tones of kindness went to her heart, and he learned her friendlessness and her sorrow. He led her to a safe Asylum, where she remained until she came to the Rosine. While there, she became awakened to religious impressions, and after some months, left the Institution to go to a place of service, with the respect and esteem of the family and the managers. Some time during the last summer, she told our matron, she had become attached to a young man, and was engaged to be married, and consulted her about the necessity of revealing to her lover her past history. The matron advised her to use perfect candor, and said, the truth was always the right, and that if he really loved her, he would respect her the more for her integrity. Mary resolved to follow her counsel, though it would be a sore trial: but she told her mentor, a few weeks since, she had not been able to do it. The gentleman's conduct had been so marked with propriety to her, that she could not reveal her disgrace to him, yet she evidently was struggling between her sense of duty, and the delicacy of her feelings. Strong indeed must have been those convictions of duty, and great her mental struggle, when the prospect of the enjoyment of a life of happiness with the one she loved, was sacrificed to her repugnance to acknowledge her misfortune, and lessen herself in his good opinion.

On the Sabbath before they were to be married,

her lover placed the wedding ring upon her finger, and she plaited some of his hair and her own together, while she said, " I do not think we shall ever be married." But so full was his heart with the prospect of their happiness, that he dreamed not of her meaning. The day arrived that was to seal their destiny. The groom had all the preparations made at the house of a mutual friend, and, at the appointed hour, went to meet the bride. But no Mary came? Search was made, but no tidings could be obtained, until the next day, when the papers described the body of a young female who had been seen to throw herself into the Schuylkill, and who was not rescued until it was too late to restore life. The ring was on her finger, and the plaited hair in her bosom, enclosed in some poetry he had given her; but the bridegroom was death, and the wedding-robe was the shrouding waters.

Mary had been at the Rosine that morning. They had spoken to her of it being the bridal-day. She replied, " He will seek me, but he will not find me." They too, thought not of the significance of her words. She bade them adieu, and proceeded immediately to the river. The mental conflict under which she had labored for months, in one short hour was terminated.

May the profligate man who wrought this ruin be pardoned; and may the name of Mary Burk strike as a funeral knell to the heart of every man who seeks to destroy and darken thus, with crime, the purity and innocence of one of God's own temples, and may her name be echoed and re-echoed through the land, in warning tones, that our daughters may receive the impress in unfading characters—that virtue alone can bestow happiness, and that undying remorse and the consciousness of guilt will remain through life, if that pure temple be desecrated. It will be the—

> "One fatal remembrance, one sorrow, that throws
> Its dark shade alike over pleasures and woes;
> For which life nothing darker or brighter can bring,
> For which joy hath no balm, and affliction no sting."

It is a source of pleasure to us to mark the reformatory efforts around us, to observe the progress of the temperance cause, and to find that women are enlisting with steady and unflinching purpose to labor for the deliverance of the captive from the greatest slavery upon earth. When we review the list of those who have been under our care, and trace their histories, we find, that in almost all the cases where women have resumed their evil courses, it has been owing to the temptations presented to them, in consequence of the sale of liquors *everywhere.*

When each day brings its hosts of facts, of individuals and families being ruined by the effects of this liquid poison, and our citizens taxed so heavily to support these rum-made paupers and criminals, it is astonishing that our legislators should hesitate to adopt a scheme that has worked so admirably wherever it has been efficiently in operation. The depopulation of the prisons and poorhouses, must inevitably be the effect of the Maine Law, and an increased stimulant be given to the education of the poorer classes. From the reports given by President Bache, M. Cousin, and George Nichols, of the state of education in Holland, we learn, that in Haarlem, with a population of 21,000, there was not a child of sound intellect of ten years of age, who could not both read and write, and that nothing could exceed the personal propriety and apparent comfort of the people of Holland, generally. The traveller meets with no ragged, dirty, or drunken persons. In the prisons of Leyden and Rotterdam, with a population of 2,500,000, there were only 150 juvenile offenders, and many of them were commited more for the benefit of industrious training, than for the commission of crime. If, therefore, the universal education of the masses presents such encouraging facts in Europe, what may we not hope when an efficient law closes our dram-shops, and a portion of the funds now invested in poison, is appropriated to the payment of the schoolmaster. When we examine the statistics of our prisons, and find that nearly all of the 10,000 persons annually arrested in our city, are brought into this condition through the influence of liquor, and that a great proportion of them can neither read nor write, are we not individually called upon to exert our influence to promote the causes of temperance and education?

The statistics of the Rosine correspond so perfectly with those of every prison to which we have referred, that it seems to be a universal fact that ignorance and intemperance produce vices and crimes of every grade, and the poverty, disease, and wretchedness that require the heavy taxation to which we are subjected, and the numerous charitable associations that absorb our time, and create a host of respectable beggars.

Of the industrial department of the Rosine, we can speak cheeringly. The increase in the number of our customers gives the character of the work. Two of the inmates are now employed, *with salaries*, as teachers of the dress-making and tailoring, while our matron and another inmate, have charge of the shirt-making and other sewing. It is a most interesting sight to visit this scene of busy industry, and compare the past and present condition of those who now present such bright and happy faces. Some of them had never made a garment of any kind before they entered the Rosine; one did not know how to thread her needle, and very few can be considered efficient until after they have served their apprenticeship of six months, and even then, many of them cannot be put on customers' work. The majority of the inmates being merely learners, and many of them passing into other families in various domestic situations, at the end of six or nine months, prevents our workroom from being as profitable as it would be if they continued a longer time with us; but if Providence should favor us with the ability to enlarge our house, we can then receive all the applicants, and have accommodations to retain them longer with us, which would be of great advantage to them and the Institution.

From October 1st, 1852, to October 1st, 1853, the number of garments made in the Rosine, for the use of the family, was - - -	490
For customers, including 348 shirts, 102 chemises, 50 quilts, 30 night-gowns, 74 dresses, 409 vests, 87 pantaloons, and sundry other articles, numbering - - - - - -	1580
Total for the family and customers, - -	2,070
Bringing the sum of - - - - - -	$830 73

This is an advance of $273 73 earned more than in any previous year.

Our Intelligence Office continues its work of usefulness, 1920 women and girls have been provided with situations through its agency. Many of them were women of the highest respectability. We are always pleased to record the progress and usefulness of the Temporary Home Association, which was founded by some of the Managers of the Rosine, to provide a safe home and employment for *respectable females* who were destitute of homes, and without friends to give them one. Situations have been procured for 2759 women and children, from the office of this Institution, making from the offices of the two Associations, 4679 persons, who have been placed in honest and respectable employment.

When we consider the importance of saving a single individual from a position in which they may be tempted to deviate from virtue and integrity; when we trace the life of that one person through all the shades of crime in which they may be immersed, and watch their course, with all its sufferings and sorrows, until, at the close of a miserable existence, they sink into a hopeless eternity; when we reflect on how much wretchedness may be crowded into one short life, and believe that, if some outstretched hand or opened home had not presented its shelter and protecting influences to these 4679 persons, many of them might now be included in the list of wanderers from virtue, then alone can we appreciate the importance and usefulness of these two Associations, in their preventive and remedial capacities.

THE LETTER.

Having, for some time, felt the importance of a simple and brief address to the unfortunate children of sorrow for whom we have been so deeply interested the following letter was printed, many copies of which have been circulated among them.

A number of interesting incidents might be narrated in connection with these letters, but we can only speak of two of them.

In company with H. we went to the house of E., and paid a most interesting visit. She was one who, at the age of seventeen, had been persuaded to elope from the home of her widowed mother with a lover, who promised marriage, but who basely took her to a house of bad character, and in three months married another, and left her to struggle with the miseries he had brought upon her. With true pathos she told us her story, and we could have wept with her as she recounted her sorrows and trials, her convictions of conscience and longings after the better life; and then her hopelessness of attaining it, her resolutions and failures, with many incidents interspersed, that bespoke a noble and generous mind, with feelings of strong and deep affection.

When we parted from her we gave her one of our letters, begging her to lay its truths in her heart, and let them grow there till they had so filled it, that they would burst her bonds asunder, and she could stand forth, a free woman, in the true nobility of her nature.

A few days afterwards she met us at the Rosine House, and asked for another Letter.

She said, the evening after we had called upon her, a gentleman stopped at her house, on his way to the theatre. She handed him the Letter to read, and gave him the history of our visit there. After perusing it, he put it in his pocket, and bade her adieu, promising to return it some other time. When he came again, it was to ask her to obtain for him another Letter. He told her, when he entered the theatre his attention was attracted by a very beautiful girl, whom he had never seen there before, and whom he felt certain had very lately entered the list of abandoned ones. Perceiving she was noticed by him, she motioned him to come to her. He went, and taking a seat beside her, handed her the Rosine Letter.

While she was reading, he watched her countenance intently. She read, and re-read it. He marked her lip quiver, and saw her struggle to suppress her emotion. But tear after tear fell upon the paper, and blotted the lines till she could read no longer; then, clasping it firmly in her handkerchief, she rose precipitately and left the theatre. Not a word had been spoken by either, but the words of truth in the Letter had met the witness for truth in her own mind—it had performed its mission.

On another occasion, we visited a house kept by a man and woman, of the name of L——. The woman was kind and polite, but the man seemed rather surly, and was not particularly pleased with our addressing the members of his family, as he feared he might lose his boarders. They told us one of the girls was absent, and when we parted with them we left a Letter for her. After our departure L—— read the Letter, and then tore it in pieces and scattered it about the floor. Soon afterwards the absentee returned, and seeing the scraps of paper, asked what they were. One of the girls replied, telling her two ladies had been there, and left a letter for her, but Mr. L—— did not wish her to see it, and had torn it up. Her curiosity was awakened—she gathered up the pieces, arranged them on a table, and getting a fine needle and thread, sewed them together neatly, and found she could read the whole Letter. Had it been handed to her as we left it, probably she would have thrown it aside and scarcely looked at it, but the fact of his destroying the paper, to prevent her seeing it, created a curiosity and interest, which made her quite familiar with its contents by the time the pieces were all placed together. She had never heard of the Rosine before, and she addressed various inquiries to the girls who had seen us, to ascertain who we were, and the motives that could prompt strangers to visit, with such feelings of interest, those whom she felt were truly the most friendless part of creation.

Before one week elapsed, that girl was an inmate of the Rosine House. She is still there.

The Letter.

To ——

Permit us to say a few words to you. Have you considered seriously the life you are leading? Are you sensible that it is in violation of the laws of God—of your duties as a human being? Are you aware that you are responsible to your Creator for every hour of misspent time, for every action of your life—that his eye is upon you; that in the darkest hour, as in the noonday, every word, thought, and act are equally before him? You are ever in his presence! You may forget him for a while, but he will never forget you, and you must render an account for every word and deed. Consider, then, how awful is your situation, living a life of crime, debasing yourself to the level of the brute creation, despised by your companions in vice, and regarded with contempt even by those who have wrought your ruin. Think of your position in society! Consider what you are, and what you might be. A virtuous woman is a pearl above price—we only ask *you* to estimate yourself in the scale of humanity. Think of your mother (if you have one), of your relatives degraded by your conduct, of the mothers, sisters, and wives whose feelings are outraged by the men who associate with you—of the violated duties of every one connected with you in your present course—and examine seriously the path you are treading. Does it not lead down to death, not only of the body but of the soul? Perhaps you have not desired to pursue a life of crime, and circumstances more than inclination, have placed you in your unhappy position. Let it be as it may, there is yet a possibility of redemption for you. The Father who watches over you is a God of love, who will ever receive his penitent children—and there are those whose hearts have been touched by your misery, whose prayers have ascended to heaven, craving for you the capacity to see yourself as you are seen by him, and that you may be awakened to a proper sense of your situation, and enabled by his blessing to strive for a better, purer life. Do you not already desire it? do you not abhor your present condition? Would you not rejoice to abandon such a life—to leave your debased associates, and return to virtuous and respected independence? If so, you have now the opportunity. A SOCIETY OF WOMEN has been formed to give you a home, if you are sincerely desirous of acting rightly, and are willing to support yourself honestly by the labor of your own hands. You may have the opportunity of learning tailoring, mantua-making, and other trades, and be instructed in the usual duties and employments of women, while at the same time, a daily school may give you the advantages of literary culture, and the efforts of those about you shall be such as to convince you, that a right course will bring you more happiness than a wrong one, and that the endeavor to pursue the path of virtue, propriety, and industry, will surround you with those who desire to be truly your friends, and who will not abandon you while your aim is, a better, purer, holier life.

Information may be received upon the subject, by application to No. 204 North Eighth Street.

ANNUAL REPORT OF THE MANAGERS OF THE ROSINE ASSOCIATION.

April 6th, 1854.

"Sayst thou four months?" behold the fields are now
White to the harvest. Thrust thy sickle in,
And aid the noble reapers who have borne
The burden in the heat, and faint not yet;
Nor will they, till success shall crown their toil.
Oh, be not laggard then, for sloth is sin,
While crime goes unrebuked, and the weak germs of virtue
Unrefreshed by kindness and encouragement, die out."

THE Managers of the Rosine Association present their Sixth Annual Report to the members and friends of the Society, under the most favorable auspices. As year after year passes away, they find the prejudices with which they have had to contend are giving place to a more perfect faith in the possibility of the redemption of woman from her frailties and missteps, and hope has sprung up in a multitude of hearts, that many of those who have seemed to be buried in error, were not dead, but that, throwing off the chrysalis condition in which their virtues have been shrouded, they may arise, and ascend upward and onward, rejoicing in the new life into which they may emerge from the darkened period of their existence.

One of the highest manifestations of the progress of the age is in the increasing evidences of our being sensible, that we are responsible in a great degree for the well or ill doing of those around us; in fact, that we are our brothers' keepers—that through our influence or our neglect their highest welfare may be increased or lessened—that by the exercise of our humanity or our selfishness, they may be placed in positions either to be elevated or degraded.

These considerations must ever press with great force upon every one who has arisen to that state in which they feel they are bound to labor for others, both morally and physically, and in our work, which leads us continually to investigate the causes of crime, we must often feel, that as this consciousness of responsibility increases in the community, many of the sources of evil will be eradicated; that the improved educational advantages will qualify many of that class, who through neglect became the victims of vice, to aim at and attain higher positions in society; and that as the knowledge of woman's capacity is extended in business relations, she will assume and maintain a station of usefulness that will elevate her above the fashions and follies that have cramped her genius, and placed her as the dependent on man, and too often the victim of his vices.

The low price of labor in the sewing department has led many a woman to ruin, from her incapacity to earn sufficient to support herself respectably; but now, as new agents are coming forward as competitors, in the form of sewing-machines, gradually, as improvements are made, the unhealthy and ill-paid toil of the seamstress will be exchanged for other kinds of business, which her taste may ornament and refine, and which will bring a proper remuneration, irrespective of sex.

The evidences thus around us are cheering, in the awakening of many individuals to their Christian duties, in whatever sphere of action Providence has opened for them; the increase of faith in the possibility of reforming the degraded, and in the prospect of other fields of labor where a better remuneration and greater variety of occupations will have a tendency to increase the mental activity and physical capacity of woman. The needle and other domestic employments have been considered the only suitable avocations of females, while the whole field of life has been open to man in all the mechanical and artistical operations, and the commercial, legal, and theological relations. But the tastes and inclinations of woman are as varied as those of man, and to some, both the needle and housework are distasteful, and while they must choose one of them if they continue in their prescribed position, they cannot but envy the boy who may turn to whatever business his taste and capacity may lead him. He may there work out at his will his secret aspirations, and develope the genius with which he has been endowed, while woman has ofttimes turned with aversion from her allotted labor, restless and uneasy, because her interests were not in her work, and society had limited her occupation and her sphere, and in every position she felt she was considered the inferior of man, and the subject of his will, his caprices, and his vices.

In this situation, and with these longings after something more congenial with her taste, woman's work is often illy done, simply because she takes no delight in it, and she seems idle and indifferent because her feelings and circumstances differ so widely. Living thus without an object or interesting employment, her affections alone are cultivated, and with the volatility of youth, and the ignorance of the fatal consequences that must result from one misguided step, she is ofttimes suddenly thrown from her position in society, and feels herself an outcast and a criminal.

With the knowledge of these facts constantly

coming before us, and believing, that as woman is more truly educated, and impressed with the idea that she can and may make her own sphere of action, wherever her abilities and qualifications may lead her, we must rejoice in the opening of other fields of labor into which she may enter, being entirely convinced that a higher, better training will be the result, and with the unfoldings of other occupations, woman will become more sensible of her duties and obligations, and fulfil them in a more dignified manner, betokening her comprehension of her responsibility as a being, both human and divine. We therefore consider these movements of the age will have a powerful effect upon the morals of the community, for no woman who is properly trained, and impressed with the dignity of her own nature, and her capacity to fulfil the highest duties of life, would stoop to be guilty of an act either criminal or degrading.

Since the Rosine House was opened, October 1st, 1847, 325 women have been admitted. Many of them were in a state of extreme ignorance. Some did not know how to do anything well or rightly. The majority needed to be taught as little children. With these the labor has been one that required great patience and perseverance, as there was not only new lessons to learn but old habits to conquer, and our excellent Matron has ofttimes needed all the virtues in the catalogue to preserve her equanimity. The office of Matron in such an institution is no sinecure. Her duties commence with the dawn of day, and only end when all are abed, and not always then, as in so large a family there are occasionally cases of illness, that need the watcher's care and the maternal superintendence.

Our Work Room presents an interesting appearance to those who can comprehend the degradation, which many of our inmates have known, and see the change that has been wrought in their condition. Some of them are very young, and have not become intemperate, but there are few of those who have numbered years of depravity, to whom the fatal cup has not been familiar. The inflamed eyes, and bloated, wretched appearance of some of our applicants for admission, combined with their utter disregard of cleanliness, and of decent apparel, require at times the greatest exercise of faith, hope, and charity, to be able to receive them, and bestow that mantle, that covereth a multitude of sins. But a week hardly elapses before a wonderful change is wrought in the outward appearance, as a portion of self-respect springs into the mind, from a consciousness of an intention to aim at the right, and an effort to fulfil it. There is one there, who some of us knew five years ago, but she seemed so low, so habituated to intemperance, so familiar from her very childhood with the prison, and houses of infamy, that we were altogether hopeless of her and could hardly say to her, *Come!* But she did come! A few days passed, and she left us. The regularity of a quiet family, the habits of industry, and the abstinence of stimulants, she was not prepared for. Months passed and again she came. But the habits of years were not conquered, and though she began to conceive that there might be a higher life for her, yet it was seen too dimly to give her perseverance. Once more she left us, and was found in her former resorts. But the witness that had been awakened in her heart slept no longer; there were cravings, that her former enjoyments could not satisfy, and in the scene of revelry came the remembrance of the hours of exhortation, of prayer and of praise in the Rosine. Doubtless there was many a struggle in her mind, and alternations of weakness, and of strong resolve, but again she came. Over two years have passed and she is still with us. She has learned to be a tailoress, and is now employed on a salary, with sometimes a dozen girls around her, as her apprentices.

There is another there, a fine shirt-maker, who was respectably married in Canada. But she placed her enemy to her lips, and the liquid poison she absorbed became her master. Her duties were neglected for the maddening bowl, until she felt her degradation so intensely that husband and children were deserted, and her restless foot bore her to this city. Here, among those she would once have scorned, days, months, and years passed. The Almighty spared her in her desolation, and in mercy led her to the Rosine, where she has been two years, usefully employed.

Nearly three years since, a girl of almost child-like appearance came to the Rosine. She had lost her mother when only a few days old, and had been seduced from the situation where her father had placed her, by one, who in the upper ranks of life, abused the gifts of Providence by his own depravity and the perversion of others. She became the mother of two children, one of whom happily died, and the other the father took from her a few days after its birth, and she knows nothing further of its history. Soon afterwards he placed her in a house of bad character, and then abandoned her. But her Heavenly Father had not deserted her, but sent to that abode of sin, one, on whose lips was the law of kindness, and she reasoned with her on the law of God, and the heart of the child was touched (for she was then not 17 years old), and she said, "I will go to the Rosine." She came. But though young in years, she was old in iniquity. The most profane expressions were her familiar language, and she was accustomed to yield to the most ungoverned transports of temper. Idleness seemed born in her, except when an opportunity presented to torment others. This was a case, in which wisdom, patience, and perseverance were needed continually, and some of us considered it altogether a hopeless one. But there were some redeeming qualities. There was a foundation of good common sense and a heart full of affection, and this encouraged us to labor with her, ofttimes almost against hope. Several months passed, before there was much sensible improvement, but the desire was raised, to please some of those who she felt had borne with her, even against hope, and she saw and acknowledged that Providence had saved her from a life of transgression, and placed her among those who loved and pitied her, and were willing to put her upon her feet, and support her there, by their counsel and assistance. Her better feelings gained the mastery! The impious word was banished from her lip, the frightful outbursts of temper were subdued, and the once idle girl is now a competent needlewoman. During the last year she has been engaged by the week as seamstress in several families, and we have received very flattering testimonials of her usefulness. On the last Christmas day she presented one of the managers a token of her feelings, in the form of a silver napkin ring, with the words "Gratitude's Offering" engraved upon it.

A few days since, her father (who had entirely disowned her and refused to have any communication with her), called upon us, to say, that by the death of her step-mother there was a vacancy in his household, and he had now come to solicit the long-discarded child to fill it; to be the caretaker of that home she had not been allowed to enter, and to act as the mother of his two young, motherless children. It is a position of great responsibility, and when we consented to return her to the parental roof, it was affecting to witness the gratitude of the father, and the self-sacrificing spirit of the daughter. May she have strength and wisdom given to her to fulfil her duties.

A number of our former inmates are situated in families as seamstresses and in other departments, and are getting good wages, and behaving in a creditable manner. One has been during the past year, attending in a dry goods store. Another, who was several years the mistress of a house of bad character, is now going out nursing. One is employed in a clothing establishment, and one is earning good wages working a sewing machine. A young woman, who came under our care soon after opening the Institution, has lived five years in the family, where she was placed, and within a few months has married a very respectable farmer, with every promise of respectability and happiness. For another we have deposited $45 in the Saving Sund. One, whose life has been connected with circumstances of deep and touching interest, has been for some time housekeeper in a wealthy family, and has conducted in a manner to gain their affection and esteem. She has $115 at interest earned (beside clothing herself handsomely), since she left the Rosine.

The limits of a pamphlet will not permit, or we might narrate many interesting circumstances of the history of others who have been inmates of the Rosine.

But we were speaking of our work room and have made this digression. Our large family during the past two years, has been under great inconvenience for want of room everywhere, our kitchen and dining apartments are entirely too small, our chambers are exceedingly crowded, and the work room has not afforded the necessary space for the various employments of the inmates. There also, are held our meetings for worship. Within the last month, the partitions separating the rooms and the entry, have been removed, and we have now a large and fine apartment, which will very much add to the comfort and convenience of the family. But we see no means to enlarge our other departments, and have not had funds either to buy or build, but day after day, as applicants have been refused admission for the want of room, we have felt an increasing necessity for a fund, that would not only enable us to obtain more extensive accommodations, but would be a permanent income to contribute toward the support of the Institution. We felt our cause was not only *our cause*, but that of humanity; that the Association was not only doing good to those in the Rosine walls, but that it had exercised a healthful influence throughout the community; that thousands of minds through our reports and appeals had been led to reflect upon subjects and duties, from which they had turned carelessly, and have felt, they could no longer walk with the priest and the Levite on the other side, but that to this unfortunate and degraded class, they owed the duty of the neighbor. They have been sensible, that through the labors and influences of this Society, very many who had been, and in all probability would again be, charges in the prison and almshouse, were now raised to a respectable position, and were supporting themselves honestly and decently.

In this situation and with these views, we believed the period had come that we might rightly apply to the State Legislature for an appropriation. The following *Memorial and Petition* were therefore prepared, with the signatures of the Managers and some of the Members:

To the Senate and House of Representatives of the State of Pennsylvania:

Gentlemen: The Managers of the "Rosine Association of Philadelphia," a Society incorporated April 11, 1848, "for the reformation, employment, and instruction of females who have led immoral lives," beg leave to state that they have been in operation six years, during which period they have received over three hundred unfortunate women, who had been in habits of dissipation and vice—the majority of whom were homeless and friendless, without reputation or the means to earn an honest living, and have had them instructed in sewing, cooking, and other domestic avocations, while at the same time, their mental and moral faculties have been cultivated by the means of a school and religious associations, so as to qualify them to become useful and respectable members of society. Many of these women have been inmates of prisons, almshouses, and houses of immoral character; and, had it not been for the exertions of the members of this Association, they would probably have continued in the same evil courses, and still be nuisances in the community, by their demoralizing habits and influence, living at the expense of the public, and carrying wretchedness and desolation to the private hearthstone of their own and other families.

Nothing of a local or sectarian character has ever been embraced by this Association. Of the three hundred and twenty women who have been inmates, ninety-five were from England, Ireland, and Germany, eighty-five were natives of Philadelphia, eighty were from other counties in this State, and sixty were from other States of the Union; eighty were Catholics, and two hundred and forty either professing Protestantism or no religion. Very few among them knew anything either of the principles or moral obligations of any religious society. The object of the Managers has been to impress upon the subjects of their care, the duties inculcated in the "Sermon upon the Mount," but doctrines of a sectarian nature have been entirely avoided. They have endeavored (as far as possible), to remedy the defects in the early training of these women, by developing the better qualities of their minds, and cultivating a sense of the importance of virtue, industry, honesty, and truthfulness, and of self-reliance, grounded upon the exercise of these principles. Of the three hundred and twenty women who have been inmates of the Rosine, one hundred and twenty could not read understandingly when admitted; one hundred and sixty-three could not write, and only four knew the multiplication table perfectly; one hundred and twenty-six were marked intemperate, but many others drank occasionally.

The "Rosine Association" was formed in 1847, and named in honor of Rosa Govona, an Italian girl, who originated several associations in her own country for friendless and unfortunate females. It came into existence from a conviction that had grown in the minds of many persons, that all women were not really vicious who appeared to be so, but that, if they were ever reformed, it must be by their own sex removing the prejudices of society, and producing a public sentiment, which, while it condemned crime, irrespective of sex, would extend the hand of sympathy and kindness to the penitent, and endeavor to enable them to tread the path of virtue and morality.

From the privacy necessary in this reform, the Managers cannot show the effects of their labor. It is their duty, as far as possible, to blot out the memory of the past, and present to the world, not the reformed transgressor, but the useful, respectable woman, qualified to fulfil and perform the duties of life.

Of the three hundred and twenty women who have been in the Institution, two hundred and thirty-five were under twenty-five years of age. Among the number more advanced, thirteen have been mistresses of houses of immoral character. Several of these women have proved the sincerity of their reformation by entering and continuing in private families as domestics. Over a dozen have married reputably since they left the institution. Some have been restored to the parental roof, while many others are filling various situations as domestics in families.

Had not this Society opened the "Rosine House" and received these unfortunates, in all probability the majority of them would have become a public charge, and continued to be a disgrace to themselves and to humanity. More than fifty women at this time are inmates of the Home, but we cannot report the number of applicants that have been refused admission into the Rosine on account of the crowded condition of the House, as no record has been taken; but very many have not been received in consequence of our inability to provide accommodations, and the want of funds to increase them.

The Society came into existence without any endowment but faith and hope, energy and industry. They believed the effort was right and would prove successful. Year after year they have gone as beggars from door to door soliciting contributions, and have thus gathered the funds by which the Institution has been supported, except the amount earned by the family, which has been a small proportion, in consequence of the ignorance of the women, when they entered the Home, and the generality of them leaving there as soon as they are considered sufficiently trained to be placed in families.

Gentlemen—the period has arrived when we feel that we may rightfully ask of you an appropriation of funds that may assist us to pay off the debt of twenty-eight hundred dollars on our Institution, enable us to enlarge our House and accommodations, and prevent the necessity of our continuing to be street beggars.

We therefore ask you to pass a law appropriating the sum of three thousand dollars, annually, towards the extension and maintainance of the "Rosine House," subject to the control of the Board of Managers that are, or may be appointed by the Society.

With this *Memorial and Petition*, the Vice-President, and Treasurer of the Society, proceeded to Harrisburg. They also took with them the following *Recommendation*, signed by the Mayor of the City, seven of the Judges of our Courts, the Attorney-General, and a number of our most distinguished lawyers, physicians, editors, and merchants.

RECOMMENDATION.

The undersigned, citizens of Philadelphia, respectfully recommend to the Senate and House of Representatives of Pennsylvania, the application of the Managers of the Rosine Association, of Philadelphia, for an annual appropriation.

The efforts of the ladies of this Society, which was incorporated April 11th, 1848, "for the *reformation, employment, and instruction of females who have led immoral lives*," must have a beneficial tendency, not only by restoring the fallen to a life of virtuous industry and usefulness, but by the prevention of these persons being chargeable to the community through their crimes, or misdemeanors. We therefore entirely approve of their application for an appropriation.

John C. Knox; J. S. Black; George W. Woodward; Ellis Lewis; Wm. D. Kelley; Oswald Thompson; Joseph Allison; Wm. B. Reed; Wm. B. Mann; John M. Read; Job R. Tyson; Morton McMichael; James S. Wallace; Charles Gilpin; Samuel H. Perkins; Joseph R. Ingersoll; J. K. Kane; Charles McAllister; S. Murphy, M.D.; P. McCall; John T. Sharpless, M.D.; Charles O'Neill; Charles B. Penrose; John Hanna; J. M. Cooper; James Huston; Lindsay & Blakiston; Washington Brown; Townsend Sharpless; Fithian, Jones & Co.; Schaffer, Roberts & Co.; Wright, Pike & Co.; Deal, Milligan & Co.; G. W. & Lewis B. Taylor; J. & B. Orne; Samuel Townsend; F. V. Warner; Reed A. Williams; Franklin Shoemaker; John T. Smith; Thomas B. Supplee; Wolfe, Ballard & Co.; Levick, Brother & Co.; Howard Williams; Buckner, McCammon & Co.; J. P. Sanderson; Robert Morris; W. H. Crump; Samuel Jeanes; Deacon, Peterson & Co.; Lewis Audenried; Chas. A. Poulson; Charles Lennig; Fred. Lennig; S. P. Hastings; Bunn, Raiguel & Co.; Alex. Miller; Joseph I. Williams; James L. Claghorn; John H. Brown; Robt. H. Small; Julian & Mason; D. B. Hinman; Edward S. Simmons.

A copy of the Memorial and Petition, with the following extracts from the presentments of two of the Grand Juries, who had visited the Rosine House, during the past year, were presented to each member of the Senate, and House of Representatives, accompanied by an appeal, and the report of last October.

PRESENTMENTS.

In the month of January, 1853, the Rosine House was visited by the Grand Jury, and in their presentment, they say:

"At the Rosine Association, we were gratified to learn that so much good had been accomplished by an Institution so little known. The benevolence and untiring devotion of the ladies connected with it, in reclaiming a class of unfortunate females, who, before the establishment of this Asylum, were, to a certain extent, friendless, deserves the highest praise. There are a number of inmates actively employed in appropriate branches of female industry, all being in good health, and well provided for, and apparently desirous of returning to the paths of virtue. This benevolence furnishes *a Home, not a place of confinement,* to those who have been misled, and supported as it is by private contributions only, it cannot be too highly recommended to the attention and liberality of Philadelphians. The amount of good that is annually accomplished, in a quiet way, deserves and should receive the support of our citizens."

In the presentment of the Grand Jury for October term, 1853, they say:

"The Grand Inquest also visited the Rosine Association. This Institution deserves to be better known and more liberally patronized by the public, for the many instances on record of the reforms that have taken place in the lives and characters of some of the most abandoned and unfortunate of the female sex, who, by the kind and tender treatment received in the Rosine, have been awakened to a sense of their previous situation, and have made a thorough change of conduct, from that of the most immoral character to one of virtue, which always secures to its possessor, health, prosperity, and happiness."

AN APPEAL.

'Tis Woman pleads for Woman's cause,
Against the arbitrary laws
Which custom, throughout hoary time,
Has named "*a weakness*" or, "*a crime.*"
When erring *Man* has gone astray,
And victims won from Virtue's way,

Society so lenient grows
That o'er the crime a veil it throws,
Which hides the fault, and scarcely blames
"*The weakness*" in the gentlest names—
But crime is *crime* when *Woman* sins,
And punishment with crime begins.
No veil around *her* fault is thrown;
No hand outstretched—she stands alone:
No mantle can her errors hide,
Or shield reproaches from her side;
An outcast, often, from the dome
Where once she graced the hearth and home,
She wanders forth in guilt's array,
Ashamed to meet the light of day;
A Pariah—lost to caste and name,
Her portion henceforth is but shame;
The midnight revel lulls her woe,
And she degraded, sinks so low,
That years or months can scarcely pass
Till, maddened by the accursed glass,
That drowns the grief she may not tell,
She sinks within the prison cell;
Or, prostrate, under fell disease,
Her anguish knows no hours of ease—
In hopeless, deep remorse she lies,
And in the PAUPER'S ALMSHOUSE dies!
And, shall we leave her there, to die—
Or in the dreary prison lie?
Shall she, if life be spared, remain
A thing accursed—a social bane,
When, in her soul's deep fountains, spring
Feelings divine, which ever bring
Pure aspirations for the right,
Which die not, ev'n in misery's night?
Shall we thus leave her to her fate,
Friendless and hopeless—desolate?
When, at our *word*, *our sesame*,
Hearts, and a Home shall open be,
To greet the wandering child of shame,
And welcome her in Virtue's name,
Point out the path which she may tread
To earn with honor—raiment—bread!
Expand her mind with learning's store,
And culture talents waked once more;
Convince her, woman's heart and voice
Will o'er the PENITENT rejoice,
And aid her in each hour of need,
With, Sister, onward! God thee speed!
Shall we not then our efforts blend,
And each one prove the wanderer's friend?
Our voice, our aid, our influence give,
And say, RETURN—REPENT and LIVE!

Our managers were received with the highest respect and kindness by the members of the legislature, and their application was presented in both Houses at the earliest opportunity. In the Senate it was referred to the Finance Committee, who proposed to our ladies to withdraw the petition for an annual appropriation, as in the low state of the treasury it was not probable we could obtain more than a donation of $3000. A highly interesting discussion took place, during which one of the members remarked, that the object of our application was to obtain a fund that would enable us to enlarge the Institution—that we now owed $2800 on the Rosine House. The sum asked for would only clear us of debt, and leave us $200, which would not effect our purpose. He therefore offered a resolution, to empower the City Councils to give the Society $10,000, with which something might be done. This resolution was not acceded to, and another gentleman offered an amendment, and a second section to the bill, which in this form passed by a vote of 21 yeas in our favor.

AN ACT APPROPRIATING CERTAIN MONEYS TO THE ROSINE ASSOCIATION.

Section 1.—Be it enacted by the Senate, etc., that the sum of $3000 be, and the same is, hereby appropriated to the Rosine Association of Philadelphia, incorporated April 11, 1848, for the purchasing a lot, or erecting or purchasing buildings for the operations of the Association: Provided, that this Act shall not take effect, until an equal amount shall have been subscribed by other responsible contributors, to said Association.

Sect. 2.—That the Councils of the City of Philadelphia are hereby authorized to appropriate to the said Association, hereafter, any sum, or sums of money, not exceeding $3000, in any one year.

In the House of Represenatives the bill was passed by a vote of 51 yeas, nays 28.

Our friends at Harrisburg consider our application has been remarkably successful, as they have no doubt, through the well-known benevolence of Philadelphia, we shall soon raise the $3000, which will entitle us to claim the appropriation of the State, and, with this sum, we can make arrangements to enlarge our Institution, which our consolidated Councils can by law enable us to fulfil. But we cannot expect to accomplish anything without effort,—we must, therefore, endeavor to enlist the sympathies of the friends of humanity to aid us in procuring the first $3000, which is to claim the second. The work of the managers has heretofore been arduous, between the varied duties in the Rosine, the necessary visits in other places, and the begging and collecting which our poverty has made an imperative necessity. We therefore must ask the aid of our friends in every way. In Boston, it has not been an unusual circumstance, for private liberality to endow charitable institutions. Can we believe the citizens of Boston to be more generous, more humane, than our own? We do not! And with so important an object as the reformation, employment, and instruction of the most unfortunate of the human race, we hope and believe that our anticipations will be realized.

Our work-room, under the care of our excellent matron, gives the most-cheering evidence of what patient instruction can perform. Very few of our inmates have been possessed of industrious habits when they entered the Rosine, or were acquainted with more than the rudiments of sewing, but we are now entirely willing to refer to our customers for the character of our work, and are happy to say, that we have no difficulty in procuring as much as we desire.

From April 1st, 1853, to March 25th, 1854, the number of garments made in the Rosine, for the use of the family, was - - -	520
For customers, including 384 shirts, 157 chemises, 42 quilts, 50 night gowns, 64 dresses, 822 vests, 97 pantaloons, 22 embroidered articles, and sundries, numbering altogether, -	1794
Total for the family and customers, - -	2314
Bringing the sum of, - - - - - -	$1099 43
The receipts from the work-room, in the year ending April 1st, 1853, were, - - -	$623 64

This is an advance of $475 79, earned more than in any previous year.

Our Intelligence Office still continues to provide situations for *respectable* females. It was opened, because we had reason to believe, that innocent girls were often sent from intelligence offices to houses of immoral character, and thus led to ruin. At a subsequent period, the managers of the Rosine were impressed with the importance of another institution, which might give a safe home to *respectable* but friendless females, when thrown out of employment, and procure situations for them, and a public meeting was called, at which the Temporary Home Association was formed. The two societies are in no way connected, except that some of the ladies have been managers in both.

The Rosine Intelligence Office has provided homes, and employment, for women and children, -	2044
The Intelligence Office of the Temporary Home, -	3337
Making from the offices of the two Institutions,	5381

The Rosine Association has thus, either directly or indirectly, been the means of providing situations for 5381 women and children. The success attending these efforts to provide homes and employment for this class of persons, proves how much good may be done with a small amount of means; but we can never know how many of these women may have thus been saved from temptations of various kinds, to which the homeless and friendless are ever subjected. Within the year, the Temporary Home has given a temporary shelter to 278 persons, and procured situations for nearly all of them.

TREASURER'S ACCOUNT.

The receipts from April 1, 1853, to March 25, have been,		
From the work-room, - - -	$1,099 43	
Board of inmates, - - - -	51 00	
Donations and subscriptions, - -	1,730 75	
		$2,881 18

EXPENSES.

Interest on the ground-rent on the house, - - - - - -	$80 00	
Family expenses, including salaries, fuel, clothing, marketing, etc., -	2,795 26	
		2,875 26
Cash on hand, - - - - - - - -		5 92
		$2,881 18

At the period of our October Report, we were $92 17 in debt, besides the $2800 due on the house. We then remarked, that we had faith to believe, that, though the barrel might be empty, and the cruse might fail, yet they would both be replenished. That belief has been verified in a wonderful manner, and hearts and hands have been opened to help us in answer to our appeals, and we have still been able to provide for our large family. But many have been refused admission for the want of room, as the accommodations are entirely too limited for the necessities of such an institution. May we not, then, ask our members and friends to aid us, not only by their own contributions, but as collectors among their friends, that a more capacious home may be prepared to receive the unfortunate wanderers from virtue, who are truly "the poorest of the poor."

To our friends and contributors, our ministers and physicians, we desire to present our thanks, and, at the same time, congratulate them, that they, with us, have had the privilege of assisting in that work, in which Jesus gave us so glorious an example.

REPLY TO A LETTER FROM A SOUTHERN LADY.

Rebecca Dear:
Thy letter came,
And tells me thou art yet the same
Warm-hearted southern maid,
To whom my mind still fondly clings,
Of whom my memory still brings
Thoughts, which can never fade.
It is delightful, dear, to me
To know, that while I thought of thee,
And felt my spirit rove
To that bright, sunny land of thine,
That thou shouldst wish to visit mine,
And bring thy pledge of love.
How can we doubt, when thus we feel
An influence around us steal,
That binds us heart to heart,
That comes unseen to human ken,
We know not how, we know not when,
And seems of us a part,

That spirits mingle, and may shed,
Like shadows o'er the streamlet spread,
 A charm, a magic dear;
Yet, like those shadows, pass away,
Nor leave memorial of their stay,
 Upon the eye, or ear.
It matters not, that thoughts should take
The self-same hues, and always make
 On each, the same impress.
The shadows charm but by their change,
A house, a cloud, a mountain range,
 By turns the waters dress.
And should our hearts be chilled, grow cold,
Because the landscape might unfold
 To thy admiring eye,
A brighter glow, a deeper shade—
A sky in lovelier tints arrayed,
 Than mine could then espy?
'Tis variation still excites,
And both the mind and ear delights!
 Hast thou not proved it dear?
And couldst thou wish that I should be
Afraid to utter thoughts to thee,
 Because they breathed a tone
Of higher, or of lower key,
Than seemed to form sweet melody,
 Or answered to thy own?
'Tis friction makes the metals bright,
And the dim mass reflect the light;
 So with the human mind;
Attrition wears the rust away
Which time has gathered, and decay
 Is left in dust behind.

I should regret my words should seem
Harsh on thy ear, or thou should deem
 My feelings were unkind
To thee, or thine; because my heart
With the oppressed has taken part,
 And I would fain unbind
The fetters, time has o'er us thrown,
Not on one suffering class alone,
 But clasping round each one;
Our chains are not more light to bear

Because they old, and rusted are,
  And came from sire to son.

The spirit of the present age
Is progress; and on every page
  We see the march of mind,
Save on that one dark, fadeless blot,
Which, like a pestilential spot
  Within our midst we find:
We mark its influence around,
We see it hath no local bound
  Within a state, or space,
But the malaria widely spread
Infects our air, till it hath bred
  Disease in every place.

See rank injustice in that hall
Where all are slaves, and none dare call
  Themselves in truth, the free!
The lordly Southron is a slave,
His institutions dig the grave
  Of his own liberty!
How many are the toils, and pains
By which he rivets on his chains;
  He must be Argus-eyed,
And watch each wildly waving blast,
That from the North comes rushing past
  In freedom's manly pride,
Lest it should tell that hearts there be
That pant, and long for liberty,
  Not for themselves alone;
But whose petitions daily rise
Like incense to the list'ning skies,
  For hearts to them unknown!
And mark the laws through which he speaks
His despot will, wherein he seeks
  To chain immortal mind,
And level with the senseless clod,
The image of a mighty God,
  And brutify his kind.
He knows, should education give
The light of knowledge, there would live
  But short despotic sway!
The chains that bind would broken be,

And one great shout for liberty,
  Rise to the God of day.
Mark too, how varied are the laws
Made for the same offending cause
  For white men, or for black.
The white, whose situation lies
Among the learned, great, and wise
  If found off virtue's track,
Is lightly punished, as if skin
Could lighten crime, or lessen sin,
  While the degraded slave
Who never read law's written leaves,
For the same act the doom receives
  Of death. A felon's grave!
A volume scarcely could unfold,
The list of wrongs that might be told
  Arising from this plan,
Which leaves the slave no self-control,
And brutifies the human soul
  And makes man, less than man.

Return we now to that great hall
Where Northern men, with Southern, call
  On Freedom, Justice, Right!
And mark how they their trusts betray,
And barter our dear rights away
  To shield our country's blight.
Oh! could our fathers, when they rose
And wrestled with our British foes,
  And broke oppression's chain,
Believe their children e'er would yield
The right of *speech*, and basely wield
  Slave manacles again!
I feel my indignation rise,
When those who should be great and wise
  And echo Freedom's tone,
Basely our Northern rights succumb,
Are dough-faced tools—or else are dumb
  And thus *their* slav'ry own.
And tell me not, fanatic zeal
Has waked in me—for thou would'st feel
  As keenly as I can,
Did not thy habits—interests—lie

Within that binding policy
  That chattelizes man.

Thou askest "What my plan would be?
If I would set three millions free
  And drive them from my door?
And say 'Go seek your daily bread,
With me you cannot lay your head,
  You can return no more!'"
No! No! indeed! that would not be
The breathing of humanity!
  But I would proudly say,
"I know that I have done you wrong—
My conscience bids me not prolong
  Your bondage for a day.
I would not wish my friends to part,
You are entwined around my heart,
  Your int'rest is my own,
And if with me you freely stay,
Whate'er is right, my hand shall pay—
  I act on this alone!
But, if with wild and roving will
You wish to leave my hearthstone, still
  Depart in peace—depart—
I would not one free spirit bind,
Nor cramp the energies, or mind
  Of one heaven-gifted heart.—
No more the lash shall now be borne,
Nor husbands from their wives be torn,
  Nor children severed wide;
But holy ties be cherished still,
And culture teach you to fulfil
  Duties, no more denied."

Our idle demagogues have sought
To spread alarms, with horror fraught,
  And threatened vengeance dire,
And sword and rapine would alone
For your long list of wrongs atone,
  And blood, and scathing fire;
But well I know the negro heart
With kindly feelings prompt to start,
  And I can ne'er believe

The dearest boon my hand could give,
Which bids the slave a freeman live,
An ingrate would receive.
Britannia's Islands proudly show
Man may be just. What blessings flow
There, upon every hand!
Millions lift up the voice of praise—
Rocks, mountains, plains, respond their lays,
And Freedom crowns the land!

Rebecca! well I know that now
The Law will no such course allow,
But such is *what should be ;*
And were you freemen, would the law
Thus keep each noble heart in awe?
Alas! ye are not free!
Ye dare not act as freemen may!
Ye dare not bid the freed-man stay
Upon his native soil,
And use the rights which nature gave,
Rights which our natures claim and crave,—
The meed of honest toil.

Yet say not, "These things cannot be!
Address not words like these to me!
What influence have I?
I am no *Man* to rule the state,
To mingle in the fierce debate,
And bid the despot fly!
Can I with sovereign states prevail
And send glad tidings with each gale
That flies from sea to sea?
Bid them no longer boast in vain,
But wipe away Columbia's stain,
And be in truth the Free!
This is no mission for my hand!
Avarice—pride—control the land,
Could Woman then prevail?
The only weapons she can wield
Are Mercy's banner—Pity's shield—
And what can they avail?"
They can avail! for private life,
And woman, too, hath power, the strife
Which angry words may wage

Is not her forte—she may not shine
Where passion rules the soul divine,
  But she may give her gage
To feel, and act on Mercy's side,
To plead for Justice when denied,
  And hold Oppression's arm,
And point to Manly Pride, and Might,—
Her motto, "*God, Justice, and Right!*"
  In these lie Woman's charm!
And here is, too, her noble path,
For she a soul and feeling hath,
  Of high and holy mould,
Which lets not selfishness or pride
Her sense of right subdue, and guide—
  For virtue is she bold.
And she dare speak! Is not the tone
Of Love, of Mercy, all her own?
  With these she hath her hour!
'Tis mind—not sex, that bears the sway,
And Man will her behests obey,
  And yield him to her power.

Say not, "I have no influence!"
See! Woman sails o'er seas immense,
  Giving love, health, and time,
To win the Pagan from his shrine,
And teach him truths she deems divine,
  Unheeding toil, or clime.
And doth *she* doubt a Woman's power?
Storms may arise, and clouds may lower,
  Yet, with a holy zeal,
She girdeth on her armor bright,
Trusting Jehovah's arm of might
  The Pagan heart may feel.
And hast not thou a tongue, a pen,
Which thou canst wield at will? And when
  Thy noble, kindly heart,
Feels the rude taunt a foreign hand
Has cast on thy beloved land,
  Think then hast thou no part
In meriting the censure thrown?
Does not thy heart its justness own?
  Does it not urge thee then

To use the weapons given thee,
To combat wrong—win victory—
  And free thy fellow-men?
Is thy power less than hers, who goes
Where Brahma rules—where Ganges flows,
  Trusting in Israel's God?
Thy countrymen more hard to win
From wrong, oppression, shame, and sin,
  Than they on India's sod?
Thou say'st, "Our fathers o'er the main
"Inflicted on us this vile stain!"
  But tell me, have we not,
With almost superhuman stroke,
From our *own shoulders* thrown their yoke?
  Then cannot this dark blot
Be wiped away? Have we not skill
Still to work out a nation's will?
  Sit we with folded hands,
And helpless, hopeless, meanly hear
The nations round us scoff and jeer?
  The scorned of other lands!
"See!" they exclaim! "yon boasting Flag!
Beneath—white slaves uphold their gag,
  And dark ones circle round!
Yet hark! they shout for Liberty!
'Land of the Brave! Home of the Free!'
  What inconsistent ground!"
And England, too, thou sayst has slaves,
"That they are buried as in graves,
  Within the darkened mine,
Deprived of education, light,
Religion—doomed to endless night,
  With scarce a trait divine."
But tell me, have they not the right,
Whene'er they wish to seek the light—
  Enjoy the sun and air?
Can they not rove where'er they will,
And Nature's cravings all fulfil?
  No master binds them there!
"Her manufactories display
Oppression too!" But tell me, say,
  Are they still bound to bear?
No! free as air their steps may rove,
And with them go the hearts they love,

And heaven's free bounties share.
No hand dare sever man and wife,
Disturb the bonds of social life,
Or break the moral ties;
The earnings of each toil-worn hand
Are sacred for the little band
That claims its sympathies.
And were it even true, that they
Were under more tyrannic sway,
More degradation knew,
Than the vast mass who on our shore
Are held as chattels, and not more—
Were this, Rebecca, true,
Would it our erring steps excuse,
Their crimes make ours their blackness lose;
Have we not moral might
Of heart, and mind, and soul, to feel
God's revelations, which unseal
The laws of truth and right?
Were all the world beside arrayed
In wrong and bloodshed, could it shade
From His omniscient eye
Our crimes, our sins? Could it atone
For us? Must not each heart alone
Give answer to the sky?

Thou speakest of the kindness shown
Your household slaves. Its truth, I own—
Thine eye may ne'er have seen
Aught that would harsh or cruel seem,
Or thou unkind, unjust, could deem,
Wherever thou hast been;
Yet in this city, where the bound
So little sympathy have found,
Where outrage, bloodshed, wrong,
Have marked with bold and lawless hand
The tyrant spirit of our land,
With persecution strong,
Hundreds of refugees we find,
The South could neither keep nor bind,
Who with content will bear
Starvation, friendless want and woe,
As cellars, lanes, and alleys show,
So freedom they may share.

Official records tell us here,
Within the last eventful year
Canadia's shore hath seen
Full fifteen hundred cross her line,
The north star oft the only sign
Which hath their guidance been.
Could we ask greater proofs than these,
Which come with every southern breeze,
When, breaking nature's ties,
The flying slave will dangers share,
And hardships, toil, and hunger bear,
To win the cherished prize?
That in the human heart their lives
A principle which ever gives,
Alike o'er land and sea,
Its dearest, warmest, strongest thrill,
Which chains cannot subdue nor chill,
To deathless Liberty.

Rebecca, when the pen I took,
I knew not I should write a book,
But thought came after thought,
And urged me on, to claim from thee
That utterance of sympathy,
With which thy heart is fraught.
I know that in thy inmost soul
Thou hatest wrong, and would control
Oppression's iron hand;
For thou with woman's heart canst feel,
And nobly meet my bold appeal
For Freedom and our land.
My words perchance may give thee pain,
And thou mayst think it is in vain
My country's wrongs I tell.
But who futurity can span?
Let us have hope in God and man!
Rebecca, fare thee well!

REPORT OF THE MANAGERS OF THE ROSINE ASSOCIATION.

To secure from vice and degradation a class of women who have forfeited their claim to the respect of the virtuous—to prepare and maintain for them an asylum, which, by its system of religious instruction, shall elevate their moral nature, teach them how to gain an honest living "by the work of their own hands," and eventually to render them useful members of the community—an Association has been formed, and denominated the Rosine Association of Philadelphia.

President, Sophia Lewis; Vice-President, Priscilla H. Hensey; Treasurer, Mira Townsend; Secretaries, Lydia Gillingham, Anna Shomaker, E. Louisa Carr.

Managers—Mary Murphy, Martha Wilson, Anna M. Taylor, Rachel Child, Sarah J. Webb, Susanna Lower, Elizabeth Carr, Eunice Tolman, Harriet Probasco, and Ann L. Rogers.

Physicians—Drs. John D. Griscom, Henry C. Child, Hannah H. Longshore, George Truman, and James Pearce.

"Abon Ben Adhem (may his tribe increase)
Awoke one night from a sweet dream of peace,
And saw (within the moonlight of his room,
Making it rich, like lilies in full bloom)
An Angel, writing in a book of gold;
Exceeding peace had made Ben Adhem bold,
And to the presence in the room, he said—
'What writest thou?' the Vision raised his head,
And, with a smiling look of sweet accord,
Answered—'The names of those who love the Lord.'
'And is mine one?' said Abon. 'Nay—not so,'
Replied the Angel. Abon spoke more low,
But cheerly still, and said, 'I pray thee, then,
Write me as one that loves his fellow-men.'
The angel wrote, and vanished. The next night
It came again, with a great wakening light,
And showed the names whom love of God had blessed,
And lo! Ben Adhem's name led all the rest."

April 5, 1855.

The above beautiful lines so entirely convey our

idea of humanity being the embodiment of the spirit of religion, and the faith that speaks by works, that we place it at the head of our report, as the exponent of our religion, of the faith that is in *us*—our belief that manifestations of our love to our brother, our sister, are more pleasing and acceptable to our heavenly Father, than rearing temples to his praise, or oblations to his glory. The altar and the temple will be mouldered by time into dust; but the soul immortal, snatched from the defilements of sin, may become a child of God, and an heir to everlasting glory. How noble, then, is our work! how exalting, how inspiring, and how cheering is that faith, that reveals to us the Divine harmony of which *we* may form a part—that receives bliss by bestowing benefits, and increases our treasures in proportion as we dispense to others. "Inasmuch as ye have done it to the least of these, ye have done it unto me." In this simple sentence is breathed the religion of Jesus; and just so far as we have been able to live out this idea, can we realize his Divine humanity, and our own brotherhood with him.

The past season has been one calculated to awaken in every heart the germs of humanity, and call into action all the sympathies of our nature. It has even been a fashion to be benevolent, and in this as in other fashions its votaries have mingled with the crowd, made their obeisance to its behests, and then turned again with equal zeal from the Calico Dress Ball or the Dorcas Society, to the pursuit of any new fantasy that presented. But in the cause in which we are engaged there is no fashion, no excitement dependent on times or seasons. The evils against which we have been struggling are those which spring from causes that lie deep in the bosom of society at all seasons, and which, while they are the prolific source of sorrow in thousands of families, are subjects that require great moral courage to speak of in social life, or introduce in an acceptable manner before a religious community.

Many of our ministers in their teachings shrink from the subject of licentiousness, and glance at it only as a theme "unfit for ears polite," in such generalizing terms, that if understood at all by their hearers, is so classed with fashionable follies, that the remarks pass without causing a moment's reflection. We have seen our grave divines sit in solemn conclave, and resolve on the dismission from their churches of those, "who whirl the light fantastic toe," while that sin that pervades the ramifications of society, destroying the morals and health of our young men, bringing disgrace and misery to so many of our females, sorrow and shame into so many families, and the wreck of soul and body to its victims, goes from age to age almost unrebuked, and is considered a theme not to be discussed, and scarcely alluded to. But does the warrior expect to conquer by flight? Can one of the greatest evils of society be subdued by avoiding the subject? Can we perform our duty to our fellow-beings by passing lightly over the errors of one part of the community, and discarding from our society and our charities, the more feeble companions of their misdeeds? It may be so, but it is not in accordance with our ideas of moral courage, or the dictates of humanity and religion. *We* have not so learned Christianity.

Seven years have elapsed since we first met in the lecture-room of the Museum to form this Association; the devouring flames have destroyed that building, but we have reason to believe that some of those who have been snatched from ruin through the instrumentality of this Society, are among the redeemed who will surround the throne of glory forever. Five of our inmates have passed away, to whom a cheering hope had been given, and several churches in our city claim as members, those who once came as wanderers from virtue to seek a shelter and the charities of their own sex at the Rosine.

It is woman's mission thus to extend her hand, her sympathies, her aid to woman. To her alone can the penitent heart unfold truly its frailties, and claim not only sympathy, but that enduring patience with its waywardness, that will bear and forbear, hope against hope, and conquer the froward only by the affection it has inspired. We have never met with more touching instances of gratitude than some of those exhibited by different members of our Rosine family. Those alone who have known and witnessed the extreme degradation and reckless depravity that often follows the lapse from virtue in woman, when she feels herself a hopeless outcast from all that is good and lovely in life, can understand the change in her feelings, when, by the magic touches of a few fleeting months she finds herself transferred from a shameless participant in the debasing revels of a house of infamy, to a peaceful, industrious resident in a respectable family. Great indeed is the change to *her*. She cannot blot from her memory the past; but the friendless one is no longer friendless. There are those who are interested in her well-doing, who would shield and protect her from injury from others, and endeavor to strengthen her to overcome the temptations and weaknesses of her own perverted nature. They have shown her that the avenues are open to her still, not only to a reputable position in life, but through redeeming mercy, to the society of the blessed forever.

We cannot expect all who come under our care to appreciate their advantages, or improve them as they might. The impulsive, unreasoning disposition that led some of them into wrong connections at first, may bring them as applicants to our door, and take them as changefully away; but there are many who have prized their privileges, and proved by their continued good conduct for a course of years, that our toils and their struggles have not been for nought. Since our last report, one of our former inmates has been married; she is the fourteenth who has married respectably since leaving the Institution; she was in the Rosine about three years, and one year since left us to enter a tailoring establishment, where three others of our girls were located. Two of the four are now members of churches, and we have reason to believe *are consistent members*. One of these was the mistress of a noted house when the Rosine was opened, and some of the first visits paid by our managers to houses of bad character, were to her abode. She always treated them with kindness and respect, but their counsel appeared to make little impression. She afterwards left Philadelphia, and opened a house of the same kind in another city. There she pursued a flourishing career; but in this strange place, where there were none to reprove or counsel, the warning of Providence came to her. She dreamed that she was dead, with all her sins upon her. The lake of fire was before her, as her imagination had pictured its horrors, and she thought she was compelled to enter it, and endure its burning torments forever. Words could not express the agony she endured as she gazed upon that glowing sea, and exclaimed, "Can nothing save me?" There was no one to answer; but she heard a voice which said, "Nothing, but to go to Mrs. ——," (who was one of the Managers of the Rosine, who had visited her in Philadelphia.) She gazed wildly around to see from whence the voice came, and in the clouds above beheld the face of her who had reasoned with her in the days long past, and pleaded with her to abandon the evils by which she was surrounded. At this period she awoke from her dream; but the impression did not pass from her mind. It continued with her from day to day, until she sold her furniture, closed her house, returned to Philadelphia, and was received into the Rosine by the same manager whose face she had seen in the clouds, and who had been her mental companion from that period.

Three years have passed, one of which was spent in the Rosine. At this time she is residing as seamstress in a respectable family, where she is highly valued, and is a regular attendant of the church to which she is united.

Within a few days we have seen two others of our former inmates, who have both been occupying the position of housekeepers in families, and are members in good standing in their churches.

Another, who was considered almost a hopeless case for some months after she entered the Asylum, continued an inmate nearly three years. Since then she has resided in a family of professing

Christians, and for several months has been a Sabbath-school teacher, and a member of the Dorcas Society of her church. She learned the tailoring trade while in the Institution, and has had work constantly from the same shop, even during the dull season, when the generality of the hands were unemployed.

These are cheering facts, and attest the influences that have been operating in the Rosine House.

We have endeavored to avoid everything of a sectarian nature in our Institution, leaving the minds of our girls free to unite themselves, after leaving us, to whatever society is most in accordance with their feelings. We have sought to impress them with the importance of truth and honesty,—of living in the spirit of prayer, and practising love and kindness one to another. We have reminded them of the omnipresence of the Deity, and his cognizance of every thought, word, and action, and of their increased responsibility from the knowledge thus presented before them.

To the ministers of the different denominations who have attended our meetings, we are greatly indebted. The seed sown in the Rosine House has, in many instances, brought forth good fruit. It is our part to labor with the ability that is given. The blessing of the Father alone can ripen the seed, and bring the increase.

Among other pleasing facts is that of the spirit of economy and forethought displayed by some of our girls, in their desire to accumulate something for a future day. Two of them have had over one hundred dollars deposited for them by us, as they have been able to bring us the savings from their wages.

To both of these girls the cells of the prison were familiar before they came to the Rosine, and one of them is still in the family who received her when she first left the Association.

We have deposited for several others smaller amounts, and find each year the number of depositors increasing. To those, through whose hands thousands of dollars are passing, it would be almost impossible to convey the idea of the increased consciousness of respectability of these women, by having even a small amount, earned by their own honest efforts, placed at interest. It is a stimulant to increased exertion and economy. One of our depositors, who attended the school regularly at the Rosine while she was an inmate, and made considerable improvement, is a domestic in a family. They have given her the privilege of attending a school under the care of her church. Her leisure hours are thus devoted to study; and she appears indifferent to company, and to everything except her intellectual advancement and the accumulation of an honestly-earned capital.

The school in the Rosine is still continued. Many of our girls, particularly the younger ones, are very desirous of improvement, and have made considerable progress. They are generally anxious to learn to write; but very few seem aware of the importance of learning to spell, as they consider writing a letter merely a mechanical operation. One, who did not even know the alphabet, was highly delighted with having a copy-book, and tracing the characters placed before her, eagerly inquired the meaning of every word.

We believed, when we entered into this work, in the possibility of the reformation of women, and now, after having been more than six years engaged in the cause, we consider we have many proofs to confirm that opinion. We have paid hundreds of visits to houses of immoral character; we have entered the lowest haunts of drunkenness and debauchery; the cells of the prison and the wards of the almshouse are familiar to us; three hundred and sixty inmates have been under our care in the Rosine, and we still believe in the possibility of reformation, even when they have been sunk in the greatest degree of degradation. We do not mean to say that *we* can reform all these women, but that in all the Divine principle has been implanted; and that, if we could surround them by congenial circumstances for a sufficient length of time to develope the buried germ, and warm it into activity we should find that in every heart there is still the image of the Deity, and desires and cravings after the good, the true, and the beautiful. A touching proof of the continued consciousness of better things was exhibited in the reply of one, who had been mistress of a house of bad repute seventeen years. Two of our ladies visited her, and as they were departing, one of them observed her looking at her with great earnestness, and said, "What are you thinking?" She replied, "I was thinking how much joy there would be in heaven when you get there, and meet all the souls you have been the means of saving." Seventeen years had that woman lived in the violation of her convictions of conscience, and yet she could picture in her mind the joyous meeting of the redeemed amid the harmonies of heaven. It was a passing thought; but her illuminated countenance as she spoke, proved that she could appreciate the reward of a life of virtue, though the habits of years, and the weakness of her own principles, prevented her from aiming at the realization, in her own case, of her glorious conceptions.

In a visit at another house of the same character, the ladies were endeavoring to persuade a young creature to go to the Rosine, when she turned to the mistress of the house and said, "If you were in my place, would you go?" The person addressed, who was perhaps fifty years of age, replied, "Certainly I would. Had I my life to pass over again, a thousand worlds would not tempt me to live as I have done!" What a lesson was contained in that one sentence! Oh! that every young girl, who stands trembling on the threshold of vice, could have these words sounded in her ears, and burned into her mind, till she could never efface the impression of their warning. A thousand worlds will not reward for a life of sin; and she who makes the first wrong step, knows not the circumstances or feelings that may bear her on, with resistless force, until (if life be spared) year after year may become a circling round, marked alone by depraved associations and unutterable miseries. A thousand worlds will not repay the poor victim of vice for the agonies of even one hour, when, keeping the benumbing bowl from her lips, she allows herself to think. Then come the rushing thoughts of her homelessness—her friendlessness—her shattered constitution—her utter degradation—and, worse than all, that hopelessness, that closes forever from her view the pure delights of virtue here, and hereafter.

Often in our visits to these unfortunates we have said, "How do you feel, when you reflect on your present condition, and retrace the past, and look into your future?" "We dare not think," has been the frequent reply. "No woman could lead this life, if she allowed herself to think. She must drown reflection, or she could not endure existence." We have ofttimes also asked them: "In what respect have you been benefited by the life you have been leading? Have you gained happiness?" "No." "Reputation?" "No." "Health?" "No." "Have you money in the Savings Fund?" "No." "Have you a hope of heaven hereafter?" "No." "What advantages, then, have you received?" A world of misery has been frequently expressed in the countenance, and in the deep tones, as they uttered, "Nothing! nothing!"

In our Report of 1853, we spoke of a young woman, whom one of our managers found in one of those miserable places, up an alley in Baker Street, where three young girls were living together without an article of furniture but two yards of rag-carpet, a porter-bottle, and a candlestick. One of these was a girl of respectable family, who, by a train of misfortunes, had become an outcast, and at the time she was discovered was barefoot and bonnetless, and without clothing, except the few articles on her person. She was taken to the Rosine, where she remained about a year, during which time she made a profession of religion, and her relatives manifested (through our interference) a willingness to acknowledge her, and treat her with kindness.

Over two years have passed since that period, and she is now in the bosom of her family, enjoying the comforts of wealth and luxury. In a letter received from her a few days since, addressed to our member who found her in Baker Street, she says, "Let me thank you for the happiness I now enjoy. Oh! how often I think of this day, and the one in which we first met. I feel as if I could not be thankful enough to our heavenly Father, for sending me so kind a friend as yourself. Upon my heart is written the law of gratitude. Your lessons of wisdom will I make the mottoes of my life.

"Remember me to Mrs. L., the matron, and all who are interested in me, and beg them to ask for me the blessing of heaven."

Various circumstances connected with our Rosine labors, from time to time, bring under our consideration subjects, that seem important to be placed before the notice of the community. During the pressure of the difficulties arising from want of employment last winter, and since that period, the quantity of young girls loitering about the streets, or being nominally match or fruit merchants, must have attracted the attention of all observers. Some of us who have had opportunities of knowing the fate that is usually consequent on such a vagrant life in children, rarely see them thus misemployed, without feeling as we pass them, that they are doomed to sin and disgrace, and to perpetuate our immoral houses, and pauper and prison population. We have had girls in the Rosine, whose career of vice commenced in this manner before they were twelve years of age, and in such cases, little short of a miracle can produce a reformation. One of them, who had long been known to one of our managers, a bright, black-eyed girl, was lately received into the Rosine. Her mother once had three daughters. She resisted the advice of those who counselled her to place them in families, where they might be brought up rightly, and employed them as venders of small articles about the streets. The three girls, one after another, became the victims of vice, and the two elder ones have gone to meet their misguided mother at the bar of judgment. The youngest came late one evening to ask admission into the Rosine. She said she was utterly friendless, and though the weather was quite severe, had not slept beneath a roof for three nights. She had hidden up alleys and under sheds, to avoid being taken up by the police, while her wretched condition excluded her from even the meanest abodes of vice. She was admitted, and upon examination found to be literally a mass of vermin. Her clothing was devoted to the flames, and for a week she was raving with mania-potu. We hoped with returning sense would come a consciousness of her degradation, and a desire for better things, but before a month elapsed the cravings for liquor and tobacco, and her old vagrant habits, revived, and she stole away, to re-enter that career that has probably ere this lodged her in the prison or the almshouse.

In the year 1850, our Managers presented the following petition to Councils:

TO THE SELECT AND COMMON COUNCILS OF PHILADELPHIA.

GENTLEMEN:—The Managers of the Rosine Association, impressed with the importance of guarding the morals of the youth of our city, and believing that one of the most fruitful sources of crime and exposure to temptation, is the vending of articles through our streets by children, beg leave to suggest, that some efficient plan be adopted for the suppression of this growing evil among us. Most especially do we plead for the little girls, that some steps may be taken to save them from the ruin that almost inevitably follows the exposure consequent upon such a course, and your petitioners ask, that such practices may be prohibited by a suitable ordinance.

Nothing, however, has been done. The evil has been increasing, and the consequence must be a proportionate increase of vice and immorality in our community. Our only hope is, that our energetic Mayor may find or devise some law that may reach such cases, and be the means of saving our children from the temptations to which the depravity or improvidence of their parents subjects them.

Our work room continues to be an object of great interest and advantage. Here many are found busily employed, who, until they entered the Rosine, had made little or no progress in the arts of the seamstress. Some have said they had never made a garment in their lives, many had never darned a stocking, and to this utter ignorance of how to work rightly in any department may be attributed the ruin of some of our inmates, as they have not been taught to aim at excellence, and therefore were not calculated to fill any useful station in life. Our worthy matron, by her judicious instructions and good taste, aided by the beautiful work of the stitching machine, has elevated the character of that department, until we are prepared to say, that the work accomplished at the Rosine stands unrivalled. The labor of teaching many of our inmates is a wearisome task, as, though they desire to improve, and become neat and industrious, yet idle and careless habits have so grown with them that they have become a second nature, and until principle can be engrafted upon them it is difficult to inspire the energy that is necessary to promote any great progress. Yet every year more work is performed than in the preceding, and should the time arrive that we may have a larger building for our operations, we can then retain those who desire to stay a longer period, and pay them a just reward for their labor.

Our plan has been, in receiving our inmates, to stipulate that they should remain as apprentices six months. After that period, if their services became valuable, and they wished to continue in the Institution, we have allowed them a satisfactory compensation. Within the past year, $203 41 have been paid as wages to inmates in the sewing department.

By a resolution of the Board, a few months since, for various reasons it was concluded to change the period of apprenticeship from six months to a year. To women who have led a dissolute life a year of probation is not too long to wean them from improper habits and associations, and accustom them to practices of industry and self-control, without which, on leaving the Rosine, they must still be liable to the same temptations that formerly led them astray.

A large proportion of the women who come to us have been accustomed to deadening their sense of shame, and the horrors of remorse, by resorting to the inebriating glass. To these a year's seclusion is highly important, not only to destroy the old habits, but to create new ones, of a more useful and elevating nature. In our teachings we endeavor to impress them with the consciousness that they are ever in the presence of the "all-seeing eye," that they are weak and variable, and governed by impulse more than reason, and that he alone who gave them life, can give them strength to resist temptation, and keep them in the better way.

From March 25th, 1854, to March 20th, 1855, the number of garments made in the Rosine, for the use of the family, has been - - - - -	810
For customers, including 289 shirts, 477 chemises, 41 quilts, 68 night-gowns, 78 dresses, 139 vests, 230 pantaloons, 700 sheets, 40 pillow-slips, 158 yards of embroidery, and sundry articles, amounting altogether to - - - - - - -	3826
Total, for family and customers, - - - - -	4636

The crowded condition of the Rosine House prevents our receiving many who apply for admission, and also excludes the introduction of other departments of labor, that might be productive of profit and advantage. We can only have one work room, and therefore must be confined to one species of work, while the number who sleep in our chambers is much greater than is conducive to health, and our dining-room and kitchen, are entirely too diminutive for the convenience of the family.

In connection with our work room we must say a few words more. To ladies who have been brought up in the lap of luxury, whose pleasure and enjoyment it has been to order whatever their taste may devise, it may be difficult to convey the idea that a debt, which may appear a trifling affair to them, may be of great importance in a family where all that is not received for labor, must be solicited from door to door. We desire to appeal to the sense of justice and humanity of some of these ladies, hoping their bills will be speedily settled, and they will understand, in the future, that our instructions to our Matron are, to deliver work done in the Rosine only upon the payment of the bills. It is a very unpleasant task to our Matron to refuse to let the articles be taken from the House until the work is paid for, but some persons are either so forgetful, or neglectful, that this rule is absolutely indispensable.

The late Dr. Elkinton (for some years an alderman), in a communication to our Board of Managers, stated that he had frequent applications from women who had been domestics in families, to institute suits for the recovery of wages from their employers. Similar complaints have come frequently to us, also from those who are employed as needlewomen. One of our former inmates, who goes out as seamstress into families, by the week, has a claim of six dollars, for three weeks' sewing, against a lady, who rides in her carriage, with every appearance of luxury around her. This account has been standing nearly two years. A few days since the poor girl called upon the lady, and stated to her that she had been there very frequently for the money; that another lady owed her eight dollars for sewing, and several others smaller amounts, which she was unable to obtain; and now, said she, my feet would be to the ground, had not a friend given me an old pair of gaiters. "Oh Mary," said the delicately nervous lady, "do not talk so—I am not well, and cannot bear it!" But no money was forthcoming, and the seamstress may go barefoot, or get shoes where she can, but she must not trouble the fine lady with the story of her necessities.

Some time since we received a young woman, who stated that she was an orphan, and had formerly rented a room, and taken in sewing. It was only by the closest economy and industry that she could meet her expenses. On one occasion, she had been busily employed on some work which occupied her a whole week. Late on Saturday evening she finished her task, and took it home, calculating to pay her rent with the proceeds, and provide for the coming week.

The lady examined the work, said all was right, but she could not pay her for her labor. The unfortunate girl turned away to hide her tears. She had tasted no food that day, and was without a cent to procure any. Her landlady was pressing for her money, and faint and dejected, she knew not which way to turn. Indignation and grief, by turns, possessed her mind, until a feeling of recklessness grew upon her, as she thought of her unrequited toil, and her struggles to earn an honest living. Oh! (said she, in recounting the events of that evening), had any one have given me but 12½ cents, it would have saved me from ruin! I had become desperate, and what have I been since, but a blot in the creation.

If women would but reflect on the fatal consequences that may result from such culpable neglect and injustice towards those whom they employ, they would shrink from the survey of their own conduct, and feel they have *no right* to engross the time or labor of either seamstress or domestic, without a positive knowledge of their ability and inclination to pay their just demands.

An Irish girl was brought by one of our members from a house of ill-fame, who had lived with a family from the time she came into the country, without receiving anything but promises for wages, until she was almost destitute of clothing. She was then advised by some one to sue her employer, and consequently lost her situation, and was without a recommendation to get another. On some pretext she was defrauded of her wages, and wandered for several days from house to house, asking in vain, for employment. She had no money to pay the fee at an Intelligence Office, or to procure board or lodging, and having no friends who could give her a home, she sought a shelter at night wherever she could find a place to creep in, and for three days was entirely destitute of food. Almost sinking from exhaustion, as a last resort she sold herself to prevent starvation, and remained in the abode of sin two weeks, when she was found by one of the managers of the Rosine, and taken to the Institution. That girl is now well and respectably married.

This subject of *wages* is one that demands, and should receive attention. Who of us are willing to feel that by our careless thoughtlessness another individual may be tempted to crime; that by our injustice the soul of a fellow-being may be sunk in sin, and perhaps lost forever? Under such circumstances are they alone responsible? He who reads *their hearts* and *ours*, alone can cast the balance.

Our *Intelligence Office*, for respectable females, is still in operation, and has been the means of providing homes and employment for 2492 women and children.

The Temporary Home which sprang from the necessity felt by our managers for a house of prevention, as well as one of a remedial character, is still pursuing its course of usefulness. Its object is to save the friendless and unprotected female, of respectable character, who is thrown out of employment and a home, and furnish her with a safe shelter until a suitable situation can be procured for her. This Institution has given a temporary home to 297 persons within the last year, and provided places for 5616 since the Home was opened.

Thus, through the instrumentality of the two associations, 8108 women and children have been placed in positions to maintain themselves honestly and reputably.

Our friends may remember, that in February, 1854, the managers of the Rosine Association made an application to the Legislature for an appropriation, and the following Act was passed:

An Act appropriating certain Monies to the Rosine Association.

Section 1.—Be it enacted by the Senate, etc., that the sum of $3000 be, and the same is, hereby appropriated to the Rosine Association of Philadelphia, incorporated April 11, 1848, for the purchasing a lot, or erecting, or purchasing buildings for the operation of the Association, *Provided, That this Act shall not take effect, until an equal amount shall have been subscribed by other responsible contributors, to said Association.*

Section 2.—That the Councils of the City of Philadelphia, are hereby authorized to appropriate to the said Association, hereafter, any sum, or sums of money, not exceeding $3000, in any one year.

Our friends in the Legislature were aware that we owed a debt of twenty-eight hundred dollars, and that if we received an appropriation of $3000, which was the sum proposed to be given, it would cover the debt, but not aid us materially in procuring a larger building. Therefore, the second section was added to the bill, under the supposition that we would immediately apply to our Councils for the annual appropriation, which this Act empowered them to give us. The Act of Consolidation took place about the same period as the passage of this law, and in the unsettled state of our city government, it was not deemed advisable to present our petition to Councils, until within the past month.

The subject is now before them, and we hope they will fulfil the expectations of the members of the State Legislature. About five hundred dollars have been subscribed by different persons, to assist us in raising the sum required to claim the appropriation from the State, and a kind friend, of whom we borrowed $1500, to aid us in the payment of the House we occupy, has given us $1000 of that amount, for the same purpose.

Those only who have been beggars for seven years, can understand how unpleasant it must be for us to be forced to solicit contributions for the support of an Institution, *year after year*. Yet, we feel the same necessity for exertion, and even more, than formerly. We are unable to receive many of the women who apply for admission, for the want of room; and our Treasurer, when the Matron has needed flour, tea, coffee, etc., has ofttimes turned from the empty treasury to the street, to collect funds, before she could meet the demands for the family supplies.

About four hundred women have been inmates of the Rosine. They have generally come from immoral houses, the almshouse, or the prison. The shelter and charities of the Association, are as much needed as ever. We thank those who have hitherto aided us, and must ask for a continued support, while we hope, in some future day, to occupy a larger and more convenient building, and receive a suitable income to support it.

Is there not some benevolent individual, whose heart has been touched by the miseries of these poor outcasts, who can, and will endow the Institution, and thus entitle themselves to the blessings and gratitude of these, the poorest of the poor.

Treasurer's Report.

The Receipts from March 23d, 1854, to March 20th, 1855, have been

From the work room, ...	$1,319 65	
Board of inmates, ...	14 00	
Cash, donations and subscriptions, .	2,232 24	
		$3,565 89

Expenses.

Ground rent, insurance, gas and water rent,	$163 00	
Family expenses, including fuel, salaries, clothing, marketing, &c., . . .	3,385 69	
Cash on hand, ...	17 20	
		$3,565 89

This amount of expenses includes $203 41 which has been paid to inmates, *for work*, in the sewing department.

Auditor's Report.

Having been duly appointed by the Board of Managers of the Rosine Association, as a Committee to examine the accounts of our Treasurer, Mira Townsend, we have attended to the duty assigned us, and found them to be entirely correct.

Priscilla H. Hensey.
Harriet Probasco.

March 10, 1855.

We stop the press to acknowledge the receipt of $39 40, from the Relief Committee of the 13th, 14th and 15th Wards of this City, per two members of the committee. This sum came very seasonably, to enable us to pay for two barrels of flour, for which we are indebted, and to purchase *another*, which is now needed. A barrel of flour, per week, is used in the Rosine House, the number of inmates being now 44, but sometimes over 50. Had we house-room and funds, we should probably have a family of double the number, but at present we are constantly forced to refuse admission to applicants. This balance of the fund collected for the poor, speaks well for the liberality of Spring Garden, and the industry and thrift of her population.

THE YOUNG MERCHANTS.

About eight o'clock one morning we were told a gentleman wished to see us in the parlor, who declined sending his name. We found a very respectable-looking young man there, but a perfect stranger. After the morning salutation he appeared embarrassed about proceeding, and finally said, he did not know how to begin his story, as he must expose himself, to accomplish what he wished. He was encouraged to proceed, and stated, that the afternoon before (the Sabbath), he with another young man, had gone to a house of bad character, and while there, had met with a young girl about seventeen years old, who had come only a week before from the country, and had been lured innocently into the house, as she was seeking employment, and had been detained there. The young man said, he had been exceedingly interested by the tale she so ingenuously told, and he inquired if she wished to continue there? She replied, no! But they tell me here, my fate is sealed for life. He assured her it was not the case, and asked if she would go to a situation in a family if he could procure her one? She had seen so much deception in the few days she had been in that house, that she answered him doubtfully, but he desiring to know her earnestness, said, "If you will go, I will find you a home in a Quaker family." "Then I will go," said she unhesitatingly. Without reflecting on the possibilities of the case, and urged on by his zeal to save a young, beautiful, and artless creature from what he knew must be a life of perpetual misery, he made an engagement to meet her at 9 o'clock the next morning, in Franklin Square, and take her to this Quaker family. When he left the house, and began to think seriously about it, he felt considerably embarrassed, and tried to banish the whole affair from his mind. But all night long it staid with him, and that sweet, innocent young face still kept looking at him, and pleading with him to save her, every time he closed his eyes till sleep was entirely banished. But what was he to do? She had only trusted him on the faith of the Quaker family, with whom he would place her, and he knew but one Friend's family in the city, and they were old and childless people, and he thought would probably have no sympathy for such a case, and besides he could not bear to expose to them his own misdoing. His mind was troubled, and when the time arrived for him to go to his store the next morning, he was as much in the dark as ever. As he proceeded down the street, his eye rested on the name on a door, and he remembered he had seen the gentleman who lived there, and that he wore the Friendly garb. But they were not acquainted. It was then almost eight o'clock, and he had promised to meet her about nine. There was no time to lose. He must break his word, and leave her to endure all the horrors of a degraded life, or expose himself to somebody. He paused, but yielding to the better feeling, his hand was on the bell, and in ten minutes he was relating the story to one who was an utter stranger. We listened, and then asked if he knew us? "No!" "Did thee ever hear any one speak of us?" "No!" "Does thee know anything about the Rosine Association?" "No!" It appeared he knew nothing about us, or our operations, and to our inquiries of how he happened to call on us, he simply answered, "He did not know where else to go." We told him it was all right, and Providence had sent him, though he came to us blindly, and putting on our bonnet, we accompanied him to Franklin Square. We sauntered there for some time, but the young girl did not make her appearance. Taking the direction of the house, we then called for another manager who was a Friend, and parting from the young man, pursued our way there. On entering, we found her in the parlor, and taking a seat on the sofa beside her, told her, a gentleman had sent us, whom she had promised to meet in Franklin Square, and then inquired why she had not fulfilled her engagement? She said the other inmates of the house had told her he was only jesting, and persuaded her not to go. We assured her he was in earnest, and had sent us for her, and asked if she would go with us? She said she wished to leave, but could not until the next day. In answer to our inquiries, after some hesitation, she acknowledged the reason she could not go, was, because a young man had left his watch and gold ring with her, and she could not leave until she delivered them to him. We told her we would make an arrangement, by which she could return them to the owner; and with this assurance she left the house with us. We took her to our own home, and leaving her there, went immediately to the young merchant's store, who owned the jewelry. He was a stranger to us, and looked very much embarrassed when we asked if he knew Emily ——. He replied, "He had seen her." We then mentioned our name, and number, and said, she is at our house and wishes to see thee! "Oh, I cannot go there!" he exclaimed, "I know your Husband." We assured him Husband should not interfere, and made the arrangement to receive him without the presence of any of our family. He came. The young lady returned the trinkets, but he urged her to keep the ring; we at once objected. The ring could be of no use to her. It would only be a badge of her dishonor, and would ever be a painful memorial to her. After some plain remarks to both of them, and portraying to her the consequences that would probably have occurred, had she continued in the house where we found her; we then represented to him, our ideas of the impropriety of his conduct, and appealed to his moral sense for the condemnation. He said, no one had ever counselled him upon the subject before. His mother was an excellent, pious woman, and she had always laid great stress upon integrity, and given him a large allowance of pocket money, that he might not be tempted to be dishonest. He had two uncles, one a clergyman, and the other a physician, both in high standing. "Did not thy mother," we asked, "warn thee against improper associations, and licentious habits, or thy uncles advise thee on the subject of thy moral, or physical health?" "No," he answered; "my uncles said, 'Sam, you must be a good boy!' and their counsel ended there. My mother would have thought it very indelicate to say a word upon the subject; so that I have been left to take my own course without any restraint!" "Does thee think it indelicate for me to talk with thee ?" "Oh no! but my mother would not have done it." He then said, the way he happened to form the acquaintance with the young lady, was thus: He and another young man were walking, when they concluded to go into a cellar, and get some oysters. They called for a glass of beer, and then for a bottle of champagne, after which they were ready for anything; and a proposition was made to go to the house of Mrs. S——, and they went; "but," he added, "I see the subject in a very different light now, and I will give you my pledge, that I will never enter a house of immoral character again, unless I go for a good purpose!" "I am glad to hear thee say so, but I would like thee to give me the temperance pledge too." "I cannot do that!" he replied; "all the young men I know, drink sometimes!" "If they do, does that make it right?" "No! but young men generally take a glass in company! I know it is a bad practice, and leads many a one to ruin; but I suppose you will allow me to take a glass of beer, or cider?" "I only wish to refer thee to thy own story. You started to take a walk, and the first conclusion was, to get a plate of oysters. Then you called for a glass of beer; then for a bottle of champagne, after which you were 'ready for anything,' and the proposition was made to go to the house of Mrs. S——, and you went. In the first place, the practice of frequenting oyster cellars is a very bad one, and leads, as in this case, to many an evil. The oysters led to the beer, the beer to the champagne, and then you were 'ready for anything.' Now, what is the consequence? Thy character lies in my hands, and were I so disposed, I could ruin thy reputation. Then think of this poor unfortunate girl. She (with many another), is the victim of the glass of beer, and the bottle of champagne. The stimulating glass excites other evil passions, and the morals, the health, and the happiness are all sacrificed. It is not only the poor degraded girls who suffer, but many a man passes through life with a ruined constitution, and entails upon his offspring scrofulous and other diseases, that result from the indulgence of vicious and ungoverned propensities. I have known the health and happiness of whole families destroyed in this manner, while the weakened intellect, and blunted moral sense of the individual, showed the fearful retribution that often follows deviations from the path of virtue. But," we added, "we do not wish thee to give *us* a pledge. Think of it for thyself, and when ready, make thy vows to thy Heavenly Father. He alone can give thee strength to keep them." We continued thus in conversation, probably an hour and a half, and parted, hoping we had spent a profitable evening.

Though Husband was not permitted to be present, of course we told him the whole story, and his surprise was great the next morning to see the young Merchant call upon him at his place of business, and request a private interview. He then narrated to him the events as they had occurred, and the conversation of the previous evening, and added, "I never had anything to make so great an impression on my mind. It has changed the whole course of my ideas. I laid awake all night thinking of it, and this morning it continues with me. I cannot attend to my business, so I resolved I would come and talk with you." They had a long talk, and a serious one, and Husband gave such counsel as he thought would be beneficial to the young man. He found, like most young men, he had good and kindly feelings, but he had not been taught to bring his impulses under the government of his reason, or the high and holy principles that would have led him to lay every action upon the altar, and ask, "Lord is it right in thy sight? I am professing to be a Christian. Am I living in the purity enjoined by thy law?" His mother, with false ideas of delicacy, had neglected to impress upon the mind of her child the importance of purity of thought and deed, and his uncles had not deemed it needful to warn him against the dangers and temptations to which the unguarded youth must ever be subjected, in the heart of a large city.

A week passed away, and one evening the young merchant called. "I have come," said he, "to give you the pledge you asked for! I could not do it then, but I am ready now."

But we have not forgotten Emily, poor child! We kept her several days with us, and, upon learning her story, thought the best plan would be to return her to her friends. We ascertained that she had a sister, who was comfortably married, and to this sister we resolved to consign the object of our care. We delivered her safely, and, for a season, occasionally heard of her and saw her. Three years had elapsed, when, returning from a visit to the country, a woman in the stage attracted our observation; and, after some conversation, we discovered it was the sister of Emily. Of course, we had many inquiries to make, and were informed that Emily was well married, and living nicely, and would be very glad to see and welcome her former friend to her own house.

About the period of our hearing this pleasant intelligence of Emily's marriage, we received another call from the young Merchant who was the means of our becoming acquainted with her. We had taken an opportunity of conversing seriously with him, on the impropriety and criminality of frequenting houses of immoral character, and found him to be warm-hearted and generous, and desirous of doing good to others, but not prepared to abandon the evil practices himself, which he knew could only bring misery in all its forms to the unfortunate victims of licentiousness. He came now to ask us to go to another house of the same character, to see another young girl, whom he had met the evening before. We went, and found a young creature, whose sweet, modest face claimed feelings of interest from every one who looked upon it, and whose gentleness of manner, and lady-like deportment, bespoke her to be accustomed to polished and refined society. She told us the same story she had given to him the evening previous. Her father was a wealthy man, and lived in the country, some distance from the city. He had married a second time, and her stepmother was disagreeable to her. She, and a younger sister, had been a year at boarding-school, and the time had nearly arrived for them to return to the paternal roof, but her aversion to her mother made her unwilling to reside at home, while her mind had been corrupted by some of her school associates, who had, through pernicious books and improper conversations, conveyed to her the idea, that a life of dissolute liberty was one of enjoyment, and her antipathy to be under the home government, combined with these false representations, made her resolve to leave the school and her sister, and cast herself into the great vortex of licentious depravity. Poor child! she was but sixteen—her knowledge of life was confined to the home circle until she entered that fatal school, and she was totally ignorant of the wretchedness, the falsehood, and the degradation of those with whom she voluntarily sought to mingle. She knew not that the midnight revel and the inebriating cup were madly sought to drown the misery (whose depths cannot be told) of the poor victims, whose happiness she had heard so highly pictured, and whose life she had imagined was one long dream of love. Taking with her scarcely a change of clothing, she left the school, alone, and came to the city. In the railroad car, she saw a colored woman, with whom she entered into conversation, and asked if she knew where there was a house of the description she sought. Guided by this woman, she entered the home of sin and wretchedness.

Scarcely a week had elapsed, when our young merchant saw her, and became at once interested for her. He drew from her this history of herself, but more she would not reveal. The next morning he called upon us, and, when we met her, she repeated the narration, but who she was, where she came from, who were her friends, or what school she had been at, she kept a profound secret.

But that one week had revealed to her the follies and errors by which she had been misguided, and she was prepared at once to go with us, as soon as she understood our mission. We took her also to our own home (as we have done many another, whose errors or misfortunes we have wished to hide), and kept her with us a few days. As she seemed desirous to conceal her history even from us, we avoided making inquiries that might lead her to unfold what she was not prepared to reveal, but we pictured to her the miseries from which she had escaped, and the downward course which is the usual lot of those who enter on the road to ruin. We told her some of the circumstances that had come under our knowledge, connected with others who had been led astray, and endeavored to impress her with the conviction, that Providence, through his agents, saved her from the dreadful fate that must have been her portion, had she not thus been snatched from a course of life that is revolting to every feeling of delicacy, and depraving in all its associations. We besought her to return speedily to her school, and account for her absence in the best manner she could, and to remember that her father had a right to select whatever lady he thought proper for his wife, and, if she could not give her affection, it was her duty to treat her with proper respect. Our own feelings were so deeply interested for her, that we urged her, with all the earnestness in our nature, to pursue the path of virtue, and return at once to her friends.

She had only been with us two or three days, when, upon returning home after one of our collecting excursions for the Rosine, we found she and her little bundle of clothing had disappeared. She had promised us, she would rejoin her sister at the school, and, doubtless, made use of our absence to leave the house, alone, that we might not discover her real name, or the locality of her friends.

She had paid very dearly for her indiscretion. May it prove a lesson, not only to her, but to others, and may it have its influence in awaking the minds of parents to their responsibilities, in regard to the early instruction of their children, on the importance of moral and physical purity, and, not like the young merchant's mother, avoid the subject from a false feeling of delicacy, and thus allow their offspring to receive impressions from corrupting sources, that may lead to depraving associations, demoralized habits, and physical and spiritual death.

Some months since, Husband went on an excursion to one of our flourishing inland towns, and, upon his return, he told us he had met our friend, Samuel ——, the young merchant, for whom we had both felt so interested. "He is married now," said he, "lives in a fine house, and insisted on my visiting there." They spoke of the circumstances we have recorded, of the changes produced by the conversation and events of one single evening in the coloring of his life, and he exclaimed, "Mr. ——, your wife has been to me a guardian angel."

We feel somewhat abashed at repeating the expression, but do it, simply hoping, that it may encourage some timid heart to perform its duty.

REPORT OF THE MANAGERS OF THE ROSINE ASSOCIATION.

Extract from the Constitution of the Rosine Association.

To secure from vice and degradation, a class of women who have forfeited their claim to the respect of the virtuous—to prepare and maintain for them an asylum, which, by its system of religious instruction, shall elevate their moral nature—teach them how to gain an honest living "by the work of their own hands"—and eventually to render them useful members of the community—an association has been formed and denominated the "ROSINE ASSOCIATION," of Philadelphia.

October 25th, 1855.

President: Sophia Lewis, 119 Wood Street; Vice-President: Priscilla H. Hensey, 8 Marshall Street; Treasurer: Mira Townsend, 220 Race Street.

Secretaries: Lydia Gillingham, 35 N. Fifth Street; Anna Shomaker, 486 N. Sixth Street; E. Louisa Carr, 440 N. Fourth Street.

Managers: Mary Murphy, N. W. corner of Twelfth and Arch Street; Martha Wilson, 19 Clinton Street; Elizabeth Diament, 20 Wister Street; Rachel Child, 104 Arch Street; Sarah J. Webb, 244 Green Street; Mary Thain, 95 New Street; Elizabeth Carr, 440 N. Fourth Street; Eunice Tolman, West Philadelphia; Harriet Probasco, corner 6th and Wager Streets; Ann L. Rogers, Cherry, 2 doors west of 15th Street.

Physicians: Drs. John D. Griscom, Henry C. Child, Hannah E. Longshore, Jane V. Myers, George Truman, James Pearce.

The return of the beautiful season of autumnal fruits and flowers brings us again together. Some of us have remained at our field of labor throughout the summer, but our members generally have inhaled the genial breezes that are wafted over hill and vale, invigorating the system, and renewing the capacity for extended usefulness. But these rural pleasures have not been enjoyed by our Rosine family. Many of them in life's early spring have gathered the daisies and buttercups in the luxuriant meadows, and strolled beside the purling streams in all the careless happiness of childhood. They may visit the country again, but to them life can never wear the sunny garb in which innocence clothed it. The glorious orb may shed his rays as brightly; the flowers may blossom with as rich perfume; the rill may flow as gently; its soft murmurings may rest upon the ear, telling the tale of its birth amid rocky clefts, and of its wanderings through leafy dells; yet, to her who has strayed from the path of virtue, in whose soul the poisoned arrow is resting, the full cup of enjoyment can never be handed, even by bountiful Nature. The streamlet will speak of its purity, the flowers of their innocency; not reproachfully, but in the foamy bubbles of the rivulet, in the dew-drops that spangle the opening blossoms, in the note of the bird that carols its joyful anthems, there are feelings awakened that cluster their smothering influences around the heart, and vibrating through the brain, bring the one fatal remembrance, and the unuttered exclamation, "I am not as thou art!"

The benumbing qualities of the inebriating cup and the ever-present consciousness of degradation, may deaden the sensibilities of the unfortunate victims of vice, and create an apparent apathy and indifference towards the good and the beautiful, but the Divine impress planted in every bosom still lives within them; and as the sparks of virtuous desires and self-respect are rekindled in their minds, their appreciation of the true, the good and the beautiful, revives; and though the cloud still must rest upon their spirits, and the showers of grief ofttimes bedew their pillows, yet, as they learn to live the true life, they can rejoice in that Divine beneficence that followed them into their low estate, and has opened a path for them (as for the prodigal) to return to the Father's house. The memory of the past cannot, will not die. It is the penalty for transgression; yet so tempered is mercy with judgment, so universal is the feeling that God is good and his mercy endureth forever, that though the penitent may feel that every man's hand has been against her, yet can she acknowledge that for her also the flowers bloom, the streamlets flow, the birds carol their harmonious lays, the sun shines, and the rain and dew bestow their blessings; and that she, too, in a degree can appreciate and enjoy the harmonies of nature and the beauties of the creation around her.

Among our inmates are many who are yet in the early spring of life, on whom the spoiler has laid his hand, but whose sensibilities have not been deadened by intercourse with the vicious, or whose habits of intemperance have dimmed their aspirations after the pure enjoyments of the higher life. These cases awaken the deepest interest, as we contemplate the position into which a misstep has cast them, and the fatal consequences arising from it, casting a shadow over the whole future life. Man may err equally, the same crime may stain his soul, and in the sight of his ever-present Judge, his guilt may be of a far deeper dye, yet society is so lenient to his transgressions that he scarcely meets reproval, and rarely loses his social position in the circle in which he moves. The stamp of infamy that is placed on woman's brow, if she be tempted from the path of virtue, and the hopelessness of ever regaining the world's approving smile, deprives her generally of the capacity to struggle, and the energy to overcome the discouraging circumstances that bind her to the racking wheel, which at every revolution sinks more deeply its poisoned shafts into her soul. But the libertine, who led his victim (often unsuspectingly) into the web which he has woven to ensnare her, turns from the foul dishonor he has heaped upon a young and trusting heart, and emerges from the dark path of ruin and the glorious temple he has desecrated, to receive from those, professing not only morality, but religion, smiles and words of welcome to what ought to be the sacred sanctuary of virtue, the domestic hearth, where the daughters cluster, and the sons' expanding minds should learn the lessons of a holy purity. Case after case of this nature presents itself before us. A very short time since, our newspapers related the history of one, a lovely young girl of seventeen, who had been persuaded to leave her secluded home, some miles from the city, with one whose respectable standing introduced him to her father's fireside (that of a wealthy farmer), where, with the serpent's tongue, he lured the only daughter from her mother's arms, and brought her here, professing love and honor, and in one short week abandoned her, to hide her shame amid the more abandoned. In less than two months, she was brought in a state of inebriation (with others whose names are linked with infamy), before a magistrate, who learned her story and sent her to our care. The cloud has passed over her. She may return to her father's house and make the acknowledgment, "I have sinned before Heaven and in thy sight!" but for her no fatted calf will be killed, no rejoicing that the lost is found. She is a woman, and society will not acknowledge that her stains can be washed away; while he who thus wrecked the happiness of a young and guileless girl, and brought sorrow in that once blest home, retains his position in an honorable profession, is a welcome visitant in respectable families, and again may woo and win the lovely and the pure.

Were it proper, we could cite other cases of

recent occurrence, where our pity and condemnation of the unfortunate girl has been mingled with feelings of indignation against the seducer, and of regret that some of those who make a religious profession admit unreservedly such persons into their homes, and the society of their sons and daughters, who are not prepared to excuse the erring female, or admit her among the circle of their friends.

We seek not to palliate crime, or lower the standard of the virtue to be required of woman, but we desire to place the subject before our friends in its true bearings, and ask that justice and mercy may be accorded to both man and woman, that each may occupy their proper position, irrespective of sex, and that the woman who strives to regain, by her appropriate conduct, the approbation of the good and reputable, may receive the helping hand and the "God speed thee!" from all those whose privilege it may be to aid in this, the work of angels; for surely, there can be no higher mission given than that of Jesus, who came to save the lost, and whose memorable words were, "Go, and sin no more."

In the records we have received of Jesus, we find no fear of compromising his character or dignity by associating with any, however low their condition. Satisfied with the purity of his own mind, and his desire to do them good, he walked fearlessly, while those who based their reputation on their society, exclaimed, "Behold, he eats with publicans and sinners!" As the precepts of Christ become better understood, and his mission appreciated, and men and women are more imbued with his spirit, there will be less need of "Rosine Associations," and individual duties will be more faithfully performed.

Since we wrote the last sentence, we were called to a gentleman who came to ask us to visit a young girl he had met in a public place, whose history he had partially learned. She is an orphan (the daughter of an intemperate man), brought to poverty by the misconduct of her father. She came to the city to seek employment, and is now living with a family. With the natural instincts of youth for social life, she has sought in her leisure hours the leafy shades of one of our public squares. There she has occasionally met with a young man who wears the garb of a gentleman, but whose profligate conduct disgraces his respectable lineage. Ignorant of the world, and unsuspecting of the wily tongue of the flatterer, the Christian brother who called on us justly estimated her danger, and felt that by our interference and counsel she might be saved. She will probably never appreciate his precaution or our feelings of interest, for she suspects not the deadly mine that is under her feet, nor the treachery that may lure her to irreparable ruin. Within the past two weeks we have visited two houses of immoral character, with the hope of saving two young girls, who, like the one above alluded to, had left their rural homes in the hopeful buoyancy of youth, to seek more remunerative employment in the city. Like her, they formed acquaintance with "the stranger," and their homes are among the unfortunate and degraded.

Some time since, a police officer claimed our attention to a young girl. She, with a friend, both of them eighteen years old, and just out of their apprenticeship, came from the neighborhood of Pottsville, with the hope of higher wages than they could get at home.

The day after they arrived, they walked around to see the city, and entered Franklin Square. While gazing upon the beautiful fountain, and expressing their admiration, they attracted the attention of two men, who fell into conversation with them, and learned they were strangers, and the object of their coming to the city. With an appearance of the greatest kindness, they informed the unsuspecting girls that they knew two ladies who needed their services, and would employ them, and offered to conduct them to the promised places. On leaving the square, they separated, and of the history of one of these girls we have no farther knowledge. On the records of the prison or almshouse her name may most probably be found. The other was taken to a low boarding-house by one of the men, and introduced as "his cousin from the country." She speedily saw she was entrapped, and confided her story to one of the girls of the house, who informed the policeman who came to us. The case was immediately attended to. The young woman was brought out of the house, and placed under the care of one of our ladies, who in a few days sent her back to her friends. It was ascertained that the man was well known to the police, and had been a convict.

When we opened the "Rosine House," it was with the belief that the benefits of the Association would not be confined to the inmates there, but that the feelings that prompted the formation of the Society, and opened the doors of the "Rosine" were latent in other hearts, and, as opportunity presented, would spring into life, and show themselves in deeds of virtue, and prove that goodness and benevolence are everywhere, and only await the moment and opportunity of development. It has been the general opinion that woman's heart was more seared against her erring sister than that of man; but when we look into the cause of this apparent coldness, we find it in the position in society in which woman has been placed. She has been the dependent on man, and though many men have chosen to associate with women of doubtful character, yet they have rarely been willing to be accompanied by their wives, daughters, or sisters, and have even desired a veil thrown over such associations.

Women, therefore, who wished to claim the golden opinions of their male friends, and saw that they visited such persons in privacy, and spoke not of these communications in the home or social circle, naturally imagined that the society men were ashamed to acknowledge was not exactly proper for them; and hence they have turned from them with coldness and aversion. But the Christian woman, standing upright on that base where Jesus stood, fears not to do the right, and nobly dares to go where duty calls, or, when opportunity presents, take the unfortunate wanderer by the hand, and aid her as she may, either physically or morally. It is emphatically woman's duty to aid the cause of woman. Man may feed, and clothe, and convey religious instruction, but woman's tongue must speak the words of sympathy and encouragement. Woman's mind and efforts must prepare for and procure the employment absolutely needful to maintain steadily the tottering mind, that scarcely believes in the possibility of its own restoration to a respectable position, and requires a heart full of love, and faith, and hope, and patience, to sustain it, and bear with its weaknesses, its waywardness, and its despondencies. When our inmates leave the "Rosine," and enter the various situations that may open for them, we feel that our work is not accomplished, but that we ought still to be the friends, the confidants, the counsellors, ever ready with word and deed to aid their necessities as best we may, and strengthen them to meet wisely the discouragements that must occasionally encircle them.

From the nature of the business engagements of men, and from the delicacy and sympathy needed in such cases, women are naturally better qualified and prepared to fulfil this important and holy mission.

We hail the advance of public sentiment respecting woman's duties and privileges, and feel that the day is past in which she must turn from her erring sister, as from a thing accursed, in order to maintain her own reputation. In this respect the "Rosine" has accomplished a great work. It has proved that the pure in heart may safely enter the abodes of iniquity, and feel that the mission there is acknowledged by God and man. It has proved that woman can, and in many cases will reform, if the circumstances around her are such as to inspire a hope that her efforts and aspirations can be crowned with success. Some of those who were once "Rosines," but are now filling important and respectable situations, feel that the day of miracles has not passed. When they recollect the degradation in which they were once immersed, and contrast that period with the present—when they remember their alienation from all that was good, and their outcast condition, and see themselves now surrounded by kind hearts and true ones, they can scarcely realize at times that any train of circumstances could produce so great a change; and the utterance from their lips has been in mingled tones of wonder and gratitude. One of those who left the "Rosine" three years since, and has been situated very advantageously, lately left the establishment in which she was located, because the conduct of some with whom she was associated was not entirely correct. "I feel," said she, "that I need the society of the good and elevated, and fear that my principles might be weakened by being in company with those whose conversation has a downward tendency." Another, who is at the head of the female department in a large manufactory, where she receives six dollars per week, lately came to one of our Managers, to consult her relative to making a change in her place of boarding. She, too, felt the importance of improving society, and the disadvantages that might result from associating with such companions as she might be liable to meet in a common boarding-house. "You are," said she, "the only friends to whom I can come for counsel." This feeling of our continued interest and protection we have found in many cases to be a great safeguard to our girls; and the thought of what the ladies would think, or how they would feel, has operated to produce beneficial results, and an increased responsibility.

Our work department has proved an efficient aid, not only in a pecuniary way, but from the advantages resulting to our inmates, by qualifying many for situations as seamstresses, whose impaired health and other circumstances would prevent them from engaging in active domestic avocations. Were the

"Rosine" considered merely a workshop, and our inmates expected to remain for a series of years after they had acquired sufficient knowledge to make them valuable, the Institution might probably be maintained by the labor of the family. But the reformatory influences have ever been considered of the first importance, and the labor as one of the necessary adjuncts to qualify for present and future usefulness. The object has never been to retain our girls in the Institution after they were prepared to go into the world and support themselves, but that the Rosine House should be a school where the weak, the ignorant, and the erring might be instructed in everything good and useful, applicable to their situations. We find many who enter the Rosine are ignorant of the simplest duties of life. Some tell us they have never made or mended a garment, and these must be taught as children, and perhaps never make sufficient improvement to be put upon customer work while in the Institution, therefore their labor is only profitable to themselves in the increased happiness they enjoy from continued occupation and the knowledge acquired, which qualifies them to earn the bread of honest industry.

The number of garments made in the past year, from October 1st, 1854, to October 1st, 1855, has been:

For the use of the family, - - - - - -	854
For customers, including 337 shirts, 398 chemises, 83 night-gowns, 44 dresses, 95 collars, 64 wrappers, 281 pillow-cases, 173 bolsters, 520 sheets, and sundry articles, amounting altogether to -	2600
Total, for family and customers, - -	3454

Beside the articles made, there has been 115

yards of embroidery worked, 681 button holes made, and 356 yards of stitching done for customers.

When we consider the ignorance and idle habits of many of those who come under our care, and the patience necessary to be exercised in their progress towards improvement, we feel there is cause for congratulation on our success in this depart-partment.

We have generally about half-a-dozen girls who have served the appointed time in the house, and wish to remain there, whose services are considered worthy of compensation, both as a reward and encouragement. To these we pay $1 per week, which enables them to provide their clothing, and, after a season, deposit something in the Saving Fund. One of these has now $24 deposited for her. Two girls, who have been living at service, have each deposited over a hundred dollars. One of these is still living in the family to which she went upon leaving the Institution. We have deposited for her $140. We can ask no better proof of the good conduct of these women, than the fact that they continue for years residents of the same family, and are accumulating a fund by their honest industry. One of our former inmates was lately married. She had lived four years in the same family, and had won a character which will surround her with friends in the rural home to which she has been removed.

The business of the household department, comprising cooking, washing, ironing, etc., is all done by the inmates, affording thus a school in which they are taught the practical operations of a family, and prepared to be useful in whatever situations they may be placed. The neglectful habits in which many young girls grow up, and the want of judicious, systematic training to qualify them to fulfil their duties, is a fruitful source of the difficulties that lead them into an abandoned life. Many of the daughters of the poorer classes of society, through a mistaken pride, are kept at home under the influence of improper examples and associations, and without the domestic teaching that would fit them for industrious usefulness. As they approach womanhood, they become dissatisfied and ungovernable, and are then frequently hired by the week into families. But the idle, careless habits generated at home usually prevent them from retaining their situations; and the frequent changes produce an unsettlement that is detrimental to the moral character, and prevents that close application to business habits without which no one can hope to succeed. Among our inmates, there is always a large number who have been left orphans early in life, and have never experienced parental care or a mother's judicious training; while another portion have been the offspring of those who have degraded themselves by inebriation or other evil habits, and have thus cast around their children a noxious and pernicious atmosphere. We have had in the Rosine, at the same period, a mother and daughter, both equally degraded; and, in a late prison visit by one of our managers, she found there the mother of a very interesting girl who had been twelve months in the Rosine, and who had herself formerly been several times a prisoner. On six different occasions, two sisters have been inmates at the same time, and, of one family, we have had an aunt and four of her nieces, *all sisters*. They were from the South, and had grown up in ignorance and poverty.

The beauty of their persons contrasted sadly with the barrenness of their minds, and the pride that made them shrink from honest labor, proved the laxity and injudiciousness of the parental training. One after another as they dawned into womanhood they became the prey of the spoiler. Of these, one has gone to render her account to Him, who sees and knows the weakness and temptations of His children, and judges not as man judges. Another passed a year in the Rosine, and, since that period, has filled a position in a wealthy family, that is honorable to herself, and satisfactory to her employers. She has been for a year or more a member of a church, that numbers among its communicants two others of our former inmates, one of whom is married to a worthy and respectable mechanic.

We have spoken in our Reports of our contracted domestic arrangements, of our small dining-room, kitchen, and yard, of our crowded chambers, and our "one room," which is in turn the inmates' parlor, work room, and church. We have also stated, that, with the hope of procuring a larger and more convenient building, into which we could welcome an increased number of the unfortunate and erring ones, we applied to the Legislature, February, 1854, for an appropriation to aid us. This was granted on certain conditions.

AN ACT APPROPRIATING CERTAIN MONEYS TO THE ROSINE ASSOCIATION.

SECTION 1.—Be it enacted by the Senate, etc., that the sum of $3000 be, and the same is, hereby appropriated to the Rosine Association of Philadelphia, incorporated April 14, 1848, for the purchasing a lot, or erecting, or purchasing buildings for the operation of the Association: Provided, That this Act shall not take effect, until an equal amount shall have been subscribed by other responsible contributors to said Association.

SECTION 2.—That the Councils of the City of Philadelphia are hereby authorized to appropriate to the said Association, hereafter, any sum, or sums of money, not exceeding $3000 in any one year.

Our friends in the Legislature knew we owed a debt of $2800 on the house we occupy, and that an appropriation of $3000, which was the sum proposed to be given, would only pay that amount, without enabling us to effect the desired purpose. The second section was therefore added, authorizing the City Councils to give us an annual appropriation of $3000, with the idea, that, with this assistance, the friends of the cause of humanity would be stimulated to aid us in raising an amount that would locate the Association in a larger and more convenient building, with an income sufficient to support the Institution without the continued beggary to which we have been subjected.

In consequence of the unsettled condition of our City government, we did not make application to Councils, until April, 1855, when we presented a petition in accordance with the above Act of the Legislature. The embarrassed condition of the City finances operated to prevent Councils from donating the amount allowed by the Legislature, but they granted an appropriation of $1500, for which we received a warrant a few days since—to be paid when the City is in funds.

A friend, whose heart and purse are ever open to the unfortunate, gave us $1000 toward the $3000 required to be subscribed to obtain the legislative donation, $500 was subscribed by other individuals, nearly all of whom are our annual contributors, which makes the amount required to obtain the State appropriation.

We are thus enabled to fulfil the conditions, and shall place the funds, when we receive them, at interest, until a sufficient sum is raised to make it prudent to proceed in whatever manner may be deemed advisable towards procuring more extensive accommodations.

We have still a debt of $1800 remaining on the house we occupy, $1300 of which is on a ground-rent. We should be unwise, in our present circumstances, to attempt either to buy or build, and thus involve the Society more deeply in debt. But we hope the day is not far distant, when a sufficient fund may be raised to warrant us to make arrangements to rear a mansion, sacred to Mercy and Virtue.

TREASURER'S REPORT.

The receipts from October 1st, 1854, to October 1st, 1855, have been:		
From the work room, - - -	$1,266 95	
Donations and annual subscriptions,	2,505 94	
		$3,772 89

EXPENSES.

To balance due October 1st, 1854,	$373 47	
To ground-rent, insurance, gas, and water-rent, - - - -	165 00	
Family expenses, including fuel, salaries, clothing, marketing, &c.,	3,122 51	
		3,660 98
Cash on hand, - - - - -		$111 91

Under the head of Salaries, we ought to note, that $184 75 was paid to inmates, who are working for wages, all of whom have been over a year in the Institution.

We desire to acknowledge the reception of $50 from T. W., of Baltimore, also $30 from "a Lady, in another State." These tokens of the interest felt in the cause of humanity, by persons at a distance, is an evidence of their appreciation of our efforts, and of the progress of that fraternal benevolence that is not confined to any location, but extends its sympathies, unasked, to the unfortunate and erring.

We also wish to present our thanks to our contributors in money, goods, or labor. The cause is yours, as well as ours! We are your agents to do what you cannot do! to use your means to effect a great result! with your aid to maintain a Home, where the erring and unfortunate may come to seek the protection and counsel they need from their own sex, and that training that may prepare them, after a season, to re-enter the world under those favorable auspices that may lead them into the enjoyment of a higher life than perhaps they have ever known, and open to them the pathway to eternal glory.

We cannot present you the history of any wonderful achievement—all we can expect to accomplish must be gained by slow and patient efforts, by the exercise of love and kindness, and by that faith that constantly remembers

"That drops of water turn the mill.

And also, that

"One by one the stones are laid,
By which the massive arch is formed;
And one by one the tints were made
Which Raphael's heart, and pictures warmed."

We cannot show you our work! We wish to hide it! We cannot show you our children! We do not want you to know they ever were ours. We want you to meet them in the field of useful labor, without a knowledge that they ever were otherwise than they now are. We hope we shall all meet them in Heaven, where their frailties, and ours, will be remembered no more.

More than four hundred women have been inmates since the house was opened. Could we turn to many of them, and show their present condition, their respectability and usefulness, and the propriety of their conduct, our friends would feel with us, that we have not labored in vain.

Our Intelligence Office at the Institution, for respectable females, is still in operation. We desire to call the attention of our friends to that, and also to our work room. Two thousand five hundred and eighty-six women and children have been provided with homes and employment from the Office. How many have been saved from ruin, by its agency, we cannot tell.

Our members and contributors will please pay their subscriptions to the store-keeper, at the Rosine House—the treasurer, Mira Townsend, 220 Race Street, to either of the managers, or to our collector, Priscilla Nicholson.

The Annual Meeting is held on the first Thursday in April.

FORM OF A BEQUEST OF PERSONAL ESTATE.

I give and bequeath to the Rosine Association of Philadelphia, and their successors, the sum of dollars, towards promoting the objects of said Society.

FORM OF A BEQUEST OF REAL ESTATE.

I give and devise to the Rosine Association of Philadelphia, or their successors, all that (here describe the property), together with the appurtenances, to hold to the said Rosine Association of Philadelphia, and their successors, forever, for them to dispose of and convey in any manner which will promote the objects of said Society.

BLACK EYES.

E. and myself had been at an Alderman's Office to endeavor to procure the release of a woman we had found in the prison the day before, and were going to another Alderman's, about another woman, when we went up —— street, and intended to pass by a house of bad character which we had visited some weeks previously, but when we came to the step, a beautiful little girl two and a half years old, stood in the door. It was the child of Emma! Poor Emma. She was the daughter of a respectable farmer in Bucks County, who perfectly understood the nobility of wealth, but had small sympathy for lovers without it. Emma was only sixteen, but she had fallen in love, or imagined she had, with a young painter, who had come to renovate the old building with his brush and paint-kettle, and surely, there seemed to be magic in that brush, or in the eyes that watched and directed its operations, for they wove a destiny for Emma she had little foreseen or dreamed of. We cannot enter into details, but the father banished the young painter from the house, and the daughter ran off with him, expecting to be married, but they were not. In the course of a few months the lover deserted her and shipped to California, and she sought a shelter in the house of a married sister, who received her unwillingly, but permitted her to remain, subject to the daily taunts and reproaches which mortified pride heaped upon her. When her babe was a few weeks old she left the unwelcome shelter, and with the infant in her arms returned to her father's house. She hoped that he would receive her, and even if he banished her from his heart, would allow her the protection of his roof. But there was a home for her no longer; she was harshly repulsed, and with her wailing babe she turned from that door with which all her cherished memories were entwined, and received that denial that doomed her to be an unsheltered wanderer. She came to the city, supposing she could find some employment, and went from house to house making the inquiry. But there was not one willing to receive a girl not seventeen, with a babe in her arms, whose respectable dress and appearance bespoke the lady unused to labor, and she passed from door to door faint and wearily, till hope seemed to die within her, and she was ready to sink from exhaustion. In this condition she entered a house, and made the oft-repeated inquiry. They told her they had no work; but they saw she was young and attractive, and they offered to take her as a boarder. It was a house of immoral character. Doubtless there was a struggle of the keenest anguish in her mind. She had never erred but once, and sadly indeed for that was she paying the penalty. But then she had no home. There, one was offered. Of the horrors of that abode she had no conception. She staid. We became acquainted with her and her history some time afterwards. As the babe grew it became very beautiful, and the mistress of the house learned to love it, while the mother looked upon it as the cause of her trouble, and felt it a burthen. Some months passed away, and a contract was signed by that unfortunate mother to give her innocent babe to the mistress of a noted house of ill-fame, to grow up amid all the debasing influences of the society clustered around her.

Emma married, and went to live in New Jersey.

We have never seen her since, but the child remained, and this was the little adopted one that claimed our attention, and put out its little hand to speak to us, and said "Come in and see my mother!" We were hurrying along, feeling we had not time to stop, but the child enticed us, and we could not resist its artless invitation. We entered, inquired of the mistress of the house for Emma, and then plead with her to give us the child. She said she could not part with it, but gave us her hand to seal her promise, that if she died first, we should have it.

During our conversation with Mrs. H., we made our observations on the company present. Three young men and one girl sat at a table playing cards; three other young men and two girls were sitting there. They were all strangers to us. We inquired of the mistress what had become of all the girls we had formerly seen there, sometimes 15 in number. She replied, they are nearly all dead! And where are all the girls we used to see in the houses about here, three or four years since? "All gone!" said she. We asked after several by name; she had not seen them for some time! Probably they had died in the prison or almshouse! "And where is that beautiful little Harriet we tried to save?" "Oh she died last week of small-pox in Ball Alley. She was taken sick here, but when I found it was small-pox I sent her away. You know I can't have sick people here!" Harriet was a bright, beautiful girl of sixteen, innocent and fresh from her country home when she first entered that fatal house. Three years had passed away, and all the fruits of her degradation had been gathered by the mistress of the house, and she had been cast into Ball Alley to die, without a friend to smooth her pillow or offer a word of consolation or hope in her last struggling agonies. "There are but two or three girls left in the neighborhood of all those you used to see in your visits here," said Mrs. H.

We had been in seventeen houses of the same character in that *one quarter of a square*, all of them tenanted by young girls, usually several in each house, and in this short period of time *all were gone but two or three.* Here was the testimony of one engaged in this horrid traffic of souls and bodies, and who was still living on the miseries and degradation of her own sex. Could but the voice of warning be sounded and fall upon the ears of the young and innocent throughout our country; could they be made sensible that the probable consequence of deviations from the path of virtue was a degraded life of shame, and a death of misery in the prison, the almshouse, or Ball Alley, would they not turn with horror from every temptation, and shudder at the fearful gulf in which one misstep might involve them!

From this conversation with Mrs. H., we turned to the persons sitting in the room, and made some remarks to each of the girls, in the hope of awaking the conscientious feelings which we knew could only be sleeping within them. The one at the card-table seemed considerably affected, and asking a young man to take her place, arose, and seemed desirous to explain her circumstances to us. She heartily condemned the life she was leading, and acknowledged an attachment to a young man whom she could not abandon, but hoped the day was not far distant, when she could return to the path of virtue. As we addressed each of them, we presented one of our printed Rosine letters, and told them we were members of the Society, and considered it a part of our duty to visit such houses, and endeavor to save the unfortunate girls; but we did not feel that our mission was confined to them, but that it was equally our duty to strive to benefit the young men whom we might meet there. One of the young men at the card-table refused to receive our document, and held back his hands when we offered it; but we urged him to receive it, assuring him it would not hurt him. "I have read enough of these things," said he, "and of the Bible too." "I have read the Bible through three times," said another youth at the table, "but it never did me any good!" "Ah," said the first one, whom we will designate as Black Eyes, for they were dark, bright, and intelligent, "I know the Bible from one end to the other, but there are some parts of it I do not believe to be true. The Book of Job, and some other parts, are only fables." "Well," said we, "even supposing they are not true, what then! Have not each of you a conviction in your own minds that tells you what is right, and teaches you that frequenting such houses as this, and playing cards, and drinking, and all other evils, are wrong? And even if we admit that the story of Job is an allegory, written for the benefit of a past age, is it not full of instruction, and may we not be strengthened by its perusal? We have read the Bible too, and believe it to have been of great use to us." Black Eyes shook his head, and added, "I once believed it, but I do not now." He then quoted the passage where Michael and the Archangels are spoken of, and other parts, showing his familiarity with its pages. It would have been of little use to discuss the truthfulness of the Bible then, therefore we avoided it as skilfully as we could, and endeavored to draw their minds to the practices produced by the religious sentiment, instead of cavilling about doctrines or beliefs. One of them said, he would like to be religious, but he did not know how! We told him there was one brief sentence, that whether he believed in the Bible, or not, would explain the whole duties of religion; and as he brought them into practice, perhaps some of the passages that now seemed unsound to him would become truths, and be revealed to his mind, and become a living Gospel to him. This sentence was,

"Cease to do evil, and learn to do well."

By abstaining from the first part, he would soon learn to practise the latter, and when he ceased from doing evil, and learned to do well *always*, he would know all about religion; but he could never understand it while he frequented such houses, and indulged in the immoral habits consequent upon it.

Black Eyes remarked that he believed in spiritual communications. We inquired if he believed in the constant presence of spirits? He said he did. We then asked if his mother was living? He replied both of his parents were dead. "Were they religious people?" "They were!" "Of what society?" "Methodists." "Was thee brought up a Methodist?" "I was!" "Was thy mother a good woman?" "She was?" "Suppose then her spirit is watching over thee, how must she feel to see her son here, in this place, in this company?" He was willing to leave this question without reply, and commenced talking about Paine and

Voltaire, and their opinions, seeming to have been puzzling his brain about creeds and theories, while he was living in violation of the purity they inculcated. We advised him to lay aside all these books, and occupy his mind with other subjects than metaphysical speculations, for it was evident that he was not in a condition to be benefited by them, and had given way to a scepticism that had loosed even the moral obligations to his mind. We gave him our views of the beauty and simplicity of religion. We were all the children of one Father, whose ear was ever open to hear our supplications for knowledge and wisdom, and who, as we endeavored to obey the impressions of duty made upon our own minds, would enlighten our understandings to see and know what was right for us; and if we lived in the simple fulfilment of these obligations as they arose before us, we believed the wisdom would be given, that would benefit us more than the study of creeds and doctrines, that ofttimes have a tendency to bewilder the mind, and fill it with controversial speculations.

The whole company appeared to be interested in the conversation. The card-table was removed, and nearly all those present joined, in an animated manner, in the discussion of the moral and religious duties. None had sinned through ignorance, and no one endeavored to exculpate themselves. The girls evidently felt the ban of society had been placed upon them, and though they were not prepared to abandon their present position (through their attachment to the men with whom they associated), yet they all hoped the day might come that they might return to a virtuous life.

After spending an hour or more thus conversing we said, we hoped none of them would forget this conversation, as there was food for reflection in many of the remarks that had been elicited. Our interview with them had been altogether accidental, *apparently*, as we had not intended to stop there, but we now believed it was *providential*, and we hoped the time would yet be, that they would all be prepared to come to us, and say, that from this hour they had never entered an improper house, or been guilty of an immoral action; and this young man (laying our hand upon the shoulder of Black Eyes, who was seated next to us), we hope to see some day in the pulpit. The remark was unquaker-like, but we made it, and a thrill passed through us as those large, dark eyes were raised and fixed upon us with a painful earnestness, as if trying to read our innermost thought, but no word was uttered. Some minutes afterwards he desired to speak with us aside, and then said, "You told me you hoped to see me some day in the pulpit. "I have been there!" "How, as a minister, a preacher?" "Yes," he replied, "I have! I was stationed two years in Illinois, and I have been two years near this city." "Tell us then," we asked, "was the Bible a true book to thee, then?" "It was!" "Were thy sermons from the convictions of thy own spirit, or were they like a parrot's chatter, by rote?" "Oh!" said he, mournfully, "they were, they were! Religion was a truth to me then! It was an improper connection with a female that caused my ruin!" "How?" said we; "did she lead thee astray?" "We were both wrong," he replied; "but I will come and see you. I wish some further conversation with you!" We gave him our name and number, desiring the impressions of that hour might continue with him, and grow and ripen, until as a "brand snatched from the burning," he might again be able to stand as a pillar in his Father's house.

The mistress of the house was in the room the principal part of the time we were there, and listened attentively, though she did not join in the conversation, and as we bade her adieu, she said, "I will endeavor to get out of this way of living as soon as I can," and we have since understood, that her husband and she have moved to another house, and are now living privately.

In this manner we have had many conversations with young men whom we have met in these houses, and in some instances have had reason to believe the opportunity has been blest to them, as they have called upon us afterwards, and expressed their gratitude for our friendly counsel. One young man who called two or three times to see us, married some months afterwards, and brought his wife to introduce to us, relating to her with a great deal of feeling the history of our first interview.

We passed from the house of Mrs. H. with the impression that we had been sent there, and that the baby girl had been the angel appointed to invite us in. How little we know the agencies around us that impel us to make our resolutions and intentions as things that were not. We had felt when we arrived at the door that we had not time to stop a moment, yet we had staid an hour and a half, and departed with our hearts filled with gratitude and wonder, as we retraced our own past lives, and the occurrences that have schooled and prepared us for our mission, to the prisoner, the outcast, and the depraved. Solomon's desire, is truly ours—for wisdom—that wisdom that cometh from above.

The wonderful, the beautiful,
  Are marked on all around,
In floating clouds—on changing earth—
  Within the teeming ground—
Born in the crystal flakes of snow,
  And in the rays of light,
Living in falling drops of dew,
  And in the eyes of night.

The wonderful, the beautiful,
  Are in the flower and tree,
Are on the mountain, in the vale,
  And o'er the waving sea—
Are in the thought, and in the hope
  Of gay and sunny youth,
And in the eye and on the lip
  Of bold and honest truth.

The wonderful, the beautiful,
  Fill up the earth and air;
They picture Heaven in our souls
  With beams of light from there.
But he hath power surpassing all,
  Around—or far—or near—
Who, clothed with love for all mankind,
  Creates a Heaven here.

CONCLUSION.

We have arrived at the last page of our book, and feel that, perhaps, a few more words are needful, by way of explanation. We hold a spring and autumnal public meeting, and at each present a report of the year preceding that period. Our reason for making each an annual report, is this—part of our contributors get the pamphlet published in the spring, and others the one in the autumn, and when we meet our friends, we like to tell them all we have been doing the past year. And now we present the history of eight years. Momentous ones they have been to many individuals, who, through the agency of the Rosine Association, have been saved from the path of destruction, and stand as monuments of Divine mercy.

In regard to ourselves, we can offer no apology for intruding upon our friends, but the simple truth. We are weary of the beggarly life we have been forced to lead, to sustain the Rosine House; and, like the drowning man catching at a straw, we thought if we could send a little messenger into the world, that could talk for us, and perform our begging, and stimulate those who were able to put their hands to the work, and join with the noble men and women who have stood by us and aided us year after year, that perhaps there might come a season of greater retirement, when we could have leisure to attend to some other duties that are pressing upon us.

Are we reaching after straws? Let that be as it may, we have not amused our friends with fancy sketches; we have given them not only Reports, but realities—solemn truths.

THE END.

www.ingramcontent.com/pod-product-compliance
Lightning Source LLC
LaVergne TN
LVHW020127110826
845151LV00001B/302
* 9 7 8 1 4 2 5 5 4 0 5 3 1 *